PERGAMON INTERNATIONAL LIBRARY
of Science, Technology, Engineering and Social Studies
The 1000-volume original paperback library in aid of education,
industrial training and the enjoyment of leisure
Publisher: Robert Maxwell, M.C.

THE CONSTRUCTION OF MADNESS,

*Emerging Conceptions and Interventions
into the Psychotic Process*

PGPS—59
Peter A. Magaro

THE PERGAMON TEXTBOOK
INSPECTION COPY SERVICE

An inspection copy of any book published in the Pergamon International
Library will gladly be sent to academic staff without obligation for their
consideration for course adoption or recommendation. Copies may be
retained for a period of 60 days from receipt and returned if not suitable.
When a particular title is adopted or recommended for adoption for class
use and the recommendation results in a sale of 12 or more copies, the
inspection copy may be retained with our compliments. If after examination the lecturer decides that the book is not suitable for adoption but
would like to retain if for his personal library, then a discount of 10% is
allowed on the invoiced price. The Publishers will be pleased to receive
suggestions for revised editions and new titles to be published in this
important International Library.

PERGAMON GENERAL PSYCHOLOGY SERIES

Editors: Arnold P. Goldstein, *Syracuse University*
Leonard Krasner, *SUNY, Stony Brook*

The terms of our inspection copy service apply to all the
above books. A complete catalogue of all books in the
Pergamon International Library is available on request.
The Publisher will be pleased to receive suggestions for
revised editions and new titles.

(continued on p. 223)

THE CONSTRUCTION OF MADNESS

Emerging Conceptions and Interventions
into the Psychotic Process

Edited by

PETER A. MAGARO

University of Maine

PERGAMON PRESS

OXFORD · TORONTO · NEW YORK
SYDNEY · PARIS · FRANKFURT

U. K.	Pergamon Press Ltd., Headington Hill Hall, Oxford OX3 0BW, England.
U. S. A.	Pergamon Press Inc., Maxwell House, Fairview Park, Elmsford, New York 10523, U.S.A.
C A N A D A	Pergamon of Canada, Ltd. P.O. Box 9600, Don Mills, M3C 2T9, Ontario, Canada
A U S T R A L I A	Pergamon Press (Aust.) Pty. Ltd., 19a Boundary Street, Rushcutters Bay, N.S.W. 2011, Australia
F R A N C E	Pergamon Press SARL, 24 rue des Ecoles, 75240 Paris, Cedex 05, France
W E S T G E R M A N Y	Pergamon Press GMbH, 6242 Kronberg/Taunus Pferdstrasse 1, Frankfurt-am-Main

First edition 1976

Library of Congress Cataloging in Publication Data

Main entry under title:

The Construction of madness.

(Pergamon general psychology series; 59)
Based on the Symposium on Schizophrenia, University of Maine, 1974.
1. Schizophrenia – Congresses. I. Magaro, Peter A. II. Symposium on Schizophrenia, University of Maine, 1974. [DNLM: 1. Schizophrenia – Congresses. WM203 S9894c]
RC514.C615 1975   616.8'982   75–23298
ISBN 0–08–019904–6
ISBN 08–019903–8 pbk.

Printed in Great Britain by Express Litho Service (Oxford)

Contents

Contributors

JAY E. ADAMS, Westminster Theological Seminary, Philadelphia, Pennsylvania.

BENJAMIN M. BRAGINSKY, Department of Psychology, Wesleyan University, Middletown, Connecticut.

DOROTHEA D. BRAGINSKY, Institute for Human Development, Fairfield University, Fairfield, Connecticut.

BERTRAM P. KARON, Department of Psychology, Michigan State University, East Lansing, Michigan.

ALAN E. KAZDIN, Department of Psychology, The Pennsylvania State University, College Park, Pennsylvania.

KENNETH E. LUX, Private Practice, Rm 58–59, 27 State Street, Bangor, Maine.

PETER A. MAGARO, Department of Psychology, University of Maine, Orono, Maine.

KENDALL A. MERRIAM, 4 Church Street, Richmond, Maine.

Peter A. Magaro (Ph.D. University of Illinois) is Associate Professor of Psychology at the University of Maine, Orono, Maine. His primary interest is in the area of schizophrenia and he is the author of *Research in Schizophrenia: An Integration Theory Resolution* published in 1975 by Lawrence Erlbaum Associates. Dr. Magaro has directed token economy and milieu therapy programs. The interest in therapy systems in institutions has led to the development of the Prescriptive Treatment Model and work on the efficacy of current treatment procedures.

Preface

Madness is as American as John Wayne, Urban Renewal and Evangel-ism. Madness, however, is unique in that its presence is known by its absence from the cultural interchange. Madness is hidden from the societal discourse by being the inverse of the ideal. If the culture idealizes work and productivity, madness is identified as the lack of such activity. If the society values morality determined by a faith in the supernatural, madness becomes a demonstration of the conse-quences of a lack of faith. The cause of madness has consistently been seen as the inverse of the dominant ethic. Using a term of George Mead, "Images of Man" construct an ideology of madness and the preferable method of intervention. These images are the models of pathology. How we think about what we don't know becomes the matter from which madness is constructed.

The reader is envisioned as a student of the current human situation who is attempting to understand his culture and its activities, especially those activities directed toward those considered mad, mentally ill, disturbed, crazy, insane, maladjusted or "a candi-date for the funny farm". Whatever the euphemism, the degree of civilization of a culture seems related to how those so identified are treated. In that sense, this book is addressed to all those engaged in the understanding of madness as treater, treated, participant in the mental health industry, or interested cultural observer. We are thus speaking to the student of human nature in an attempt to derive a greater understanding of two human activities: psychopathology and therapy. The following chapters are expressions of the many roads one may travel in conceptualizing madness and devising a treatment fitting the conceptualization. Hopefully, the reader will find where he acts and why.

The book presents what are, in the editor's opinion, the most viable conceptions of the nature of man as applied to pathology and its treatment. The contributions presented here explicate the follow-ing models of psychopathology: Experiential, Social, Mystical, Moral, Learning, and Psychological. The Experiential chapter is the statement of an individual filling the traditional description (as well as picking up the usual labels) of one who is mad. He presents an

ix

explicit challenge to those who would so label without thinking and an implicit statement of a man in control of his own treatment. Many years from now treatment may be dominantly conceptualized as an individual matter which can only be inhibited by the intervention of another. For now we assume, with faith and nothing more, that someone has to receive "help" from another to become "sane". The author questions whether all this help is really helpful; he searches for other ways to view his experiences, and a better notion of who might provide further understanding.

The Cultural Context chapters present the relevance of culture, present and past, for understanding madness and its treatment. The first chapter places the past conception of madness into its cultural context. The striking oddity of these treatments becomes more understandable, but certainly not justifiable especially for those extreme treatments which led to extensive mangling of the individual. The second chapter mirrors the conceptions of our present treatment behavior and questions if they are not as ill-informed as those of the past. The currently accepted intervention systems, with their assumptions of the nature of madness, are analyzed as potentially ignoring the actual state of the inmate, who is more aware of his position in the social—political—economic matrix of the society than is usually recognized.

The Spiritual Vision chapters present the views of two men who clearly spell out their notions of our nature and the forces affecting us. The positions expressed are not common themes in the current therapeutic discourse, but they stem from a focus of interest which has wielded a powerful influence throughout time — that of morality. Both authors capture the sense of an experience which is beyond the ordinary and which may be the element that man requires for a meaningful existence. Making the spiritual explicit and bringing it into a relationship between treater and treatee is their vision of the answer of what is commonly thought of as pathology. Both writers hesitate to use the traditional terms and have only applied them for the sake of communication. Their sincerity in what they believe and their efforts to incorporate those beliefs into the usual conception of therapy deserves serious attention.

The last two chapters are intelligent discussions of two current treatment systems. The behavior modification chapter is an up-to-date statement of the state of the art and presents the method in its most viable form. The image of behavior modification as stuffing M & M's into people at specific times for certain behaviors is intellectually bankrupt. The sophistication which has evolved in the field since that time is described as an effective intervention for those disposed to benefit from such an approach. The last chapter is by a psychoanalytic therapist speaking of his procedure with a sense of its problems, and the techniques he has found useful. His awareness of the psychoanalytic method comes from intimate experience, rather than a forcing of the therapeutic experience into a reified theoretical jargon.

The occasion which brought us all together and resulted in this book was a Symposium on Schizophrenia presented at the University of Maine. Thanks must be given to Victor Des Marais, who, as Director of the Psychology Department's Community Mental Health Center, had the administrative skill and patience to tie together the thousand strands of an intense experience. The symposium was a "happening" in that the differing views presented here were merged into a sharing of the understandings we each affirmed. The audience composed of students, professionals, public, and patients, joined us in a quest to understand. We all left with the sense that this experience could be shared with others who also are concerned with themselves and their madness.

The contributors represent differing views of madness (some do not even like the word); but what is more important, they each have a commitment to their view which removes it from the abstract and creates a meaningful interchange called therapy. Whether it is effective is another question, but until we know what we do and why, the result can never be adequately evaluated. The contributors have stated what they do and why. Hopefully, this book will assist the reader to define madness and its treatment for himself.

PETER A. MAGARO
Orono, Maine

I

The Experience

CHAPTER 1

The Experience of Schizophrenia

I am classified by the Veteran's Administration as a paranoid schizo-phrenic, which is my chief qualification for writing this article. A friend of mine who is studying psychology told me that in one of Laing's books, he mentions a psychiatric conference held in the late nineteenth century. One of the "attractions" of the conference was a therapist and catatonic patient on the stage of the auditorium. During the presentation, the "therapist" prodded, poked and stuck pins in the catatonic woman to show that she had no "feelings", while all the woman wanted to do was pull at a lock of her hair and be left alone.

In many ways I feel like that woman. I am an exhibit requested to reveal my thoughts, emotions and experiences, however painful they might be. Since I am a poet as well as a schizophrenic, I want to relay to you a poem that I wrote recently, before I had heard the Laing story, that will illustrate something of what I feel. It is called "Danc-ing Bear".

> Here I am
> the dancing bear
> of this schizophrenic circus
> what tricks shall I perform for you?
> shall I gibber and scream?
> take off my fur?
> communicate with cats and birds?
> or cry?
> I've done them all before
>
> No, I'd better not do any of that
> it's bound to embarrass you,
> tell you something you don't want to know
> you'd rather have
> my personal history, family history, case history
> diagnosis, prognosis, cognosis
> the size of my skull, the size of my pill, the size of my cell
> am I paranoid, reactive, undifferentiated?
> can I remember my dreams?
> do I lie still on the couch?

will I come along quietly?
NO, NO, NO,
the answer is NO!!!
God damnit, I am a person
I eat, shit and fly
    just like you do
I read, talk and make love
    just like you do
I feel, fear and shiver
    just like you do
God damnit, I am a person!

This gives you a strong indication that I am a whole being, not just a schizophrenic on display. I hope that it might help you see the patients or clients who consult with you in terms other than that of their "disease" or "problem". This is the main reason I am writing here, to help you see "mental health consumers" who usually approach you as supplicants begging for charms and potions, as your equal as human beings.

The term "mental health consumer" is a rather curious one, which brings to my mind the image of a slavering, fanged beast down on all fours, gnawing at the leg of a psychiatrist. Terminology is extremely important—I have, in the past several months, heard four different mental health professionals refer to people coming under their care as "real nuts", "dodos", "schizos" and "schizies".

Of course, the most damaging term, made popular by Alfred Hitchcock's film of the same name, is "psycho". My wife is still afraid to take a shower when she is home alone because of it and many people impute most violent crimes to "psychos". I hope that most of you, being well read in professional studies, are aware that actually mental patients commit significantly less crime and especially less homicide than does the general population. But, nevertheless, most people, sometimes including you, toss off words like "psycho" as some people toss off the words "queer", "bitch", "nigger", and all the other demeaning slang words. It hurts us just as much, but more damaging than being hurt, repeated often enough it makes some believe we really are the ugly, one-dimensional stereotype that the careless word implies.

One of the first papers I did in graduate school was a study of the effectiveness of the black reform groups SNCC and CORE. Since I was far from their field-of activity and not much had been published about them in 1967, my paper did not come up with any startling revelations, but I did substitute the word Afro-American where ordinarily I would have said Negro. This was just before the word black became the accepted term. Now I am not about to declare "Schizophrenic is Beautiful", though some of my friends claim I am a "schizophrenic chauvinist" but I do want to point out how labels affect thinking.

Let us try a simple experiment with some common psychological phrases that you all know. For the words usually found in the following sentences, I'll substitute the words "human beings". "Approximately 1% of the population are human beings." "Some human beings require 1000 milligrams of Thorazine a day to remain calm." "All human beings will be back on the ward at 9 p.m." "Human beings being treated by Dr. X will be charged $35.00 per 50 minute hour."

That simple substitution of terms makes your thinking about your clients infinitely more complex. I think you must find it much more comfortable and easier to put a "schizophrenic" or "manic depressive" in a psychiatric prison camp or charge them outrageous fees because they are an easily defined, quantifiable "thing" rather than a complex human being like yourself.

I'm going to let you read another poem which tells how I got my label. It is entitled "A. S. A." which is the acronym for the Army Security Agency.

My official
Veteran's Administration Certification
is
Acute Paranoid Schizophrenic
(Chronic)
30% Nervous Disability
(Service Connected)
when I'm out
and 100%
when I'm in

It's worth $77 a month
to me
but I would rather find
the *causus belli* of my sanity
but they won't let me
see my records
the doctor's privilege
extending to the VA clerks
but not to me

I wasn't always crazy, you know
once, I was an all around
American Christian crew cut boy
but that was before

that skinny kid
called the Army recruiter in Salem
said he was a friend
(even though he
was 1-Y)

Tested and inspected
like good grade meat
at the Boston Army Base
I was called aside
by this bald-headed sergeant
who asked
if I would like to take
a special test

He said if I passed
I would be in the
Cream of the Army
and could go to Europe
where my girlfriend was
it would only cost me four years
so I signed
what the hell
I was 1-A
and had been refused admission
to the Graduate School of Public Administration
at the University of Alabama
(I was going to
change the South)

Seven days into reception company
they told us that they had been
watching us
for a long time
something clicked
in my mind
people who had spoken to me for no reason
or had asked me odd questions
so I determined to outwit them
and be Superspy

Two months later
at Valley Forge
Mr. Bazzle sat me down in Occupational Therapy
where I was trying to weave
myself back together
and said, "Merriam, you
ain't no spy, you're sick,
sick, you understand."

I was noticeably confused
the next week
when the Psychiatrist Doctor Captain
called me in
"Son," he said, "I've got a letter here
from your Company Commander Captain
at Fort Dix.
Now, it seems you *were* in A. S. A.
and it seems
you *were* under some observation
or 'being watched'
as you call it,
and son,
he would like to know
if you want them to continue
your background security check."

What could I say?
I was already
Acute Paranoid Schizophrenic
(Chronic)
30% when I'm out
and 100% when I'm in.

The ironic, but I suppose not to be unexpected these days, part of
it is, that my Army records indicate, from the portion of them I got
recently, that I had been undergoing a security check of some kind
from 1 March 1964, or approximately 16 months before I had any
personal notion of enlisting in the Army.

My Army psychiatrist, now practicing outside of Philadelphia,
called my fear of being spied upon and thoughts that I was being
tested, "feelings of alien control". A friend has more recently disagreed and said she thought that I must have had some unconscious
awareness that it was going on and when finally told, rebelled, was
socked with a heavy dosage of drugs which really screwed me up.

Whatever the real truth about my first hospitalization, I am now a
paranoid schizophrenic, at least according to the Veteran's Administration. Three of the four times I've been hospitalized I've been
taken by police. The last time I was sprayed with Chemical Mace
because I was walking along the main street of Lewiston, a nearby
city, naked. Now some of my friends claim I was an early streaker,
but I can assure you back in 1972 it was not a laughing matter.

When I am in a "schizophrenic state" or "high" as the young
people would call it, I see visions, taste, smell, hear and touch things
which apparently are not really there. I've seen visions of incredibly
beautiful women and seen friends turn into monsters. I've tasted

water that was like the worst of poisons and smelled the concentrated incense of thousands of fir trees. I have had the strength to knock an orderly out cold and another time fallen helpless and crying out in anguish.

I've spent about 9 months in the last 7 years in mental hospitals; about half of the total time was spent on locked wards. I now take 100 milligrams of Thorazine nightly in order to sleep, but there have been times in the hospital when I've been given as much as 1600 milligrams a day to counteract my "schizophrenia" and, believe me, that is enough to knock you flat. I've been strapped down, straitjacketed, and sat on to be kept under control, and only then with difficulty.

After reading the last three paragraphs, you probably think I am a strange creature — both dangerous and frightening. What I told you perfectly fits the one-dimensional stereotype of a madman but like all other human beings, I have more than one dimension. I put my pants on one leg at a time, I get overdue notices from the power company and I like Italian sandwiches (with lots of onions) like most of you do.

Besides being a paranoid schizophrenic I am a writer, a husband and lover, a competent historian, a union member, a war tax resister, and a good cook. When I am not "insane" I like to work, to write, to smoke my corncob pipe, to dance and to make French bread. In other words, most of the time I am a normal human being with the same hopes and desires, aches and fears that you have—in most ways I am very like you.

But there are differences and I do not deny them. Somebody told me at a New Year's Eve party that I went to, that it takes a kind of genius to go mad—to disobey the world's regulations and make your own world with laws and behavior all your own. I agree to some extent. I tend to think that schizophrenics have broken some kind of barrier in the brain. Some researchers have said that most people use only 5% of the brain actively, anyway, and I think that the electrical or chemical storms in the brain which produce or are produced by "insanity" may open new channels in the brain which enable or force us to see "visions" and hear "voices".

Though many psychologists, psychiatrists and metaphysicians have tried to determine the root cause of madness, they have not done so. It is, in my opinion, probably a combination of genetic, biochemical and environmental influences and I have learned to distrust anyone who says there is one simple answer.

In my own case, until the past spring, my treatment has been almost entirely within the biochemical realm. In both the Army hospital that I was in and at the Togus Veteran's Administration Center (Maine's only Veteran's Hospital), there was an extremely heavy dependence by the staff on the administering of tranquilizing drugs, almost to the exclusion of any real therapy program. Part of this problem is due to the number of people in the hospital in proportion to staff; partly due to the medically trained psychiatrists who tend to know less, or at least do less, about the psyche and depend on medication for pacification (psychologists were generally kept in a very secondary position); and partly due to laziness of the staff who tended to congregate in the ward office and pay little or no attention to the patients, except at medication times—by far the most observed part of the daily regimen.

I once asked a nurse at Togus who was being paid $10,000 a year, if she would be there helping us if she were not paid and she said, "No, of course not." (In fairness I should point out that some VA patients with service-connected "nervous disabilities" receive compensation when they are hospitalized, though I don't think too many go there for that reason. I certainly don't, though it is ironic that I can earn more inside the hospital than I seem to be able to outside.) We had a saying about the staff at Togus, "Only the patients have the patience to stay here 24 hours a day, the staff can't take it more than 40 hours a week." That is, of course, less than 2 days of the patients' week.

This brings me to a point that I wish to make very strongly. That treatment in most public mental hospitals is at best inadequate and at worst maliciously dreadful. I know that you don't have *the* answer to schizophrenia but you do have some treatment modes to make life somewhat more comfortable. You professionals know best what types of treatments and personnel are available and if you allow the continuance of hellholes· and the quacks that run them then you must shoulder a large part of the blame for the very real pain these institutions cause.

The following poem shows my anger and anguish, but, I think, by and large, true, so I trust you will hear it out. It is called "Murder in the First Degree".

> If any of you have weak stomachs
> or weak minds
> I strongly suggest that you leave the room
> because I am going to accuse you
> of murder
> murder in the first degree

the murder of my brother
Parker, age 18
on Friday, November 13, 1970
alone, at home
he put a 30.06 to his head
and blew the top of it off
he was taking tranquilizers
he saw the local psychiatrist
and was imprisoned
nine months in that
horrible gothic prison
called Bangor State Hospital
he saw a psychologist once
he saw a social worker once
when my parents came to see the
doctors
they couldn't even speak decent English
Christ! Psychiatry and psychology
are built on words and symbols
and you bastards permitted
this State Hospital to be run
by cheap foreign doctors
trained in Europe
before Freud had finished publishing
they couldn't even speak decent English
how were my parents supposed to know
what to do?

You, AMA, APA, MSW members
what have you done in the last ten years
to tell people what these psychiatric prisons
are like?
Have you lobbied in the Maine Legislature?
—No, I know that, I was at the
L. D. 965 hearing and none of you
were there
Have you lobbied in Congress?
No, you don't want a national health care plan
—you make too much money
sucking our blood
My brother lived in a ward with 50 beds
50 beds all alike
50 nightstands all alike
Bile green walls
Barred windows, brick walls
medicated out of his mind
so he and 49 other zombies
could be watched by
one minimum wage orderly
You, Mr. Phd., Michigan State University

You, Mr. Phd., Penn State University
You, Mr. Phd., Private Practice
tell me why 60% of all psychiatrists
are on Manhattan Island
you trained them
you went to school with them
You make $25,000 a year
why is it you let a few quacks
run all the state hospitals
that's where we schizophrenics end up
we can't afford
James Taylor's $36,000 a year
McLean Hospital
We can't afford your private clinics
your university centers
when the police take us
its to
Augusta State
Bangor State
Togus VA
its 1600 milligrams of Thorazine
straps and straitjackets
no door bathroom stalls
line up in the cafeteria
line up for medication
line up for raking leaves

Eight hours strains you,
what in hell do you think 24
does to us?
Social workers average $10,000
Psychologists $25,000
Psychiatrists $50,000
and we can't even collect
unemployment for being in the hospital
You all think Bleuler was right
dementia praecox
does sound primitive
Schizophrenia
is ever so much more scientific
and for that you charge us $35 an hour
and you pay your war taxes,
to help the FBI's and ICBM's
keep us secure
For Christ's sake
do you wonder why
I remember the bit of lead
being dug out of the wall
of the room I grew up in
that I think of the blood

and the shattered skull
the blue police lights
and my father's shattered heart
Do you wonder why I think
of borrowing Ric's
38 Police Special
or the neighbor's Luger
to join my brother?
We schizophrenics are 1%
of the population
we are psychics, shamans, and windigos
we have broken barriers in the brain
we have seen great and terrible visions
we have eaten manna
we cry and scream
we kill no one
please don't murder the rest of us.

I suppose what I have to say after this will be anti-climactic but I will go on to give you a few more glimpses from the inside and a few recommendations that I have for improvement of the system. In many ways I just want to forget what happened to me which I think may be the reason that not too many mental health "consumers" have turned into crusaders.

What would be the effect if twenty-five ex-mental patients took sledge-hammers and crowbars and marched on Bangor State Hospital (one of Maine's two State mental hospitals) and started knocking it down brick by brick? You know and I know that they would immediately be made patients, subdued with drugs and thrown on locked wards. Contrariwise, if twenty-five of you professionals did the same thing, you would be arrested, but soon bailed out and have a nice dramatic court case in which you could eloquently make your point.

What I am saying is though we know intimately the pain of being on the inside we lack the power and what is just as important, the feeling of power which is necessary to make the changes. Most of you have the power of your positions, your salaries, and your connections to protect you. In most cases we do not.

I think you would find that most ex-mental patients earn a very low income on their own, that they do not have positions in the establishment, especially not the mental health establishment, and by and large their self image is so damaged by hospitalization and feelings of inadequacy that they can not risk the hostility and political power that would be brought to bear against them if they insisted on a treatment revolution.

You have a lot less to lose. You have friends and associations to protect you, you don't have to fill in that "Have you ever been hospitalized for mental reasons" blank on job applications, you probably think that most of the time you are competent to do your job, you have access to case files, professional studies, consultants—we have none of those—that is why we have not until now tried to change and probably will have difficulty changing the system which you are paid to run.

Let me propose a minor revolution that you could instigate that would change the lives of a number of schizophrenics. As you probably know, meaningful, well-paid work is one of the essentials to staying out of the hospital. As you may or may not know, many schizophrenics are highly intelligent and sensitive people. There are fifty or more "mental health professionals" in the audience. Why don't you professionals seek out schizophrenics, train them and then give them your own jobs?

I think it could work very well, welfare mothers in Washington, D.C. have made outstanding, empathetic social workers with very little training. All of you must be aware that one of the real successes in the drug crisis has been the use of ex-drug addicts as counselors. Do you not think the same might be true with ex-mental patients? Are any of you willing to try my revolution? You came into the mental health field with some vague idea of helping people. Are you willing to go far enough as to give someone your own means of livelihood?

If there is to be a revolution in mental health care it first must be a revolution in your minds. Now, I don't seriously expect any of you to give me your job or jobs to my ex-mental patient friends; you haven't progressed that far in your thinking. But let me give you ten simple tasks which, if you each carried them out in the next year would go a long way towards a dramatic change for mental health care in Maine.

1. Find a good job for one ex-mental patient.
2. Convince a psychologist or psychiatrist you know to take three patients into therapy free.
3. Spend one week of your vacation as a patient on a locked ward of a mental hospital.
4. Convince your local legislator that expenditures for mental health care should be doubled.
5. Write one letter to the editor or take advantage of free radio and/or television time to counteract the current false stereotype of mental patients.

6. Convince one employer to eliminate any questions on his or her job application about former mental illness.
7. Bring a current mental patient home from the hospital to your home for a weekend.
8. Force one bad mental health professional to resign or mend his or her ways.
9. Talk to one high school class about their chances of facing mental illness and how to cope with it.
10. Write a simple explanation why someone should not commit suicide.

I want to use the last part of the article to tell you about the steps I personally have been taking away from madness. In January 1971, a letter appeared in the *Maine Sunday Telegram* telling about the Pine Tree Schizophrenia Association.

I wrote a letter to the address given and was contacted by one of the members. They arranged a trip for me to New York to see Dr. Allan Cott, a psychiatrist who is one of the leaders of the Mega-vitamin treatment. I was given the HOD (Hoffer—Osmond) test, a verbal test which is supposed to quantify incorrect thinking and which they use to determine how many milligrams of the vitamin, chiefly niacinimide, to give the patient. Usually they give some kind of a urine test and a 6-hour blood sugar test, but since I had scored so low on their scale they didn't bother.

I went home and began taking the vitamins, which didn't do much. In 2 weeks I called Dr. Cott as instructed and he asked me how I was getting along and I said OK so he said, "Double the doses." I did for a couple of days, but then I got to thinking that it seemed kind of ridiculous to be taking fairly massive doses of what was supposedly a biochemical treatment which assignment of chemicals were based on a purely verbal test and no chemical tests.

So I stopped taking the megavitamins and refused to pay the bill for the office visit. Only naturally, I kept getting bills and finally a letter from a lawyer demanding payment, but I never got an inquiry from the doctor how I was doing healthwise. This confirmed some of my suspicions about psychiatrists.

In the Spring of 1972 I ran into an acquaintance in a bookstore in a nearby town. He was a psychiatric social worker at Pineland Hospital (Maine's institution for the retarded) and we got talking about mental illness, treatment, etcetera, and finally discussed the fact that I was taking Thorazine. He said that he had recently read some references to the fact that the long term use of Thorazine could damage the liver. Since I had been taking it steadily for 6 years I got a little concerned. So I wrote a letter to the Togus VA Center asking for several medical journal references about this problem so I could read them for myself.

I got a very patronizing letter back saying essentially, be a good boy, take your medicine and shut up. Naturally that was the wrong thing to tell me, so I stopped taking my Thorazine.

Also during the spring of 1972 I found out about a group of ex-mental patients who were meeting in Portland (Maine's largest city). Of course, I didn't find this through any professional channel but through an ad in an underground newspaper. I started going to the group as time would permit—gradually made some friends and found out that almost everyone had had bad experiences with their therapists and in the hospital, but we mainly spent the meetings just listening to each other's tales of pain.

Of course, the HELP group only met a couple of hours a week, what really dominated my thinking at the time was the Thorazine or rather the lack of it. The first week after I stopped taking it, I slept very little, but gradually I got so I was sleeping fairly normally, though much less than when I had been taking the Thorazine. At the same time I began to go into an enormous surge of creativity. This took the form of writing, mostly letters but also several articles and poems. It would be nothing to crack off a 2000 word letter in a couple of hours, writing just as fast as I could type. I go over some of the stuff from time to time, since I kept carbons of most everything, and it is all quite sensible and good writing; in fact some of the best I've done.

But I felt, though I didn't acknowledge it, that I was getting higher and higher as the residual Thorazine wore away. But, of course, it was a good feeling—a type of manic state. Finally I spent a week in the middle of June as a camp counselor. There were a lot of conflicts during the week and it was rainy and cold, so I got even less sleep than usual and 2 days after I came home on Summer Solstice Sunday I was walking into Lewiston nude.

All the bad things happened. I got sprayed with mace, thrown in a jail cell, interviewed by a psychiatrist and committed, taken to the hospital in a straitjacket and put on a locked ward.

The hospital experience was generally bad with a few very high intervals. One of the most absurd was the whole Eagleton Debacle which occurred while I was on a locked ward—I voted for him and Shirley Chisholm the next fall. I never will forgive McGovern for that.

My mainstay was my wife who, though I kept rejecting her, partly because she had been forced to commit me and partly because I thought I was in love with someone else, kept visiting me and enduring my nastiness and finally when I was released took me home even though I threatened to leave anytime.

Gradually, I calmed down, or the Thorazine did it for me, and began to write and study again. I began to go to the HELP group more regularly and as I got to know the people better we began to give each other more support and advice. Also about this time I began collecting books dealing with madness and psychotherapy and began finding out there was no simple answer to my problems or anyone else's.

One of the books that I picked up, because I have a great interest in Russia, was *A Question of Madness* by Zhores Medvedev. The book deals with his imprisonment in a psychiatric hospital in Russia for political reasons. Though the author has a very patronizing air about the regular patients in the hospital which I found offensive, one thing struck me forcibly. He said in one place that some friends had come to visit him on Saturday but were turned away because it wasn't "visiting day".

The same thing had happened to me at Valley Forge Army Hospital and I immediately began making some comparisons. I tell you this not to claim that I actually was a political prisoner of some sort but to demonstrate how much I wanted to think that, that I wanted to be a rebel rather than someone who is sick. A number of times this has occurred after I have read or seen something that strikes some chord of my experience. I think, subliminally, if I must admit the truth that I hope someday, somebody will walk up to me and say, "Yes, Mr. Merriam, it was a test and you passed successfully, and now you're all right." That, somehow, is easier to accept than the fact that my brain, which I do and have to trust so implicitly, has failed me and misinterpreted signals and misdirected action.

But anyway, I went along faithfully taking my tranqs and reading about psychotherapy including about the death of psychoanalysis and the success of Lithium in treating Manic Depression and hoping that some similar drug cure-all would come along for my schizophrenia.

Then about a year ago, an old college friend came up for a weekend from New Jersey. He is now working as a psychiatric social worker and undergoing psychoanalysis. In fact, he lives in a totally psychoanalytic environment. He lives in the house of his therapist, he has 3 hours of analysis a week, 6 hours of group therapy and 3 hours of Yoga and frequently spends weekends in marathons. This costs him about $5000 per year.

I spent the whole weekend putting him down, putting Freud down and putting biochemical genetics up.

But I started thinking about it. He seemed a changed person, not nearly as tense as he had been the year before, so I thought there was something to it. Naturally, there not being any directory or other good way of finding a therapist, I asked my friends in the HELP group for someone and told them that I was specifically looking for a psychologist and not a psychiatrist. They recommended someone whom a member of the group had had good luck with. So I called him up and made an appointment for job counseling—something I was also very concerned with at the time.

Also about that time a little incident gave me courage. I was at a party talking with a woman and somehow we got around to talking about my illness, and after some hesitation I mentioned the Lewiston incident. She really astonished me by saying, "I'm sure you had a very logical reason for doing that." Later on when we were discussing how much medication I take, she said, "I can see that that must be a real problem; it must cut the top off your creativity and make you function at a much lower level than you are capable of."

This kind of insight which has not occurred to me often seems to come more frequently from nonprofessionals than professionals. Most recently my Yoga teacher, after a discussion of my almost constant thoughts of suicide, said that she had had the same thoughts when she was younger but that she had finally come to the conclusion that she was thinking about doing things to herself that she would never do to anyone else and that really she had the right to be well treated, especially by herself.

Now every time I think of suicide, her simple illustration comes into play like a check valve and I am really able to deal with it for the first time.

I do not mean to imply that the psychological help I am getting currently is not useful, it certainly is. I have an hour of therapy every 2 weeks and my psychologist, after doing some testing, spends the sessions dealing with current problems and doing a history, something the VA has never done to any extent.

He explained that the Lewiston incident was very logical indeed; that I was trying to leave my life totally behind and start out with nothing—it is just that my behavior happened to conflict with society's norms. He is pointing out that the rigid behavior and high achievement expected by my parents was so good that it was actually bad and now we are dealing with the dominating effect of religion in my early life.

I have recently heard some people put down all therapists. I cannot agree with this. I do think there are some who are criminally bad, but that there is a need for some of us to have professional guidance in the self-discovery that we need to deal with life. I must say that now under therapy, I find this discovery, for the first time, exciting rather than frightening.

I do not mean to leave you with the impression that everything is coming up roses in my own life or in that of the other mental patient friends that I have, but I think there is hope. But it is going to take a hell of a lot of work on your part and ours. I have proposed ten simple things earlier on in this article that you could do to raise your consciousness. I am also in favor of the abolishment of insane asylums, lower treatment fees, a professional register with client comments, and a publication for mental patients by ex-mental patients. These are more difficult tasks and we ex-mental patients are organizing to do them ourselves. If you want to help, do so, especially if you are willing to work yourself out of a job, because I hope that will happen.

I am particularly interested in seeing a set-up where ex-mental patients do crisis counseling to keep people out of the hospitals. I think we can do it best, because we have empathy, experience and are not community authority figures. Our very powerlessness will be a big asset. We will be able to do it if we can get a piece of the change that pays you and you do not take the program over. We are human beings and hopefully can help the 1% of human beings who feel the pain and power of schizophrenia.

I would like to close with another new poem. It's entitled "On Cold Mountain":

> Up on Cold Mountain
> the devil has roared by
> searing my soul with his cold fire
> his white angels
> have stabbed me with their
> icy glass daggers
> tied me down with white cloths
> locked me in a white cell
> yet my mind was not imprisoned
> with his pain and poison
> it roamed from Siberia
> to the Enchanted
> listened to whale chants
> and

tasted forbidden wine
You put me on Cold Mountain
You are paid by Cold Mountain
Cold Mountain is your master
Cold Mountain is my prison
you intend to build terraces
and plant soil holding trees
to preserve Cold Mountain
so you can continue
to offer up our bodies
I intend to tunnel under Cold Mountain
and plant charges
to call on wind and river
to wear Cold Mountain away
if my mind still wanders
it is still escaping from Cold Mountain
I pray you understand this
and why I must tear your altar down
and you must give us up
as your sacrifice
and go back to tilling the fields
while we, your prisoners,
carry Cold Mountain away
on our backs

II

The Cultural Context

CHAPTER 2

The Cultural Context of Madness and its Treatment

No matter how complex the situation, there are always explanations which are intuitively correct and make good common sense. They are simple explanations that seem to naturally follow considering our understanding of ourselves and our world. Once the underlying assumptions are clear, most behavior is perfectly understandable, however, being understandable does not mean being correct. Let us look at the conceptualization and treatment of an individual's problem a decade ago and in the present. A 45-year-old married woman whose children have grown and left home begins complaining that life is meaningless, she is not getting enough attention from her husband, and she wants to start a new life. The husband prescribes a healthy dose of paragoric and takes her to the doctor for hormone injections to ease her "time of life". Considering the view of the nature of women a few years ago such a solution makes good common sense. Ten years later in the midst of women's liberation, it would not be good common sense to administer paragoric or estrogen for "women's problems". The conception of the problem would be an oppressed unfulfilled person who has never developed her own individuality or independence. The solution may be to rehabilitate the husband or obtain the woman a satisfying employment opportunity.

Obviously then, common sense is the logical consequence of an accepted set of values and assumptions about the world and its inhabitants that form the conceptual milieu of a culture. From actions which administer to women in pain to deciding whether or not to place someone in an institution, there are reasons which justify actions. These reasons descend from our cultural beliefs in the conditions of the environment and the nature of man. They are based upon a belief system which extends from being relatively accurate and observable to being purely unobservable and generated almost totally upon one's faith. Where resides the concept of mental illness and schizophrenia? Let us back up a little and briefly explore the question of epistomology.

If while building a shed we handle and nail the boards together, we concretely and directly observe the parts that fit together to something more than its parts, the building. One does not need too many assumptions here as one could understand through direct sensory experience the elements that comprise the whole. Probably building a rocket for those putting the parts together takes on the same concrete understanding. Now, those who do not share in the direct sensory experience of fitting the rocket parts together will stand in awe. It is in a sense incomprehensible even though we may know some of the principles that create the propulsion and guidance system. There is much in the physical sciences and a great deal more in the social sciences which are not clearly understood on a factual level, hence, the introduction of the theory to create bridges of understanding. Most of our knowledge of society, in terms of what causes what, is a matter of much theory and little fact. The pressing need to understand ourselves in relation to our society can not wait for facts. Hence, we sometimes do not differentiate between understanding for its own sake and understanding based upon demonstrable principles (Hampton-Turner, 1970).

The culture abounds with understandings accepted as truths but which are nothing more than beliefs assumed to be based upon facts. Most of these truths are only consensually validated explanations which form a history of common sense. This history changes sometimes through the discovery of new facts, but usually through the emergence of explanations which are more compatible to the economic, political, and social milieu. The changing mode of explanation is seen through the constant emergence of dominant theories or theologies which at any one time are accepted as the most accurate explanation of the nature of man. These accepted beliefs define what social conditions are beneficial to man and which are destructive. A belief in the nature of man includes those characteristics which are responsible for his acceptance, success, failure, and rejection in the society. What, therefore, is man? Is he good, evil, an expression of childhood, his society, his genes, physiology or physiognamy, his spirit, soul, greed, altruism, learning, emotions, or a force beyond man such as God? Such explanations of the nature of man are rarely explicit in our devising of social rules but they are the basis we use when constructing social institutions.

Wrightsman (1973) has attempted to measure dominant conceptions of human nature strongly arguing for the study of concepts of human nature as the main enterprise of psychology. "For most of us, human nature is a pervasive and useful concept. We rely upon it

frequently to justify our own behavior and the behavior of others."
(1973, p. 69). Through a brief view of contemporary literature,
social philosophy and psychological theory as well as some specific
work with a philosophy of human nature scale, Wrightsman (1973)
offers six different beliefs about human nature. All people maintain a
concept of human nature, however, individuals differ in the content
of their belief. Some will think of man as trustworthy, strong willed,
rational, selfish, etc., as well as any combination of beliefs while
others may assume the opposite (Wrightsman and Satterfield, 1967).
Also, the beliefs of individuals become much more similar when they
are grouped by various social factors such as geographical residence,
religious preference, occupation, or economic status. In short, there
are specific constellations of beliefs which exist in specific times and
although temporarily influenced by dramatic events (Wrightsman and
Noble, 1965), they are mainly stable over time (Baxter, 1968).

We would expect that the more deviant the individual behavior,
the greater would be the necessity to apply concepts of human
nature. If you observed someone going to the store for a quart of
milk, you would not usually explain the behavior by degree of rationality, strength of will, or man's need for order. A simple hypothesis that he is bringing milk home to feed the cat would suffice.
However, if while obtaining the milk, he also robbed the store, one
would more likely explain that behavior by a concept of human
nature rather than applying the explanation that he wanted the
money to buy the cat in order to feed it milk. If the robber also
spoke of the Devil making him rob to obtain the money to feed the
cat who was a spirit from another world, the human nature concepts
dealing with rationality, strength of will, trustworthiness, etc. would
seem even more applicable. That is, as the behavior becomes more
deviant, the more concepts are called upon to provide explanatory
closure of the situation. What we don't know, we will understand
and a concept of human nature provides a manner to form this
understanding. He robbed the store because man is basically untrust-
worthy, selfish, and has a lack of will power. He spoke of the Devil
because he was irrational and could not control himself. The belief in
human nature which stresses rationality and will power easily infers
that deviant behavior is a result of a lack of these traits. If human
nature in the natural normal state is rational and possessing will
power, the deviant or derranged is the abnormal state exhibiting the
inverse of these qualities. If our concept of human nature was of the
irrational with little control over needs, the mad robber would be
seen as sane. Incidentally, Foucault (1967) places this change in the

belief of human nature when the irrational was replaced by the rational to the Age of Reason during the seventeenth and eighteenth centuries. Prior to this time, a belief in man as irrational and impelled by forces beyond his control was acceptable and not reserved solely for the deviant.

A belief in human nature is not applied equally to all members of a society. Groups in power usually assign their adversary as being of a different human nature than themselves. For instance, the Japanese of WWII were of a different species than Americans. Their nature changed, however, after the war when we became partners in industrial progress halting the "Red Menace". Blacks were considered to have a nature resembling beasts of burden which drastically changed after the integration struggle. However, the differentiation in assignment of human nature which most concerns our discussion of the concept of madness is the belief in human nature of the social classes. Treatment was and is different for the lower and middle classes. One of the reasons for the differential treatment methods is the differential concepts of human nature of the two social classes. The middle class is traditionally more powerful and in control of the events that effect them. The lower class (which in this discussion mainly refers to blue collar workers and low income groups) may be seen as an adversary group which does not share the same values, goals, genes, etc. That the lower class has received different treatments for madness than the middle class has been clearly documented (Hollingshead and Redlich, 1958). Also, different treatment methods have been applied because they were thought to be more appropriate to the characteristics of lower class individuals (Riessman, Cohen, and Pearl, 1964; Goldstein, 1971). We will attempt to show that the cultural concept of social class differences is based upon ideas of the different human nature of the social classes.

As often stated in recent years (Szasz, 1961; Braginsky and Braginsky, 1974), mental illness has no objective truth demonstrated by scientific fact or predictable laws. There is behavior that is different than usual, but that is all. How the culture conceptualizes it, explains it, makes it understandable will determine how we treat it. How we understand madness and its consequent treatment method, therefore, will be mainly determined by how we understand man. To demonstrate the force of the belief in the nature of man upon the formation of social institutions and explanations of insanity, let us use the vantage point of a historical perspective to recall a small slice of our treatment past within the context of the cultural conceptions of man dominant at the time. We will briefly review a period of time which revived an interest in the mad and the manner of restoring him to society. We will attempt to assess the ideas of that time which influenced the manner in which this revival occurred.

A Brief History

The age to be recalled has been called the Age of Individual Worth or the Age of Revolution as it is bracketed by the French Revolutions of 1789 and 1848. The French Revolution of 1789 has traditionally been viewed as a dividing line in history, an event which marked an end to the old political, social, legal, and judicial institutions and brought forth a new era characterized by an emphasis upon individual rights, representative government, and nationalism (Breunig, 1970). The philosophies had been born during the eighteenth century but it was not until this time that they became a reality. For the first time, representative governments were formed which significantly shifted political control to the middle class. Along with the shift in power, a new social conscience was being expressed. Those having political force began to create new institutions which would benefit the have-nots of political power. In other terms, the needs of the populace became the topic of concern rather than the means of control. There was also a dissatisfaction with materialism that led to the promotion of an idealism which projected a romantic vision of a State benefiting the greatest number of people without qualification to their productive worth. Although heard for centuries, the terms liberty, equality and justice now became a social movement represented by political parties (Gottschalk and Sach, 1973). Within the framework of such interests, the State was being seen as a provider and guaranteer of basic rights including the right to survive.

There were many social factors which laid the groundwork for the first of the French Revolutions. A major factor was that of economics. Prerevolutionary France was steadily increasing its wealth with a rising industrial production and an increased volume of foreign trade. The problems stemmed from the distribution of wealth. For while the nobility, clergy, and merchants prospered, the peasants and workers were beset by increasing poverty and rampant inflation. The peasants were destitute and had serious grievances against their landlords, the nobility, who cultivated most of the common lands. The workers received some wage increases but inflation lowered their purchasing power at a time when basic commodity shortages were threatening. Rioting had broken out in several cities to protest higher taxes and the price of bread (Breunig, 1970). Another factor that led to the unrest was that although the State economy was rising, the monarchy was broke. It had incurred heavy debts from previous wars but it also was guilty of mismanaging funds. Because of this mismanaging funds, further taxes to retire the outstanding debts were very unpopular, particularly with the middle class. Another cultural element adding to the press for change was the intellectuals who were opposed to the established regime and all its institutions (Brinton, 1957). Philosophically, the spirit of Rousseau was extremely active and the idea that an orderly society could occur without a monarchy was becoming acceptable. The middle class understood the writings of the philosophies but mainly in terms of their own needs for more power and less governmental restrictions upon their activity. The nobles also looked to a change in their situation which was perceived as not sharing in the wealth of a nation which seemed precarious due to the intrigue in the court of Louis XVI and Marie Antoinette.

The National Assembly was called in 1789 by Louis XVI to institute the new taxes needed to relieve the national debt. The monarch and indeed few of the nobles seemed to comprehend the degree of frustration present in Paris and in all of France. The wealthy middle class felt discriminated against, especially being excluded from certain government positions. The peasants who formed 80% of the population (Brinton, 1957) appeared loyal to the monarch mainly through their allegiance to the church but their extreme poverty and their grievances against the nobility created serious discontent. The major concrete force in the revolution was the Paris working men. They were near enough physically to the locale of the Assembly and discontented enough to become a forceful mob when events or rumors of events filtered out of the meetings. Thus, the working man, the peasant, and the middle class were fused into a revolutionary temper not only by economic factors but also by political-social interests which were flamed by the idea that the assembly was a plot by the aristocracy to gain greater benefits from the State at everyone else's expense. It would not be unfair to believe that all social classes were opposed to the current regime and had hopes that the Assembly was a means to further their own interests. When the king tried to forcefully intervene in the Assembly, the workers' anger towards the nobility and the price of food led them to storm the Bastille. The rioting artisans, small tradesmen, and wage earners were encouraged by the more prosperous business men and industrialists who shared the common disdain of the conspicuous consumption of the nobility. Within a month, the widespread rioting begun at the Bastille produced a France no longer controlled by the aristocracy but governed by the National Assembly.

The Assembly produced a Constitution presenting the principles of equality, liberty, and fraternity as the natural rights of all citizens. Property rights were also affirmed, indeed, much of the feeling behind the revolution was aimed at protecting property and reflected the power of the merchant class in the revolution and the consequent constitutional assembly. Birth no longer had privileges but property did and in this sense the revolution was a revolution of the middle class over the feeble aristocracy, possibly even more so than over the monarchy. The Declaration of the Rights of Men was reminiscent of Rousseau and the American Bill of Rights, but they were thought of and understood as the rights of the propertied man over both the working man and the landed gentry. The perception of Marx that the revolution of 1789 was a bourgeois revolution producing a bourgeois ruling class was not an understatement since property was held sacred and political power was invested in the propertied class (Breunig, 1970). The Constitutional monarchy created by the National Assembly (1789–92) demonstrated middle class power also in the designation of the franchise. Although claiming that all men were created equal, they instituted a system where only those who paid a certain amount of taxes, only two-thirds of the French males, were allowed to vote. This was even more restrictive than it seems since voters could only vote for electors. The electors then voted for the representatives to the Assembly. Since the electors had to own property, it was the propertied class who filled the Assembly. This restriction on voting privileges clearly split the working and middle classes producing the first bitterness that would later grow into a war between the classes.

The Assembly created a new administrative structuring of districts which decentralized the governing units. This decentralization had raised the working classes' hopes that they would be involved in local decisions. The absence of a voice in local decisions was probably more aggravating to the workers than the lack of the vote in national elections. Whereas previously the lower and middle classes were aligned against the nobility, the new equality and fraternity produced an alliance between merchant and noble that dominated the worker. Yet, there were benefits aside from voting privileges. Economic policies such as price and wage controls were established which benefited the poor and created a new sense of belonging to the new

State. However, with all the social and economic benefits, new rioting broke out.

In 1791, the new Assembly was called as planned by the Constitution of 1789. The monarchy was suspended and France was declared a Republic. The new Assembly, far from punishing rioters, condoned the mob executions of loyalists to the king and there began the period known as the Reign of Terror. During the Terror, those who did not agree with the new government were liquidated. The enemy was not from one particular class suggesting that equality was taken seriously. Almost 85% of those sentenced to death during the Reign of Terror were peasants and workers. 2639 were sentenced in Paris alone while total estimates run as high as 20,000 (Greer, 1935). During this time there was the Conspiracy of Equals which attempted to overthrow the State in order to form a socialist State abolishing private property, but the time was not yet ripe for instituting the equality which was being proclaimed. However, even with the confusion at home under Robespierre, nationalism was rediscovered in the form of a pride in the Republic that increased military effectiveness. The success of the citizen army against larger professional armies was seen as an individual effort arising from each man fighting for a personal cause. The Reign of Terror ended in 1794, and in 1795 the Assembly voted to have five Directors govern France (Wells, 1920). This regime lasted for 5 years and during their tenure all that was produced was much confusion, profiteering and disillusionment. The time was ripe for a change, one that would produce a stability in a country that had been in constant upheaval for 10 years.

The Napoleonic era began with a strong leader and a needed sense of order. Napoleon created a stable State seemingly destined to carry the ideas of the Revolution throughout Europe. He created a functioning administrative system, an enumerated system of jurisprudence, a stabilization of finances, and the epitomization of a national patriotic spirit. He also censored speech and political activity, but his reign was symbolic of national leadership being determined by ability rather than birth. Brunn (1965) considers the whole appeal of Napoleon as an intense aspiration for order, however, Napoleon also inspired the idea of the philosopher prince who embodied the principles of the enlightenment imposed upon a nation with a strong hand. The strong rational leader wished for by Voltaire and Kant was being found and approved of by the masses. Bonaparte, therefore, did not subvert a revolution as much as extend it into the continuity of the previous century. His rescuing France from social strife and foreign threats did no damage to the hero image but the main appeal was providing a sense of reasoned organization pursuing an orderly life (Bernard, 1973). Napoleon seemed to justify the Revolution as evidenced by the acceptance of the Napoleonic code throughout Europe inspiring Goethe to consider Napoleon as the expression of all that was reasonable and legitimate in the revolutionary movement. The pressure against Napoleon was the cooperative effort of the rest of the European nations led by monarchies to contain Napoleon's imperialism. Waterloo was their victory and led to the imposition of a new monarchy upon France.

In the period after Napoleon, 1814–30, the Bourbons were restored to the crown. The days of an absolute control by a monarchy were over in France even though Louis XVIII attempted to restore such a State and considered the constitution his "gift" to the nation. Because he began his reign with the support of the rest of Europe, he maintained more power than would have been given to a popular sovereignty. Louis formed a conservative tyranical government which supported the nobility and opposed the gains from the revolution including the power obtained by the middle and upper classes. Radical movements were known but were basically unsupported probably because radicals were severely repressed (Breunig, 1970). Charles X succeeded Louis XVIII in 1824 and attempted to restore the absolute monarchy. He immediately dissolved the Assembly, established an electoral assembly which deprived the wealthy bourgeois of the vote, and censored the press. Another revolution occurred and Louis Philippe became the next constitutional monarch (1830–48). After this revolution, the principals of the initial Revolution were the minimal that were acceptable to the new government. The new constitution represented the final triumph of the bourgeois over the nobility but the working class was still excluded since suffrage again was extended to only a few property owners (Breunig, 1970). The new monarch himself incorporated the values of the propertied class and proposed policies favoring manufacturers and tradesmen leading to his full acceptance by the Bourgeois. Lesser artisans and working men suffered another disillusionment. Within the context of equality, the working class identified a new enemy, the middle class, who controlled and benefitted from the new economic policies. The new aristocracy controlled the growing industrial system which abused the poor while the State did not offer any protective regulations. It should be remembered that industrialization did not occur as rapidly in France as in England hence when the population drastically increased in the first half of the century, from 29 million in 1815 to 36 million in 1851 (Cobban, 1965), the migration was to the city where living conditions were not much better than the farm. The radicals and socialists who made up the minority opposition party in the assembly urged a further extension of the electoral base, but they were defeated. Class wars did emerge in the beginning of this reign but they were bloodily repressed.

Almost 20 years later, the urban and rural working classes were again experiencing severe problems. As in the initial revolution of 1789, a poor harvest, increasing inflation, and large unemployment led to a hunger riot. The urban working class wanted a change and were to risk the turmoil and personal suffering that change so often meant. They were convinced they were entitled to greater benefits as part of their natural rights as citizens. By 1848, there was enough momentum by the working classes to take to the barricades creating the situation which forced Louis Philippe to abdicate. The new assembly was the battleground between the radicals who were supported by the Paris working class advocating social reform, and the moderates who were supported by the majority of the French (Breunig, 1970). One of the first projects of the new assembly was the establishment of Public Work Projects to ease the unemployment problem. This project amounted to hiring 120,000 workers. Since there were not enough jobs for such a large number, they were paid a dole to end unemployment. Next, universal suffrage for males was granted. The new elections, with nine million people eligible to vote, elected a conservative assembly, finally demonstrating the conservation of rural France as contrasted with the urban French advocating radical politics in the Assembly. The new assembly abolished the works program and again the workers went to war. This time they were severely beaten by a coalition of the nobility, peasantry, and middle classes. The class lines were rigidly drawn and the fighting was the bloodiest street fighting of the nineteenth century with estimates of 100,000 dead and injured besides those imprisoned and deported to Algeria (Breunig, 1970). The moderate middle class won and order was established. The lower, working class was completely defeated, class lines were irreversibly drawn, and the group most eager for significant political change was removed from the political arena. Marx described the 1848 Republic as the bourgeoisie finally becoming visible in demonstrating their rule over the working class, and in the process beginning the formation of a class consciousness which continues to the present.

These last revolutionary jerks brought France back to the early Republic of 1792 taking nearly 50 years to finalize the first urge toward a new social order now embodied in the constitution of the second Republic. The previous period never really accepted poverty as a social problem except as it interfered with the functioning of the State. After the Revolution, the humanitarian tradition of the Enlightenment combined with the Rousseausian influence centered upon the amelioration of poverty as the central object of social thought (Cobban, 1965). The goodness of the people was part of the romantic doctrine and the people were defined as the urban poor. Moreover, the Revolutions of 1848 were not now only limited to France. The dominant ideas of the Revolution were so entrenched in European culture that there was an epidemic of revolutions throughout Europe at this time (Black, 1967). In the first 4 months of 1848, revolutions occurred in Palermo, Austria, Prussia and lesser German and Italian States. They were called the Revolutions of the Intellectual showing the transmission of common ideals and principles across languages. The march of a new obtainable set of goals for man and society was unleashed. Universal suffrage became the passion for radicals and liberals throughout Europe. The working class was seen as needing protection from the State which would be accomplished through new institutions.

The values held by the middle class were also accepted by all and were part of the new social order. The idea of a social conscience can almost capture this new spirit as the responsibility of the State for all members of the society came to be an accepted value. This responsibility was to be extended to all those not sharing in the wealth of the society. However, although the State was to accept responsibility, the individual was not to create chaos. Undoubtedly the severe measures of the middle class to contain the working class stemmed not only from selfish economic interests but also a need to maintain a clear social order (Durant and Durant, 1967). The conviction was still present that the continuity of political and social institutions was to have precedence over the individual. The need for order at this time was probably greater than a need for liberty and the peasantry which had the most to lose under a strong monarchy was the strongest advocate of an orderly society. During the elections of '48, they sent a monarchist to the assembly and later overwhelmingly elected the younger Napoleon because of the resemblance in name to the epitome of a strong leader. The majority urged a liberty for all, but this liberty was contained within a stronger sense of moral responsibility and order.

A revolution was also occurring in England, but one that was more enduring and beneficial to the lower classes than the French Revolution with all its glamour. Osborne (1970) called it "The Silent

Revolution", an apt description of the social changes during the expansion of the Industrial Revolution. Throughout the beginning of the first half of the nineteenth century societal changes were made, not by changing governments but by new legislation. Hartwell (1967) reports that there was a greater distribution of income in 1850 than 1800. The *per capita* income increased and the average real income doubled during this period. Prices seemed to decline while wages held constant, suggesting a tight labor pool and an increase in the standard of living. Also, contributions to poor relief funds seemed to have decreased while receipt to the working poor increased, reflecting greater care for fewer poor. Quality and type of food increased with meat a common meal for the working family for possibly the first time in history. Real wages dramatically increased from 1800 to 1850 (Deane and Cole, 1962), creating an optimism in the benefits of the system. New industries such as steel and construction produced high paying jobs, although the agricultural workers often watched their children starve. The very poor were further depressed in 1815 when the Corn Law increased the price of grain to the benefit of large landowners and merchants. Within that milieu of contrasts the industrialized worker, while wanting more, could see they also had more, especially if they were not domestics or agricultural workers.

As with France, the population increase in England was immense, doubling between 1780 and 1840. Cities grew drastically with 25% of the population living in cities by 1831. Lancashire for instance, increased 98% in population (Osborne, 1970). This population explosion was a cause for concern so the poor were urged to refrain from early marriages and to emulate the sacrificing middle class by delaying the production of children. The rural poor shifted into the cities which demanded large pools of labor whose lives revolved around the factory. Laws were established to facilitate industrial production such as the breaking of old family patterns that might inhibit the worker from performing in a consistent machine-like fashion. Such legislation subjected the worker to economic factors beyond his control and created a dependence upon the industry or the State (Osborne, 1970). The suffering of the transplanted worker, however, was at least matched by the opportunities for advancement. Never before in history were there so many chances for humble men to advance themselves through industry (Osborne, 1970). The Horatio Alger story was born here and much of the new middle-class power originated in such men within one generation. Every man was considered able to change his status and supporting those who did not was seen as a burden. Perhaps because of this, relief to the poor was increasingly being resented, culminating in 1834 with the abolishment of the Poor Law in favor of work house relief. The economic policy of *laissez-faire* and social creeds of individualism were built upon the idea that man would progress with unbridled rights disciplined by moral values.

As in France, the manner in which income was distributed was still questioned. The suspicion existed that the capitalistic system caused suffering for those who had no control over their destiny. Many writers argued for a better wage for labor and less servitude to the wealthy. Socialism was first introduced as a term in 1825. One rare man, Robert Owen, ran a successful cotton factory by sharing the benefits with labor. The unions finally formed during this period, albeit without employer approval, and succeeded in producing modest improvements in wages and working conditions but only for a special class of skilled workers. Unskilled or easily trained workers continued to work at a subsistence level (Osborne, 1970). The construction workers and artisans who had middle class goals achieved worker solidarity through benefit clubs, savings banks, and eventually trade unions (Osborne, 1970). With all these efforts, however, it is not really clear how much poverty and unemployment was decreased during this time.

Liberals and radicals did urge greater reform but the power of these groups was minimal and had little influence. The majority of workers had a faith in government reform which was not unrealistic. The belief that the State was responsible for its people had enough periods of ascendancy to create a sense of involvement with the present industrial State. Utilitarianism was born as a middle class movement to provide government leadership in alleviating problems of the poor. The passage of the Reform Bill of 1832 displaced many rural officials with representatives for the more populous urban population. This more representative franchise gave a voice to urban legislation and in this manner was considered to be the most important piece of legislation since 1688 (Osborne, 1970). As in France, it was the rioting working class who were responsible for the passage of the bill, even though workers were still denied representation in the House. The Chartist movement (those who wanted civil rights expanded) began and while its leaders were mainly middle class radicals, they did have the support of the workers. Yet as workers became a political force, class antagonism did not develop as it did in France, probably because living conditions were much better due to the wealth of English trade during this period. In any case, there was no

movement toward a French type revolution. Violence did erupt
sporadically but riots seemed to be a condition of Industrial life since
the late 1700s. The Gordon Riots of 1780 sacked London for a
week while the Birmingham Riots of 1791 punished everyone including their supporters before it was brutally stopped. Riots never
threatened the *status quo*. The only noticeable result was either imprisonment or death for the protesters, depending on the seriousness
of the riot. The consciousness of the working man as belonging to a
specific interest group was fragile and they were beginning to channel
their grievances into political demands. It is not surprising that the
working class and the poor were not in the mood for violent revolution. It was the middle class radical and poet who most often presented the tragedy of the working class. Wordsworth wrote of the
danger of commercial ties replacing personal ties between men, and
Coleridge warned of systems of thought such as the popular econo-
mists who looked at men as things. However, these obtuse concerns
were of little interest to labor.

The formation of clear political parties in the nineteenth century
and the dominance of the legislature over the monarchy supported a
belief in the English political system as a system which could be
responsive to the needs of people. The Reform Bill clearly established a two-party system which proposed legislation as part of the
party platforms. Also, the federal administration became more efficient at this time, with specific bureaucracies being formed to meet
social problems with some corrective legislation. Examples of legislation passed by the new political system were the restriction of the
power of poor-law authorities to break up families and exploit
pauper children, the extension of the jury system, the correction of
abuses in educational and charitable endeavors and child labor legislation. The desire to help animals and children through law would soon
apply to all less fortunate including the criminal and the mad. The
courts and prisons were reformed in the sense of being less punitive
and more efficient. The idea that all unfortunates were to be cared
for led to the formation of the Society for the Prevention of Cruelty
to Animals in 1824. The rationale for the Society was that preventing cruelty to animals would lessen brutality in human beings
(Osborne, 1970). Those involved in increasing humane concern toward animals were also involved in passing social legislation increasing the humane concern for workers.

The middle class was horrified by the abuses industry was heaping
upon their employees especially child labor practices. Child labor had
always been common on the farm and probably more punishing, but

in the city with 500 placed in one building, they created a pitiful sight. Their conspicuousness led to many laws culminating in 1833 with an effective factory law which restricted use of children and established a means of policing industrial practices. The law also required the State to educate working class children, another illustration of middle class concern for the plight of the poor. Probably the goals of education best mirrored the dominant values of the time. The lower grades were to implant a sense of morality and religion in working class children, not with the emphasis on faith and spirituality but on the Puritan ethic stressing self-control and obedience. The higher grades had these same goals plus an expanded but divided curriculum. The upper classes were given courses dealing with culture and the lower classes were trained in work skills. Possibly this condescending attitude toward the lower classes is best summarized by the name of a philanthropic organization of 1813, "The London Orphan Asylum for the Reception and Education of Destitute Orphans, Particularly Those Descended from Respectable Parents." Besides education and occupation, there were sharp distinctions drawn between the classes in terms of speech, clothes, and interests. The classes became separate in residential location, so that manners, speech, and general overall life style were class related. The lower class developed their own language similar to the present colloquialisms which were dissimilar and considered inferior to middle class speech. The worker remained docile and obedient probably because his needs and pleasures, while not as grandly met as those of the middle class, were sufficiently met so that they did not feel totally deprived. The really destitute were not plentiful or powerful enough to demand consideration of the possibility that poverty was beyond the individual's control.

The actual basis of the welfare State was laid in this period as was the rationale for nationalization of industry. Political ideology at this time not only admitted the existence of problems in society, but clearly addressed them in the confidence that a solution was inevitable. The factory, railroad, and mines Acts of this time all acted to place industry under some form of governmental control which would provide for public good rather than private interest. Public health policies provided regulations to protect wives and servants as well as controlling prostitution and lodging houses (Osborne, 1970). The small powerless groups were also protected. Slaves were freed in 1833, tithes were commuted in 1836, chimney sweeps were protected in 1840, primary schools were given government funding in 1833. Consistently, private interests in businesses were being subordinated to the interest of individuals by the State. The theory of unbridled *laissez-faire* economics was losing its appeal. The need to use the power of the State to alleviate social problems was gaining in popularity. Regulation was not seen as bad but beneficial to those needing aid. Societal changes were being made based on a new concept: man's responsibility to man, more commonly known as humanitarianism.

Through this brief glimpse of the revolutionary events that comprised this half century of history, certain ideas became rallying cries either in the form of political parties or in artistic movements. During the Restoration (1814—1830), the opposition party to the royalists and the monarchy were the liberals. Liberalism was born during this period as a belief in the freedoms of the Declaration of the Rights of Man as well as the freedom of an economic system of *laissez-faire*. Popular sovereignty was another goal of the liberals although the term had a severely limited meaning, as did the ideal of equality before the law which was also a widely shared desire. Liberalism was a constant force during this period. It advocated the ideals of the Revolution but usually in an alignment with the material goals of the propertied class. The common urge of all liberals seemed to be the construction of free institutions where various freedoms would be realized (Collins, 1967). The liberal favored Rousseau's conception of civil liberty in that the individual does not have natural rights but civil rights recognized by a society. In this sense, liberals were opposed to the democrats who they considered as advocating the rule of the tyrannical mob (Collins, 1967). The liberals had a strong belief in the intellectual approach of cultured individuals who were not romantics but believed in the efficiency of the State. Possibly the revolutions of 1848 were crucial for the development of liberalism as it provided a middle ground between revolution and dictatorships but even at such a propitious time, the liberals were not able to provide effective leadership or meet the pressing social needs of the time (Namier, 1967).

Nationalism was another ism which fed into the total cultural context of this period. People had the vote, hence they became invested in their own unique fatherland. Growth and defense of a nation, therefore, depended upon one's degree of control of its destiny. As with the liberals, nationalists were opposed to authoritarian systems which deprived the individual of the vote. The common opposition to the *status quo* was to return individuality to each citizen. The liberal saw this as the natural outgrowth of the principles of the Revolution and the nationalist saw it as the final protection and expansion of the State.

Romanticism was possibly the most important element of this period. Recognizing the drifting elements of the political convolutions in France, a growing belief in the emotions and a justification of action by feeling became very important. Reality lies in the soul, not in the understanding of the intellect, therefore, a just act is not only a correct understanding but a feeling of correctness. Such determinants of action allow courageous and impulsive actions such as the barricades which would never be accepted as a rational means of fighting an army. The romantic artist believed in expressing his instincts and passions. The painting was the artist's conception of his personal universe rather than a formal representation of an existing order. A painting would stimulate emotionally as would a novel, a poem, or a concert. The concept of the artist, as needing to oppose conventions in order to create, was born of this period. Art was a subjectivism creating ideal worlds that were intuitively better than the reality of the present. Writing was not to generalize about principles of behavior common to all men but to emphasize the uniqueness of each man. The Middle Ages were idealized as a time of virtue having an alliance of man and nature. Romantics became interested in medieval poetry and the virtues of simple people who were noble and wild. The Gothic tale of terror was also popular with its presentation of the mysterious and unexplainable. Heroes were an essential part of the literature demonstrating and underlying faith that man was good and environment created evil. Correcting the detrimental environmental influences were seen as the means to create the ideal society. Allowing evils to exist by not controlling society would be irresponsible. A moral sensibility was, therefore, formed in sympathy for the unfortunate who was a victim of society (Ball, 1959). Man's best era was a time of faith and idealized romance, not as a prisoner of reason. Imagination was revered as a greater guide to truth than reason. The philosophy of Schopenhauer, although recognizing the ability or natural science to understand external phenomena in the world, considered intuition the key to grasping reality. The Romantics agreed with this presentation of intuition and expressed the point in their writings. The world was seen as being too mechanistic and limited when viewed by a rational skepticism, hence, the encounter with the unknown or mysterious had to occur in order for man to survive as a whole being. The French Revolution of 1789 was celebrated as a return to the needs of men formerly suppressed by a too highly organized and repressive society, but the ensuing Reign of Terror dashed this vision, and the Romantic poet became more conservative, feeling that stronger State control was essential if man was to fulfill his destiny and create the ideal society. Man's goodness only could be expressed through a benign control by the State that maintained a social conscience before financial interest. The Romantic movement believed in the rights of man, meeting the needs of the poor, and building a humanitarian society which considered the needs of the individual as paramount. No institution should be allowed to conquer the uniqueness and emotionality of men. As such, Romanticism was a feeling that urged man to attempt to achieve more for himself and to wax eloquently about freedom and the dangers of confinement by institutions. His individual feelings about his own condition could be more true than the social status where he was relegated. By accentuating the emotionality of the individual, his worth was increased beyond his accomplishments and the concern for another became of greater importance than the concern for the institutions that maintained the society.

The Romantic ideal behind the social conscience legislation can best be seen by briefly recalling the outstanding literature of the time. However, before doing so it should best be remembered that the Romantic poets were not the popular writers of the time. The average middle class individual expressed the urge to aid the unfortunate but this romantic vision was more a reflection of a sentimental morality. The middle class judged art on the basis of a moral imperative. Concern for the worker was part of the literature of the time, but the popular books were little nonsense stories told as scenes from the beach or on the road. The prevailing taste was vulgar, and art became familiar and unimaginative, a material object for acquisition by the middle class. The popularity of the Horatio Alger stories and Self-Help Manuals on how to be a good middle class male or female as well as the romantic medieval adventure stories of Scott stated the level of the average person's interest. History was treated in the same pulp fashion and group singing had the reputation of good music. Byron was a severe critic of the mediocre tastes of the middle class who judged the quality of a book by how expensive was its binding rather than the writing therein. He was viewed as an eccentric and consequently was read because of his reputation as an immoral adventurer rather than for the beauty of his poetry. The value of art, literature, music and education was judged by the prevailing morality tempered by pragmatic business practices. Even with this dominant coarseness of taste, some of the greatest literature in Western civilization was written during this time. Political idealism, the supernatural, nature, or the pastoral unity of the past would be the themes of the Romantics (Barnes, 1965). The Romantic emphasized the individual driven by emotions and desires. The visions of Blake in *Songs of Experience* and *Songs of Innocence*, published in 1794 and 1789 respectively, expressed mystical contact with the supernatural equating life with energy. He believed he received truth in a mystical intuitive manner beyond the grasp of reason and those who could not accept his visions were fools. Wordsworth and Coleridge published *Lyrical Ballads* in 1798 in which they attempted to express the universal passions of humanity in common language (Ball, 1959). Wordsworth presented nature with a mystical belief in the message to free men from stupidity. He saw himself as a dedicated spirit wherein his poetry presented the idea that literature can not be judged by absolute forms and structures. Art was an expression and could only be judged by intuition. If direct intuition was the foundation for expression, then only another intuition could judge it. Eventually an idealistic philosophy could be developed to provide contact with eternal truths. The artist created a gold-like expression issuing out of his moral intuition (Ball, 1959). Byron was the personification of the age. He was the proud and noble spirit who tested all the pleasures and glories of life but found them empty and so contemptuously withdrew from society. An outlaw self-stationed on a sphere above the world, he appeared disreputable in the eyes of the respectable. His dishonor was a sign of true glory and "true honor creating a champion of liberty above all social judgement" (Ball, 1959).

Shelley was a contemporary of Byron and possibly lived more as an outcast than the popular conception of Byron. He was the complete anathema of culture; deserter, adulterer, atheist, etc., and consequently made enemies of the whole society while maintaining the conviction that he was right. There was an absoluteness in his assurance of his work which was a vision of love controlling all things. Human nature was capable of perfection and only needed freedom to follow the noble impulse. Shelley opposed all social systems fearing the poetic imagination would be trampled into a lack of understanding of ultimate truths by any reasoning authority. Keats expressed the same love of the imagination providing images which seemed to reveal a truth not revealed by logical systems. However, Shelley and Keats were mainly an unacknowledged minority in their time. Scott was more popular with his realistic tales of history written in romantic prose. His adventurous tales had a strange and colorful pageantry that provided escapism but also a sense of the present as an outgrowth of history. Scott wrote to entertain creating a great deal of action and lively personalities which had the effect of rehabilitating the novel and impressing upon the society simple ideas of romantic

belief related to an optimistic belief in human nature and firm per-
suasions (Ball, 1969). Scott was a good Tory who accepted the order
of things, admired the aristocratic tradition, and the power of wealth
and place. He more than any other writer gave the public what it
wanted, blending romanticism with social morality. Dickens wrote of
the period emphasizing more the struggles of the lower class in the
drama of life with fathers and employers. He was one of the few
English writers who treated social criticism in the novel in a manner
which brought the humanness and reality of the working class life
into political consciousness inspiring further reform movements.

There was a comparable Romantic literary movement in France.
Chateaubriand was very popular writing novels which were the
French version of Scott. He was an ardent Christian who told of love
and passion in exotic settings. Lamartine was similar to Wordsworth
with the lyrical treatment of nature. Hugo was a monumental figure
who was the great voice of French romanticism, urging a return to
nature and greater freedom of form and language (Barnes, 1965).
Hugo seemed to encompass the interests and concerns of the time
bringing the fight for Romanticism in art to the face of controversy.
Balzac, with his prolific amount of literary and insightful writings
described the insensibilities of the middle class similar to Jane
Austen's treatment of the middle class in England. He also described
other social classes showing the discrepancy in material conditions
between classes but the similarity in avarice and baseness (Barnes,
1965). Lamennais wrote passionately of the suffering of the new
Messiah who were the people (Cobban, 1965). Saint-Simon, Fourier,
and Proridhon among others were all a new breed of social theorists
all influenced by Rousseau and concerned with the spiritual, psychological, and material life of the poor. With each social philosophy,
there were also attempts at communes and Utopian societies reflecting the seriousness of the intent and the spread of the social change
movement.

To summarize the age, we would first emphasize the quest for
humanism in the concept of the free individual who is good and
trying to cope with a destructive civilization. One can try and crush
the civilization and build a new one or one can try and reform.
France attempted the first and England the second. The advanced
progress of the Industrial Revolution created a lower class with an
economic investment in the system, hence, they were docile and
loyal to a middle class controlled legislature who exhibited a social
conscience. The French worker was excluded from a punitive system
that did not provide the necessary benefits. They were the fodder

and impetus of the many revolutions which furthered middle class interest and produced a more open society.

Almost every ism in our vocabulary derives from this period. Some "isms" derived from the forces released by the French and Industrial Revolutions while others were reactions to them. Although the meaning of each has changed through time, the initial idea was formulated and converted into political form at this time (Black, 1967). Liberalism, nationalism, socialism, communism, and romanticism all blended into assigning more importance to the needs of the individual than the needs of the State. Increasing the humanness of the person was a task society had to undertake to become the ideal State. Human nature was good and trustworthy, however, there was no question that human nature acquired institutions to control and change those unable to master their romantic or possibly even destructive impulses. *Man through a community* could provide the best possible world for its inhabitants, hence, the social, political, and physical environment had to be carefully structured by reasoned men. Between 1789 and 1850 France became a constitutional monarchy, a democratic republic, a bourgeois republic, an enlightened despotism, and a liberal hereditary monarchy. None of their political forms were as important *per se* as their movement to meeting more and more needs of people. The political formulas represented by the succeeding governments although judged in terms of extending the franchise and substitution of elected versus hereditary offices did not in themselves alleviate the problems of the poor which became the underlying concern. The democratic ideal was a concern for change in the distribution of wealth and progressive benefits to the poor was the pressure for continuous political change once middle class needs were met.

France fades from history after this period but its demonstration of the basic humanitarian values coupled with morality left a legacy that all oppressed people would receive. The mad were one of these groups. Their treatment, although couched in medical-sociological-philosophical terms, was a direct reflection of the view of man and the concept of the role of the society in ministering to his needs. It is to this delicate interaction between societal institutions and the mad where we will now turn. From our brief treatment of the culture we would expect a cry of freedom from the Romantic, but also a stern warning from the bourgeois to be morally responsible.

The Treatment

As the social classes differed in life styles, financial stability, and degree of institutional support, they also differed in their use of therapeutic treatments. There were two main treatment trends that emerged during the nineteenth century. The one was a development of institutions to treat the mad, while the other was the emergence of individual practitioners applying relatively mystical power. The former was mainly attended by the poor while the latter was frequented by the rich. The institutional movement expressed the social morality or social conscience of the time and had as its goal the encouragement of self-control. The mystical practitioner expressed the Romanticism of the time and had as his goal the production of nonmaterial experiences for the middle class who had by definition demonstrated a strength of will. Treatment through policies of social conscience, therefore, descended upon the poor while the enrichment of internal states was the domain of the wealthy. We shall first consider the social conscience reform movement led by Pinel and Tuke who embodied the humanitarian, liberal, utilitarian, etc. philosophies and required a liberation of the mad from their confinement of the last century. This movement did not occur just in France and England, but also in the United States with the crusades of Clifford Beers and Dorothea Dix. Each liberation took on different form depending upon the character of the country, so we will first speak of Pinel.

As we have seen, the French cultural context within which Pinel emerged was one of an overthrow of the established social order. The Revolution was directed against what was considered to be the repression by the State. Confinement was symbolic of the power of the State, and this symbol was attacked in the storming of the Bastille during the first days of the 1789 Revolution. Madness was firmly linked to confinement producing the idea that madness was the very symbol of confining power (Foucault, 1967). Tyranny with all its sadism and fearful arbitrariness in the power to confine and kill was localized by the people of Paris at the General Hospital. The Hospital, as a place of confinement, created such a fear that at one point a suspicion arose that it was spreading a dangerous disease through the air. One of the first decrees issued by the Revolutionary government ordered all persons removed from confinement except major criminals or the mad. The mad were to be examined to ascertain if they were mad and if so they were to be assigned to treatment hospitals or to the family. Since there were no hospitals, a law in 1791 entrusted the care of the mad to the family, however, this procedure was not acceptable or desired by the families, hence, the Bicetre became the place of confinement only for the mad. Note, the initial urge of the new social era was to release all from confinement, however, there was nowhere for them to go and they were returned to a confinement of their own kind, marking the birth of the asylum. Within this context, Pinel arrived and removed the last vestiges of criminal constraint. Corrthon as a member of the central committee asked after seeing the patients, "Now, citizen, are you mad yourself to seek to unchain such beasts?" Pinel replied, "Citizen, I am convinced that these madmen are intractible only because they have been deprived of air and liberty" (Foucault, 1967, pp. 195–6). It is often thought that Pinel, being a physician, used a medical approach. Not so. Although Pinel compiled an extensive and detailed nosography, he had little faith in most of the usual medical treatments including bloodletting, dunking, drugs, and other unproved techniques (Zilboorg and Henry, 1941). On the basis of an extensive understanding of the inadequacy of previous treatments, he decided to listen and appeal to their senses. Accepting the middle class values of the time, his approach was of increasing morality and individual responsibility with the goal of maximizing the freedom of the individual. Pinel did not permit religious instruction as he thought such religious images might increase madness and, in fact, the fanatics who believed themselves inspired were not even welcome as patients. As common to the time, faith in religious institutions was at a low, hence, the morality of Pinel was an ethical system based upon social principles. Family, work, honor, and other middle class values were to be enforced, and the conformity to these values would constitute the basis for cure and freedom. The asylum must act as an awakening and a reminder of a morality that would prevail from within. Within this context, Pinel effected a moral synthesis assuring an ethical continuity between the world of madness and the world of reason by practising a social treatment that guaranteed bourgeois morality as the alternative, the treatment, and the cause of insanity (Foucault, 1967). The entire life of the inmates, their keepers, and their doctors were organized by Pinel to effect the moral synthesis. There were three principal means of achieving synthesis: silence, recognition by mirrors, and perpetual judgement. The first, silence, was used with those who were projecting a false image such as being Christ. The treatment involved striking the chains and then ignoring the individual. Believing that man needed a social community, the patient would give up his delusion to find companionship. Recognition by mirrors was a means to present the individual's madness to himself. Three patients, each believing themselves to be the king, were introduced to one another and made to appreciate the absurdity of the other two in their pretense to royalty. Later this absurdity was applied to viewing themselves until they recognized the ridiculousness of their own pretense. Perpetual judgement referred to the constant supervision of each individual by the staff clearly showing each patient that he was to be judged by the keeper without any further appeal. When a patient refused to eat, Pinel with a full staff, some shaking heavy chains, came to his door and angrily told him to eat or the next day he would meet the most severe punishment possible. He ate. Pinel presented an offer he could not refuse and he had the ultimate authority to assure the consequences which would occur. The justice of Pinel was not the punishment administered to a criminal act, but it was supposed to serve as a counterthreat to the individual's own system of rewards; in this case, the benefits the patient received for not eating. Showers, baths, packs, etc. usually used to calm the body were also used in a judicial sense. "The use of the shower became frankly juridical: the shower was the habitual punishment of the ordinary police tribunal that sat permanently at the asylum." (Foucault, 1967, p. 214). The treatment was supposed to elicit remorse and guilt from which would come the desire to incorporate the values of the society. Those who did not improve, that is, who did not incorporate such values were banished from the realm of the hopeful by further confining them in cells located in the center of the institution. In effect, placing them in the same condition they were in before they were liberated. The behaviors indicating a failure to respond were disobedience, theft, and resistance to work, the three horsemen of a bourgeoisie society. In the process of administering moral treatment, Pinel justified the medical personage as the keeper of the mad. Where previously he had a minor part, he now became the essential figure in charge of entry and departure, recognition of madness, and its cure. The physician was not to be viewed as an expert in physiology, but as an active partner teaching the patient to adjust to society. Self-control and the elimination of symptoms through reward and punishment as well as the control of emotions by reasons were to be therapeutic tools (Carlson and Dain, 1960). The Revolutionary Committee established a principle of proper behavior of the mad not in terms of medical determination but as a moral and juridical guarantee. Man must be rational and abhor a repression unless it's within the framework of a morality attempting to create liberty. Later physicians not aware of from where their power arose, attempted medical treatment but the initial charge was to administer a just morality. The middle class values of responsibility and will were the strength of the individual and they were to be given back through institutions providing a beneficial environment which was still viewed as the determining factor in creating and dissolving mental disorders. The institution was built to form the most healthy environment for the individual which became the model for the moral treatment approach during the nineteenth century in America (Caplan, 1969).

Other aspects of French Revolutionary thought effected treatment methods besides the building of the asylums. Saint-Pierre in 1818, finding no success with medications advised work and the experience of nature. Saint-Pierre accepted the Rousseauian philosophy that the basic perceptions occurred with direct sensory experience and that society was an illusion which separated man from the self. There could not be a mad savage as he is immersed in reality where the imagination can not be diverted by pleasure, hence, removing man from nature was tantamount to creating madness. Gheel as a treatment concept was rómanticized at this period for curing madness by returning man to nature and his senses. Man in tune with the laws of nature will become reconciled to the ways of reason since the basic laws of nature restrain the violence of desire. Pinel agreed that the laws of nature would contain the imagination as would the laws of morality since both laws assumed the environment provided a constancy which was the essential condition to control the impulse.

The need for a social stability that led to the need for the second Napoleon also required the idea of a constancy in the environment as essential for human well-being to the point where various political and social changes were seen as causes of insanity or their cure. Spurzheim, in 1818, wrote of the English Sickness. Seeing that England still had mental disorders, although the wealthiest of countries, indicated that the freedom of choice evident in the political life created illness by providing too many choices which would not be comprehended, hence, the individual became mad. The therapeutic solution would be to install greater authority in the State to alleviate all this indecision, vacillation, and listening to so many views, many contradictory, which result in a disruption of the mind. England was also faulted for its commercialism which hindered natural liberty by the large competitive societal demands dividing man from his essence through the constant external interactions with other people in order to acquire money. The view of England from Rousseauian France, therefore, focused upon the successful mercantile State placing itself between man and nature, thus, creating madness. Once the habits of social life in a commercial civilization separated men from the rhythm found in nature, the English Sickness would appear.

However, it was not only France which had the view of civilization as a destructive psychic force. Kant also considered the savage to be healthy and society creating frustrations by its complex demands which resulted in the faulty understanding characteristic of madness (Zilboorg and Henry, 1941). In America, Rush considered that any change in political, economic, and social institution produced changes in health. The American Revolution produced good health as it was based upon correct political principles. Hysterical women who favored the Revolution were cured and even marriages were more fruitful. Those who were loyal to England had physical breakdowns diagnosed as Revolutionary or Protection Fever, arising from Excessive concern for protection of their property threatened by the Revolution. There was also suffering after the peace of 1783, as the mind was not capable of handling the new liberty. Pinel added to such societal disease speculations but in the opposite direction. He considered the French Revolution to create more psychosis due to the drastic change in social institutions. In sum, a stable and ordered democracy was necessary for health (Rosen, 1969).

The English preoccupation with the benefits of social institutions on individuals would lead to the English solution of institutional settings being the best way to solve the problem of madness. All social problems such as public education and proper diet had institutional solutions which could be delivered through appropriate legislation. A sense of charity and care for the underprivileged sector of society was part of the middle class concern which found its way into most areas of human suffering. The mad were to feel this concern with the conception of the mental disorder as a social problem (Jones, 1955), leading to the establishment of public insane asylums in 1808 followed by an Act to inspect such places in 1828. In 1845, an Act extended the conditions for certification and specified procedures for record-keeping for both public and private institutions. The mad, as with all disadvantaged, were a social problem which would be solved with State programs. Public standards were developed for the care of the unfortunate and conceptions of the mad were replaced by conceptions of a physical disorder or a lack of constructive work (Osborne, 1970).

The treatment of madness as a physical disorder had as its cultural base, the progress being made in the biological sciences. However, whereas scientific progress was directly experimental in presenting specific physiological, anatomical, and neurological findings, the physical treatment of the mad was based upon metaphysiological concepts still derived from the bile theory which was not yet seriously challenged. At one point, patients were dunked in vats of cold water to contract the blood vessels and free the bile which was inflaming the brain and causing the delirium of insanity. At another time, a common treatment was bloodletting to purify the contaminated blood. Complete transfusions were also attempted to make the cleansing more complete. A treatment that was a direct result of the Industrial Revolution was the eating of iron capsules. Since iron was seen to be such a wonderful invention being able to produce precision in machinery that was not thought possible, it was considered to be the invention that would solve the problems of man (Osborne, 1970). The implication that it should also cure madness naturally followed. Since the blood vessels were either too rigid or soft in the mad, iron mixed into the vessels would provide the proper maleability to free the bile. Another industrial product, soap, was also highly recommended to be eaten to clean out the disordered system. Soap was being recognized as an important factor in controlling disease through public sanitation programs, hence, a little inner sanitation was seriously applied to the inmate. An interesting therapy for those with a more. psychological bent was the method of noninjurious torture. This involved placing the person where a cannon could be suddenly and unexpectedly fired or where he could be suddenly dunked with ice water. Both procedures were used to bring the person to his senses which were overcome by a too active distracting imagination. If man is in a constant struggle between his rationality and his emotions, the emotions can affect the imagination to the point where reason and judgement become faulty. Shocking him back to a reasonable state through whatever means possible made sense. However, even with those who proposed a medical basis of madness, the corollary belief was that environmental conditions could modify such states. A defective brain caused insanity but the brain was maleable and proper habits and training could nurture goodness and/or sanity. A pathological condition could be modified by corrective experiences, therefore, insanity whether the result of injury, emotions, or intellectual confusion could be cured in almost every case (Caplan, 1969). Hence, the individual by knowing his individuality and the dangers of the forces in the environment could escape insanity by protecting himself from noxious situations. The milieu was the important condition to influence the maleable individual. Treatment was humane but was also sterile in the sense that there was little romance or mysticism in the institution.

Treatment implemented by legislative act was mainly directed at the lower classes where the problem was mainly considered to reside,

although in 1837, Browne, the superintendent of the Montrose
Asylum in England, thought madness was more prevalent in upper
classes but mainly when there is moral agitation (Rosen, 1969). However, most experts placed the disorder in the lower classes. Hawkes
attempted preventive psychiatry in 1857, calling for a mental sani-
tary reform involving a working with the poor to reduce the strain
created by their working conditions. Working class children were to
be helped through instruction in mental hygiene. In short, even
though incidence of madness by social class was not known, upper
social class incidence was surmised due to the assumed dangers of
society as it separates man from his nature while the more turbulent
lower· classes seemed to lack a self-control. Therefore, treatment
which aimed at man's nature or internal feelings would be a sensible
approach for the middle class but would seem a dangerous procedure
if applied to the lower classes. Most legislation aimed at solving societal problems through the developing of institutions was directed
toward the low income individual with a faith that all social programs, including the moral treatment of the mad, would be successful. Once the social problem was isolated, it would be solved by
institutions devised to solve this problem. The asylums had an expectation placed upon them they never were able to meet.

Within the social etiology framework of England which fit its
effort to build a responsible constitutional monarchy through State
institutions, Tuke practised his moral treatment and like Pinel produced a more humane approach to mental illness, however, Tuke,
unlike Pinel attempted to bring the moral synthesis to the middle
class. Tuke was a Quaker who began the retreat for those who, as he
advertised in a brochure, "had the misfortune to lose their reason
without a sufficient fortune to resort to expensive establishments all
the resources of medicine and all the comforts of life compatible
with their state" (Foucault, 1967, p. 195). The Tuke Retreat, therefore, focused more upon the lower-middle class than the poor who
were still located in alms houses and prisons. We will note, however,
that separate treatment centers according to class were not unique to
England. Paris had the Maisons de Sante whose residents were not
subjected to the asylums of Pinel (Zilboorg and Henry, 1941). Like
Pinel, Tuke established an instrument of moral and religious segrega-
tion which attempted to surround the mad with a community, as
much as possible like the Community of Quakers. Religion here
could provide the natural laws which had lost their ability to control
reason. The transgressor was placed within a milieu which provided
perpetual anxiety ceaselessly threatened by law and punishment

(Foucault, 1967). The individual was seen as responsible and only in need of the moral guidance to learn the proper behavior. The individual must feel morally responsible for anything within him that disturbs morality and society holding no one responsible but himself for the punishment he receives. Madness now could only rage under the seals of conscience rather than within the walls of confinement (Foucault, 1967). The retreat organized the guilt and elaborated the punishment. By the mad taking on the role of the keeper in observing himself as socially correct and applying punishment when due, he would leave free. Work would be a definite sign of cure as it was viewed as a constraining power which frees the mind from its wanderings and directs it to a task. Work was the main treatment as a means to provide a moral rule, a submission to a higher order and an engagement of responsibility. Another treatment was the observation of others and being observed to satisfy the need for esteem. Patients were invited for ceremonial occasions such as a tea where they were treated as strangers. Everyone would wear their best and vie with each other in politeness and manners. Behavior was minutely monitored to assure that the individual exhibited the behavior which would be rewarded in society. He would also learn to observe others and himself to clearly and impersonally be able to observe the slightest expression of madness. The value of the individual was to be his social behavior and like the mirror technique of Pinel, the observation of the other and himself as a member of a moral society was to contain the madness. The physicians used by Tuke also were more moral leaders than proscribers of medication. The patient was invited into a family in which he had all the responsibilities and rights as long as he observed custom. The patient was liberated from accounting for his inner states, only for that which was visible.

In reading accounts of Pinel and Tuke, a number of readers are probably hearing behavior modification. The treater punished or ignored incorrect behavior and rewarded the correct. That is not how Pinel would describe his behavior. When Pinel threatened the patient who would not eat, he had previously diagnosed him as someone who was extremely fearful of Hell. The reason for the abstinence was inferred to be his attempt to escape eternal damnation. Pinel proposed to present a greater consequence, an immediate strong and deep fear which replaced the more remote justice. Pinel's treatment, therefore, was to produce a counterbalancing fear that derived from a moral system that was cognizant of the individual's natural rights. Man is only ill when he loses his belief in social morality. A belief in the social contract of man was the heart of the French Revolution and the context of Pinel's conception of insanity. Possibly you say, what is the difference how he thought about it, it worked didn't it? Patients ate, lost their sovereignty, were cured, and restored to society. Remember, it did not work. The cursory reading of the Pinel liberation movement produced an image of the faithful courageous doctor curing the strange, almost bestial creatures. The close look is of Pinel having an institution within an institution. Cells within the heart of the asylum for those who resisted the moral synthesis. Those who did not eat, abdicate their thrones, repent, etc., went to the confinement of the inner dungeons. Remember the characteristics of the failures? Those who disobeyed such as the religious fanatics who believed themselves inspired and did not obey or urged others not to obey on the pretext that it is better to obey God than man. Another was those who would not work, and the last were those who would steal. The three great transgressions against the bourgeois which were dominant in the society. It was not behavior that was to change, but behavior reflecting a morality. The same principle underlay the exquisite tea parties and dinners to which Tuke invited his patients. Dressed in their finery, the patients were expected to exhibit the proper manners and social customs. The patients were closely scrutinized for social errors and when they did not occur a cure was claimed. The theme of Tuke's treatment was surveillance and judgement administered with moral authority. The acceptance by society was central to Tuke along with the religious morality of the Society of Friends. Tuke may have rewarded and punished to create adjusted behavior, but it was not just to adapt to society but to support a religious morality.

The English social conscience shaped the form of treatment of the mad. The belief in the value of man and a basic humanitarianism produced expectancies for change which grew into moral treatment and the "cult of cureability" which at one American institution reported a 100% cure rate. A time later, it was noted that cure meant counting everyone who came in and left no matter how many times it occurred (Caplan, 1969). When statistics were adjusted for those who came in and were transferred to alms houses and other public facilities, the percent of cures dropped 70%. However, within the morality of the York retreat or the asylum of Pinel, there was a faith in man's ability to change his condition to one that is most beneficial. The age of revolution shifted the responsibility for behavior from the authoritarian rule to the individual. Treatment could be performed if man is changeable, and good is only corrupted by an overly materialistic society. There still was not the great faith in the potentiality of all men as much as the belief in middle class values and forces judged as the ideal state of man. The middle class were to help, treat, change, or educate in order to create the mad in their likeness. Obviously, institutional treatment was then the bourgeoisie acting upon the poor.

We must now return to the treatment method which was reserved for those in control of their society. The question is how did the educated middle class act upon themselves especially when their behavior was not that deviant. How would the ruling classes look towards their own problems? Not in the asylums, but possibly in the medical conception or in the realm of the mystical elaborated upon by the Romantic poets. To speculate upon this question, we would look at the effect of Mesmer upon the time. Even before the Revolution, Mesmer published a work describing the effects of astrological events upon behavior. Later, he elaborated upon the effect of a magical magnetic field outside human experience which could resolve mental problems. Mesmer attracted a large following explaining how the individual was influenced by the stars which directed the flowing magnetic fluid which filled the universe. The harmony of this fluid within the individual protected against disease, hence, treatment was achieving the necessary balance by controlling the flow of fluid. The treatment object was a banquet, an arrangement of mirrors and rods, which directed the magnetic flow to the individual. Mesmer was considered a quack by the medical and academic community. In 1784, an Academy of Science committee considered the treatment worthless and possibly harmful. Interestingly, the members of the committee were members of the revolution active in hospital reform. Pinel was a member of this committee who thought the treatment worthless but also noted that many citizens, especially socially prominent women, seemed to be cured by the procedure. In fact, the procedure consistently was reported as providing cures and was heavily supported by the upper classes and intellectuals somewhat comparable to a century later when psychoanalysis was accepted by the upper classes in face of the opposition of academic psychology. The educated of this time took up the cause of Mesmerism in opposition to medical judgement and published numerous volumes citing its effectiveness (Zilboorg and Henry, 1941). Throughout the nineteenth century, the method was constantly debated, appearing in modified form as a viable treatment method into the twentieth century. Mary Baker Eddy was cured of her hysterical paralysis by an American student of Mesmerism hence providing a tie between Mesmerism and Christian Science Theology. The concept of man as subject to mystical forces was not an idea that was to die even though it seemed to find its cures in the wealthy and the intelligentsia.

Possibly by understanding the dominance of the position maintained by Pinel could be understood the undercurrent of Mesmer. Pinel was prominent in every government of the time. He served as physician-in-chief of the Bicetre and the Salpetriere under the initial Revolution and later during the Reign of Terror. He was the physician required to be at the execution of Louis XVI, and later was asked to be personal physician to Napoleon as well as both Bourbon kings. Pinel's acceptance by all regimes reflects the alliance of his treatment philosophy with the revolutionary cultures' understanding of man. Mesmer espoused the minority philosophy and had the exact opposite effect upon those in authority. Mesmer arrived in Paris the same year as Pinel. He migrated from Vienna where he discovered and defended his concept of animal magnetism, however, the opposition to his theory and practice was so vehement that he was forced to leave. Mesmer took Paris by storm, but it was mainly with bourgeois wives that he created the sensation (Zilboorg and Henry, 1941). The scientific community called him a Charlatan from the beginning although he seemed to alleviate the problems of middle class women. Most previous treatments of the mad were practised in institutions and usually directed toward the superfluous people in the society. Now those who were productive individuals by societal definitions found a means of communicating with some part of themselves which was not acceptable conversation in middle class industrial society. It has been proposed that Mesmerism was the first attempt to treat the neurosis (Zilboorg and Henry, 1941), however, Mesmerism may be more of a first attempt to incorporate Romanticism into a personal expression within a society which offered few other acceptable outlets. A poetry existed expressing the romantic spirit, but it was an underground art not having the acceptability or respectability of the adventure tales or self-help manuals. Mesmerism was a powerful movement which would not go away no matter how severe the scientific judgement. It was not a treatment for the poor or the established leaders in the profession but it was for those who were responding to the revolutionary spirit of the time which did not necessarily accept all the benefits of a wealthy industrial society. The Romantic movement did not feel that man dominated by institutions established through a reasoned analysis was adequate in meeting the needs of men. Even though social legislation was seen as adequate for dealing with the problems of the poor, Mesmerism was seen as more compatible for the rich. Both intended to change the position of man to his society. Pinel was to provide controlled liberty while Mesmer was to increase individuality. Mesmerism was a noninstitutional treatment with a mystical romantic element. It was assumed the middle class had enough will-power. What was required was greater personal freedom. This was not the same as assumptions of the nature of the lower classes.

Interestingly, Dain and Carlson (1959) consider that in America between the years 1789 and 1824, social class differences in the professional care of the insane also increased. The private hospitals advertised the psychological and caring atmosphere of moral treatment but it was only for those with some degree of wealth and middle class values. In a later time when the lower classes contained a majority of immigrants, it was agreed that moral treatment could not be expected to cure those so different from the native American (Caplan, 1969). However, the lower classes, even before the arrival of the immigrant, were viewed as not benefiting from a moral approach and consequently discharged to the jails and alms houses. In the early issues of the *American Journal of Insanity*, just prior to the middle of the century, there was an attempt to teach the public about the curability of the insane and to rouse public concern for the treatment of the ill. Preventive psychiatry was launched in this period to prevent those societal conditions which were destructive to the individual including working conditions, child rearing, education, and notation. The individual had to resist the dangers of the society mainly by a strict inculcation of self-discipline (Caplan, 1969). The first psychiatry movement in America stemmed from the English tradition mainly through Tuke, but also from the similar morality of Pinel. The early members of the Association of Medical superintendents gave all sorts of advice on cultural conditions even to attacking the intense emotionalism of the religious sects. The Church was to develop the social conscience and not be dangerous by increasing the enthusiasm of religious expressions which would derange. In effect, America during the nineteenth century followed Europe during the early half of the century, possibly with less conflict due to the unity of the society. As in Europe, the medical value of treatment was not accepted and in fact found too many times to be destructive (Caplan, 1969), hence, the production of a sound environment within an institution was the goal. Due to the newness of some of the institutions, they in many ways were more pleasant than their European counterparts but the intent of the treatment and the acceptable patient was little different than Tuke.

If we could briefly summarize, we would note that the English tradition advocated revolution through evolution of social structures. A social morality, implemented through the political institutions of a social conscience à la Pinel and Tuke, made sense as the manner to curb the deviance in man. The revolutionary period clearly focused upon changing the social environment to mold man. The man who molded was the new middle class man, and the man to be molded was the lower class man. The successful man epitomized the common beliefs in human nature also embodied in the Puritan Ethic and it was the strengthening of these aspects of man which made sense as treatment although not explicitly stated and not necessarily applied to those who were enforcing such beliefs. The imposition of the middle class belief system on others under the guise of treatment remains with us until today (Magaro, 1969). However, one must not lose sight of the fact that this time was attempting to improve the condition of the worker which can not be so readily said for past periods in our history. The needs of those not in power became almost as important as the needs of those having power. Involvement in prevention of cruelty to animals, urban squalor, orphans, sanitation, penal reform and the insane reflected a focus upon those previously taken advantage of or disregarded as superfluous during economic and political changes in society. A major tenet underlying most of the isms was that of more equitable relationships between men. The social morality of the middle class was an accepting of personal responsibility for the conditions of the society, thus humanitarian service became the obligation of all (Caplan, 1969). This obligation became social institutions devised to stamp out mental illness and everyone who was associated with the disorder was to receive the same stamp.

An Alternate Treatment Conception

A presentation of past treatment methods outside the context of the thought of the time seems quaint and humorous, sometimes masking the seriousness with which they were applied. Previous treatments are cause for mirth because we do not share the common assumptions concerning man and his madness. In just 26 years from now, at the turn of the century, many of our procedures will not make good common sense and will be cause for amusement. Possibly the question is how many casualties do we sacrifice for the few successes that will occur? Since all treatments produce positive and negative treatment outcomes, does treatment have to be conceptualized as a unitary system applicable to all individuals. The first conceptual changes regarding treatment would involve surrendering a unibelief system. It could be argued that the belief of professionals regarding the nature of mental illness is downright arrogant. It is the arrogance that states a belief as a fact, the stating of a knowledge that is considered to be beyond the common sense of a culture acquired through some expert training. A reading of our short history of the Age of Revolution finds the treater explaining madness in a jargon that is only the most popular belief of man at the time. Throughout history, the treater has been so sure of his knowledge that those subjected to his care have undergone the most extreme conditions without any question as if the treatment really is more than the imposition of a faith even though each treater within any time period has facts which prove him to be right. That the understanding of madness reflects no more than the application of common cultural beliefs to a specific subject, the schizophrenic for instance, is relatively clear.

The institution is the link between the abstract belief and the concrete behavior of the societal agent. Institutions are born to implement a belief and as the belief changes so does the institution. Institutions are not mere buildings but social systems such as schools, hospitals, welfare, industries, PTA, and psychologists. We are limiting our concern to the institutions treating the mentally ill. Most treaters have answered without asking, the question of what is the nature of man? What is it that makes men act in both acceptable and unacceptable ways? What is it in man and his spiritual and material context which creates the image of man? This may seem to be a question of philosophy and not that for the treater of the mad, however, it is the treater who mans the institutions. It is he that is the embodiment of the answer the culture provides to the question of the nature of man. The dominant answer in a culture is expressed through the institution in the form of its staff and imposed upon the inmates. The action of the treater, therefore, becomes the imposition and possibly the coercion of one set of beliefs upon another, possibly with a different set of beliefs. The imposition of one of a group of similar treatments upon individuals is a common philosophy and all occupants of the institution must conform to that philosophy. Unknowingly, we make all men fit one conception of human nature. To elaborate, we will consider the links between the cultural belief, the institution, the treater, and the patient.

Let us first elaborate upon the link between the culture and the institution. Society imposes restraints upon individual behavior through laws, police, mores, etc. Individuals have needs to be met. Institutions are built to provide constraint and satisfy needs. However, there is usually just one institution formed to meet the need. The choice of the character of the one institution is guided by a desire to provide the best manner of meeting the need and best is the professional thought which is closest to the dominant cultural thought of the time. As the time passes and the institution does not change, it is only a matter of time before the institution becomes ripe for scandal and exposé. Note, what changes is the idea of man's nature and his relation to the society. Most asylums were only performing what they were charged to do 50 years before. A custodial hospital would be a scandal today but a pride 50 years ago. A behavior modification hospital is a pride today, but probably a scandal 50 years from now. The dominant cultural thought of cause and effect in medieval times was God and the Devil. The institution was a religious exorcism of the Devil. The dominant thought of the Renaissance was humanism and the natural expressibility of man, hence, the Ship of Fools became the acceptable and exotic nature of the treatment of the insane. The Age of Reason believed in the benefits of a rational order based upon social organization and productivity, hence, the workhouse and enforced labor for the mad. The Industrial Revolution through the nineteenth century brought on a sense of a social conscience and the responsibility of the State in providing care for all its members, hence, the social legislation creating the asylum. On and on we find the institution for the mad reflecting the cultural conception of the nature of man and consequently his deviance.

The institution is established and we must now consider the link between the institution and the treater. The mental health institution such as a State hospital was a noble action. As we have seen, it was a humanitarian urge to remove the mad from chains and the degradation of the severest repression and cruelty as found in prisons and poor houses where there was little idea of even separating them from other residents. The institution was born to provide answers to the legitimate needs of its members. A morality was trained with the expectation that even those who did not share these values would surely benefit from additional training. The man that runs the institution at any level fits the societal concept of the responsible professional who can implement the techniques that fit the underlying assumptions about man in general. It is not important that the culture understands the technique. They assume the expert knows the details of how to implement the cultural assumptions. For example, if the underlying assumption regarding man's nature is spiritual, the intimacy of man to God and the Devil, society will insist that the treater skilled in such techniques rectify this balance. It is not debatable if it is or isn't a spiritual matter. The only question is who can implement the spiritual solution best. The layman is not expected to know what words are to be uttered or what incense is used. That is the role of the expert. If the nature of man is mainly based upon the effects of different physical structures, one chooses to man the institution those who are the experts in physical structure. If the nature of man is determined by childhood experiences, those who can change the effect of those experiences shall run the institution. The people or their elected representatives are not expected to know the methods of administering the solution to the problem, and even if the methods seem strange, they are used by an expert aiming at a commonly defined problem and will be supported.

The seriousness of this situation and the atrocities which will be approved under the guise of treatment become obvious when a society condones the elimination of its superfluous people. The solution to madness in Nazi Germany was murder. Between 1939 and 1945 the population of Berlin psychiatric hospitals dropped 75%. The therapeutic success was due to gassing mental patients and others suspected of being mentally deficient (Wertham, 1966). The estimate of the number of psychiatric patients murdered was 250,000 including chronics, acutes, psychopaths, children, cripples, aged, etc. (Wertham, 1966). In the case of the aged, psychiatrists even made house calls to examine the old folks, determine their insanity, and have them removed to the gas chambers. The Jews followed the mad when the method proved effective. The point here is that this treatment program, conceptualized in terms of saving painfully dying valueless people, was administered by the leading academic and hospital psychiatrists in Germany. The program was not run by SS troops who later exterminated the Jews but rather by respected members of the psychiatric profession. A reading of the names of these treatment leaders is a glimpse of a psychiatric Who's Who in Germany. The total psychiatric team shared in the common goal of extermination as exemplified in the Hadamer psychiatric hospital where, in celebration of the cremation of the ten-thousandth mental patient, the whole staff; secretaries, psychiatrists, nurses, and attendants, were all given a bottle of beer to toast their success. The culture of Nazi Germany condoned the destruction of the impure in the creation of the superman. The treaters were not only members of the culture; they embodied and acted-out the consequences of the dominant social thought. Each treater creates the interface between the cultural belief concerning the nature of man formed into an institution and the individual who is considered to require a realignment of his nature. Possibly few treaters offer the extreme solution of the German or even the isolation by Pinel, but then again our history has not yet been written.

The link between the treater and the individual is the act of imposing a cultural belief. The charge to the treater is to change the individual into a behavior pattern which is at least a facsimile of the current conception of the culturally accepted man. It is at this point where social class difference becomes crucial. Beyond the belief in human nature, there will be a belief in the nature of lower class men. State institutions mainly serve the lower class mad, therefore, the treater will treat a conception of the nature of lower class man since he is the dominant resident and the stranger. We have seen that the asylum was built for the middle class as an extension of middle-class values incorporating a belief in the nature of man. The asylum was filled by the lower classes who were viewed as sharing a different human nature, thus, moral treatment could not succeed as it was based upon the nature of the middle-class Anglo-Saxon Puritan (Caplan, 1969). The treater in the form of the superintendent attempted to maintain the middle class Tuke retreat, but the legislature recognized its failure and accepted more the idea of the physical determines of behavior with the context of an emphasis upon a material technological world. The consequent decrease in funding of the asylum in the later nineteenth century was, therefore, not just a function of its revealed treatment failures but of a shift in views of man from the moral to the material. The culture shifted to a faith in industrialization which emphasized the mechanical view of man present in the neurological explanation of behavior. The treater became the physician rather than the moralist. The individual was not to be reformed but retooled as soon as the curative physical treatment was discovered. The treater now engaged in different practices and the individual was to accept the new conceptualization of his state but also the newly formulated interventions, no matter how strange. London (1974) links the popularity of the new sensitivity therapies to the changing conception of men in the present. He views current therapies as a part of the generalized service industry which is reaching out for a more affluent population who answer their boredom with a cry for further growth. We have entered the Age of Annui and new therapeutic inventions have appeared to fit the time.

Again, the question is not which treatment is right. There is no one answer, as there is no treatment that fits all natures. The point of one treatment being correct always elicits the hottest disagreement while the present is upon us. Each time period produces rousing debate concerning methods of treatment and all demonstrating their worth through one method or another. If I could add my name to one principle in the area of mental health, I would stress the fact that: *The evidence confirming the success of a treatment decreases with the length of time the treatment is practised.* I would venture that the principle applies to all treatments in the area of mental health. Tourney (1970) has reviewed a number of psychiatric treatments, listing the success rate of the treatment over time. He found that over a 20-year period, the success rate follows a trend of moderate (approximately 40% success) to high (70–90%) to low (20–30%), and this occurs with therapies derived from medical, psychological, or learning models. A method is born, it demonstrates its truth, it cures its recipients, it expands dramatically, it becomes criticized, it is shown not to be effective, it is replaced, and it enters the annals of quaint humor.

The dominance of treatment of cultural belief would recommend a rather pessimistic picture for those labelled mad. However, there does seem to be a simple conceptual change which can resolve this problem. It is to direct treatment away from the assumptions of the treater to the assumptions of the treatee. To have the treatment process move up rather than down the ladder of beliefs. To explain further, let me back up to our discussion of institution.

Remember that the society through its legislative apparatus decides to assume the responsibility for meeting the needs of its citizens. Following the liberal English tradition we decide to invest our societal resources in an institution to meet a particular need. In this case, insanity. An institution is formed to implement the solution and an administrator is chosen to lead. This is the first mistake since the administrator is chosen due to his complete acceptance of the cultural conception of the disorder. The treater may encourage different treatments within an institution but the differences will be minor. Major differences in conception create conflict and the role of the treater-administrator is to reduce conflict and produce an efficient organization. Multiple treatment processes may be seen as creating such conflicting demands that they would overwhelm the administrator who was initially chosen by exhibiting the correct one-source thought. The result is that the individual entering the system is similar to a member of a minority entering the home turf of an organized majority. His assumptions concerning man and his relation to his society are not necessarily shared by the keepers. No one unithought institution can hope to meet the needs of all individuals who arrive with different conceptions of themselves and others. For example, a man enters an institution built upon a physiological base and espouses deep religious experiences or a sincere speaking-in-voices Pentacostal is assigned for diagnosis and treatment to an avowed atheist. The patient may see someone listening to him speak about God, but the degree of communication is zero. The basic assumption of man's relation to the supernatural is so different that he can only be relegated to the realm of the mad. Another man enters expounding upon the existential experience of multiple sensations which are permitting him to integrate himself at a higher level of being. The treater wants to modify his behavior patterns so he can better adjust to society. Again the vast difference in their concept of the experience assures the treater of the individual's need for his services.

I should mention quickly that one could say that looking at the range of treatment available in the society today, one finds such a wide choice that my objection is really a straw man. That objection is somewhat true when looking at the number of treatments practised throughout the country, however, it is not true outside of the major metropolitan cities, and what is more germane to the present discussion, it is certainly not true in our public institutions. There are not many nude group marathons in our State institutions including counselling centers, nor are there many Baptist religious experience groups, nor psychoanalytic living centers. The multitude of treatments are only available to those who can afford to move outside the legislated system and obtain private services. Private facilities have always provided what the wealthy minority groups felt were conducive to their nature, even before Mesmer. For the majority of individuals, treatment is a one-course meal without a menu. I am modestly suggesting that we can no longer think in terms of single institutions in the area of mental health. We can no longer judge efficiency in terms of one facility meeting the needs of all. Institutions must always be plural built upon the differing beliefs in the nature of man generated from the experience of ourselves and others.

The present argument is to organize an institution so the treatee could choose his own brand of medicine. As those with financial means can choose, so would I extend that privilege to every individual in the society. The multithought institution would give the individual the right to shift treatments according to his own satisfaction which is not present with the current institutional and societal conception. I believe that one nature of man producing one conception of schizophrenia and one treatment automatically provides many failures. The idea of prescriptive treatment is only a matter of presenting a choice of treatment methods which could be prescribed for different patient groups (Magaro, 1969; Magaro and Staples, 1972). The added element of the present argument is to have the patient prescribe the treatment. The goal would be to bring the schizophrenic experience back into a communicable realm of the human choice. Not everyone is on one continuum from mad to sane. We are on different mad to sane continua and we must coexist as we touch and overlap. We have an arsenal of treatments and it behooves us to learn which one is applicable to whom. Each treatment by itself can only account for one segment of the therapeutic effort which ranges from modifying poverty condition to firing destructive teachers to various types of group living to the various religious teachings to the traditional forms of therapy. To cover the field requires an institutional framework which is tolerant of many and ready to give to the individual seeking aid the choice of treatment that conforms to his own assumptions about himself.

References

Ball, J. *From Beowulf to Modern British Writers.* New York: Odyssey Press, Inc., 1959.

Barnes, H. E. *An Intellectual and Cultural History of the Western World.* New York: Dover Publications, 1965.

Baxter, G. W. Changes in PHN after one year and two years in college. Unpublished master's thesis, George Peabody College for Teachers, 1968.

Bernard, J. F. *Talleyrand: A biography.* New York: Putnam, 1973.

Black, E. C. *European Political History, 1815–1870.* New York: Harper and Row, 1967.

Braginsky, B. M. and Braginsky, D. D. *Mainstream Psychology, A Critique.* New York: Holt, Rinehart and Winston, Inc., 1974.

Breunig, C. *The Age of Revolution and Reaction.* New York: W. W. Norton, Inc., 1970.

Brinton, C. *Anatomy of Revolution.* New York: Random House, 1957.

Brunn, G. *Europe and the French Imperium.* New York: Harper and Row, 1938.

Caplan, R. B. *Psychiatry and the Community in Nineteenth Century America.* New York: Basic Books, Inc., 1969.

Carlson, E. T. and Dain, N. The psychotherapy that was moral treatment. *American Journal of Psychiatry,* 1960, 115, 519–24.

Cobban, A. *A History of Modern France, Volume 2: 1799–1871.* Baltimore: Penguin Books, 1968.

Collins, I. Liberalism in Nineteenth-Century Europe. In *European Political History, 1850–1870.* E. C. Black (Ed.), New York: Harper and Row, 1967.

Dain, N. and Carlson, E. T. Social class and psychological medicine in the United States, 1789–1824. *Bulletin of the History of Medicine,* 1959, 33, 454–65.

Deane, P. and Cole, W. A. British Economic Growth, 1688–1959. *Trends and Structure.* Cambridge: Cambridge Press, 1962.

Durant, W. and Durant, A. *Rousseau and Revolution.* New York: Simon and Schuster, 1967.

Foucault, M. *Madness and Civilization.* New York: New American Library, 1967.

Goldstein, A. P. *Psychotherapeutic Attraction.* New York: Pergamon Press, Inc., 1971.

Gottschalk, L. and Sach, D. *Toward the French Revolution.* New York: Charles Scribner's Sons, 1973.

Greer, D. M. *The Incidence of Terror during the French Revolution.* Cambridge: Peter Smith Co., 1935.

Hampton-Turner, C. *Radical Man.* Cambridge, Mass.: Schenkman Publishing Co., 1970.

Hartwell, R. M. The Rising Standard of Living in England, 1800–1850. In *European Political History, 1815–1870.* E. C. Black (Ed.). New York: Harper and Row, 1967.

Hollingshead, A. B. and Redlich, F. C. *Social Class and Mental Illness.* New York: Wiley and Sons, Inc., 1958.

Jones, K. Lunacy, Law and Conscience, 1744—1845. *The Social History of the Care of the Insane.* London: Routledge and Paul, Inc., 1955.

London, P. The psychotherapy boom: From the long couch for the sick to the push button for the bored. *Psychology Today,* 1974, 8, 62—9.

Magaro, P. A. A prescriptive treatment model based upon social class and premorbid adjustment. *Psychotherapy: Theory, Research, and Practice,* 1969, 6, 57—70.

Magaro, P. A. and Staples, S. B. Schizophrenic patients as therapists: An expansion of the prescriptive treatment system based upon premorbid adjustment social class, and A—B status. *Psychotherapy: Theory, Research, Practice,* 1972, 9, 352—8.

Namier, L. B. Nationality and Liberty. In *European Political History, 1815—1870.* E. C. Black (Ed.). New York: Harper and Row, 1967.

Osborn, J. W. *The Silent Revolution.* New York: Charles Scribner's Sons, 1970.

Riessman, F., Cohen, J. and Pearl, A. *Mental Health of the Poor.* London: Free Press, 1964.

Rosen, G. *Madness in Society.* New York: Harper and Row, 1968.

Szasz, T. S. *The Myth of Mental Illness.* New York: Harper and Row, 1961.

Tourney, G. Psychiatric Therapies: 1800—1968. In T. Rothman (Ed.), *Changing Patterns in Psychiatric Care.* New York: Crown Publishers, 1970.

Wells, H. G. *The Outline of History.* New York: Macmillan Co., 1922.

Wertham, F. *A Sign for Cain.* New York: Macmillan Co., 1966.

Wrightsman, L. S. *Social Psychology in the Seventies.* Monterey, Calif.: Brooks/Cole Co., 1973.

Wrightsman, L. S. and Noble, F. C. Reactions to the President's assassination and changes in philosophies of human nature. *Psychological Reports,* 1965, 16, 159—62.

Wrightsman, L. S. and Satterfield, C. H. Additional norms and standardization of the Philosophies of Human Nature scale—1967 Revision. George Peabody College for Teachers, 1967. (Mimeographed copy).

Zilboorg, G. and Henry G. W. *A History of Medical Psychology.* New York: W. W. Norton, Inc., 1941.

CHAPTER 3

The Myth of Schizophrenia

There is perhaps no human problem of such magnitude and significance that has remained so elusive as mental illness. Throughout
history man has tried to comprehend and cure aberrant human behavior. The theories and treatments of each era reflect the dominant
view of the nature of man during that period rather than scientific
progress in understanding mental disorders. Thus, early man, certain
that supernatural forces controlled every aspect of his existence, believed that aberrant behavior was caused by those powers taking
"possession" of a person. Since most deviant conduct was considered
to be evil, the possession almost always was demonic. Given such
origins, the treatment included a variety of exorcism techniques such
as prayer, bloodletting, sacrifice, all of which were intended to drive
the demon or evil spirit out of the possessed person's body.

These primitive notions were abandoned by the intellectuals of the
Greek era, particularly by the famous physician, Hippocrates, who
fashioned his own explanation of aberrant behavior. According to
him, all deviant conduct had an organic origin and, more specifically,
was a manifestation of some body fluid. For instance, an excess of
black bile would lead to a melancholic temperament, too much
phlegm, a phlegmatic temperament. The treatment, like the cause,
was removed from the realm of supernatural powers to the world of
human organisms. Thus activities such as exercise, parties, dieting,
massage, hypnotism and musical concerts were considered therapeutic.

Although many Greek and Roman physicians refined and elaborated upon Hippocrates' endocrinological theory, the basic organic
explanation of abnormal behavior was dominant until the Middle
Ages. With the decline of rational civilization and the ascendancy of
the Church, demons appeared on the mental illness scene again, re-
possessing victims either as punishment for sinfulness or because they
were "in league with the devil". Exorcism also reappeared as the
treatment for demonical possession, although this time in more extreme forms. If prayers and incantations did not work, attempts were

made to drive Satan out by flogging, burning, drowning, or be-heading the heretic or witch. Despite a heroic effort on the part of the clergy and medieval physicians, epidemics of madness occurred throughout the fifteenth and sixteenth centuries, and witches and heretics still could be found after the Inquisition. It was not until 1782 when the last known witch was finally execu-ted in Switzerland.

The unbridled fanaticism of the witch hunts gave way to a more rational explanation of abnormal behavior. The medical profession, separating itself at last from theological doctrine, no longer viewed insanity as the will of God, but instead, as the outcome of a diseased brain. Since those persons afflicted with mental disease were thought to be insensitive and unaware of their surroundings, violent forms of medical treatment were prescribed. The torture of the Middle Ages, then, was replaced by medicinal bloodletting and emetics.

By the close of the eighteenth century an enlightened public put an end to this oppressive medical treatment. In keeping with that era's stress upon the dignity of all humans, sane or insane, physicians emphasized the functional rather than the organic nature of mental disorders, That is, aberrant behavior was viewed as the result of events and situations in the life of the patient, such as losing a loved one or a sudden financial crisis. The treatment involved simply placing the insane in an asylum, a pleasant milieu, immersed in brotherly love, treating them with kindness and sensitivity in order to restore their power of reason and inner harmony. The key to "moral treatment", as this was called, was respect for the mentally ill as people.

Respect for the dignity of the individual, however, underwent a radical change following the Civil War in America. This change was directly reflected in the standards of care and concern for the men-tally ill. The medical profession reverted to the disease hypothesis, adding further that the disease was disintegrative, afflicting only those persons with inferior heredity. Thus, doctors saw mental illness as evidence of Darwin's theory of natural selection, as nature's way of eliminating the unfit of the species. Since it would violate philoso-phical and religious principles to allow nature to take its course, and since rehabilitation and treatment were out of the question, the only thing to be done with the insane was to provide them with custodial care in institutions.

Although some still exist, most custodial facilities were abandoned in favor of therapeutically-oriented institutions shortly after the First World War. Unlike the changes in the past, however, this approach was not preceded by any discernible change in the conceptions of the mentally ill. In fact, most present-day theories concerning mental disorders contain elements reminiscent of earlier views.

How, then, is the problem of abnormal behavior conceptualized today? What exactly are the causes of this behavior? What is being done to alleviate or cure the problem? What is the magnitude or prevalence of madness in our society today? Thousands of social scientists have spent millions of hours in an attempt to answer just these questions. Let us turn to the answers they have produced.

Prevalence of Madness

With the outbreak of the Second World War, psychologists were employed by the Armed Forces to construct tests with which they might screen out men who were psychologically disturbed or mentally deficient. On the basis of these tests, one out of every five men was rejected for military service. That is, approximately five million young American men were found to be either intellectually deficient or psychologically disturbed. More recently, Srole and his associates (1962) attempted to discover the extent of abnormality in a randomly sampled group of people. In the now famous Midtown Manhattan Study, Srole *et. al.* found that less than one out of every four people in their 16,000 person sample were judged to be "healthy" or "well". Furthermore, nearly one out of five were considered to be clearly "incapacitated" by a mental disorder.

It is no surprise then that the number of persons considered to be psychologically disturbed is in the millions, and that there are over one-half million people in mental hospitals. Moreover, Lemkan and Crocetti (1958) predicted that approximately one out of every 50 children born in the U.S. will at some point in their life be in a mental institution. Despite the annual increases in the number of admissions in mental hospitals, the percentage of the total popula‍tion who are hospitalized (admission rate) over the past 100 years (see Goldhamer and Marshall, 1949), as well as the characteristics of those who are hospitalized (see Stearns and Ullman, 1949) has remained remarkably stable. Indeed, one of the most consistent findings in social science research is that most of the people who are institutionalized for mental disturbances come from the poorest social class, representing the marginal castoffs of society.

Who Are the Mentally Ill?

One of the earliest and most influential studies of the population distribution of mental disorders was conducted by Faris and Dunham (1939). They investigated the residential distribution of all hospitalized mental patients from the Chicago area as well as the diagnostic categories for the various areas of the city. The highest rates of admission were found near the center of the city where the population was unstable, heterogeneous, and economically impoverished. The lowest rates were found in the stable, higher socioeconomic residential communities. Moreover, the distribution of schizophrenia, the most severe mental disturbance, was highest in the central Chicago poverty areas.

Nearly 20 years later Hollingshead and Redlich (1958), in their study of mental disorders and social class in the New Haven area, reported strikingly similar results. More specifically, they found that persons from the lower socioeconomic classes tended to receive more severe diagnoses (e.g. schizophrenia) and were placed in psychiatric institutions more readily than middle- and upper-class persons with mental disorders. The latter were generally diagnosed as psychoneurotic and, when in need of psychiatric care, were provided with out-patient psychotherapy. Parallel results were obtained by Meyers and Bean (1968) in a 10-year follow-up study in the New Haven region.

On the basis of these research reports as well as a host of others that support these findings, most social scientists have concluded that social status has a great impact upon the incidence and prevalence of mental illness. Regardless of the presumed etiology or source of these disorders (i.e., genetic, biochemical, intrapsychic, social, etc.), the theoreticians have attempted to subsume these data into their models of mental illness. For instance, those who assume a genetic cause use these findings to support the notion that lower social class people are in general genetically inferior, and that it is the "genetic deficit" that causes not only the mental disorder but the lower social status as well. On the other hand, an environmentally oriented social scientist would propose that dwelling in socially disorganized, impoverished slum communities "breeds" individual intrapsychic disorganization and impoverishment which leads to psychopathology. Or, another alternative would suggest that living in such communities provides little or no opportunity for the person to "learn" socially acceptable, adaptive patterns of behavior, but instead "reinforces" maladaptive, unacceptable behavior patterns.

In short, the consistent dramatic relationship between social class and the incidence of mental illness, the assignment to diagnostic categories, and the different psychiatric treatment prescribed has not lead to any reformulation of the prevalent views of mental disorders, but has merely been treated as another bit of information to be assimilated into these models of madness. Later in the chapter we will return to these findings and examine their implications from a very different perspective.

By now we are aware of who is and how many are mentally ill. Let us now explore the prevalent models or conceptions of mental illness. That is, what exactly is this problem so many people suffer, particularly, low status, marginal people?

Models of Madness

Now, as in the past, various theoretical models which attempt to explain abnormal, aberrant human behavior are being advocated. Earlier explanations included demon possession, imbalanced body fluids, diseased minds, poor moral training. Although our present-day explanations sound more scientific, they share a great deal in common with the more primitive models. The most important similarity is that despite the guise of scientific respectability, they still are as theoretical and speculative as their predecessors. That is, the theories are little more than concepts and models constructed in the minds of men who are trying to grapple with the ancient mystery of bizarre human conduct. For this reason, theories may exist side by side, often within the same academic discipline, which are contradictory and mutually exclusive. The proponents of these various theories do share in common, however, the assumption that something is "wrong" with the person who behaves in an abnormal manner, and a concern to do something to alleviate whatever it is that is "wrong".

Although there are scores of theories and hundreds of hypotheses concerning the origins, the "nature", the classification, and the treatment of mental illness, there are three basic models of abnormal behavior which encompass this theoretical hodgepodge: the medical model, the behaviorist model, and the imprisonment model (Ederyn Williams, 1972).

The Medical Model

The most dominant and most familiar is the medical model in which aberrant behavior is seen as a symptom of an underlying illness. Like other medical symptoms, such as fever or vomiting, the behavior reflects some underlying disease process. It is the function of the physician to diagnose on the basis of the patient's symptoms the underlying cause (e.g. flu or viral infection), and to cure the disease rather than to simply try to alleviate the symptoms. With respect to bizarre behavior, therefore, it is the task of the psychiatrist or psychologist to determine the cause (e.g. biochemical imbalance, weak ego boundaries, etc.), to diagnose the disorder (e.g. schizophrenia, manic-depressive, etc.) and to intervene with the appropriate treatment. Thus, persons behaving abnormally are seen as patients with an illness who must be treated by doctors, and, if they are sick enough, to be hospitalized. Not surprising then, this model is preferred by psychiatrists and other medically oriented mental health professionals.

Since the medical model has been with us for decades, it would require volumes to merely catalogue the various causes and treatments that have been proposed. The diagnostic nomenclature alone has undergone such extensive change in recent years that the American Psychiatric Association's revised *Diagnostic and Statistical Manual of Mental Disorders* (1968) included 66 new diagnostic categories that did not appear in the 1952 edition. Nonetheless, two basic approaches or themes utilized by proponents of the medical model can be discerned among the variety of subtheories, namely, the biochemical and psychodynamic approaches.

Organic Man

The entire biochemical approach is best summarized in the words of Thudichum (1884), the founder of modern neurochemistry:

> Many forms of insanity are unquestionably the external manifestations of the effects upon the brain, substance of poisons fermented within the body, just as mental aberrations accompanying chronic alcoholic intoxication are the accumulated effects of a relatively simple poison fermented out of the body. These poisons we shall, I have no doubt, be able to isolate after we know the normal chemistry to its uttermost detail. And then will come in their turn the crowning discoveries to which our efforts must ultimately be directed, namely, the discoveries of the antidotes to the poisons and to fermenting causes and processes which produce them.

Those who employ a biochemical approach today have postulated among other things the following causes of mental illness: decrease of basal metabolism, defects in oxidative phosphorylation, differences in amino acid patterns, presence of certain unidentified imidazoles in the urine, vitamin deficiencies, faulty metabolism of epinephrine, increase in serum copper in the form of ceruloplasmin, increase in toxic materials in the blood, high concentration of serotonin, and so on. In all cases it is assumed that the symptoms of mental illness (the behaviors) are caused by the action of abnormal biochemical derivatives. Some theoreticians postulate further that there is a genetic basis for the biochemical disorders, so that in the final analysis, mental illness is determined by genetic factors.

All that has been added, then, in the past 90 years is the specification of the presumed poisons (e.g., serotonin, ceruloplasmin, etc.). The structure and logic of this model remains the same as Thudichum's which in turn is identical to the one put forth by Hippocrates.

Since the cause of the mental illness is biochemical, it follows that the cure would ultimately have to be biochemical. In recent years, a multitude of psychopharmacological preparations have been advanced as *the* treatment, if not the cure, for a variety of mental diseases.

Psychological Man

The majority of the advocates of the medical model, however, do not entirely agree with a biochemical explanation of abnormal behavior, but instead prefer a psychodynamic interpretation. According to this approach, mental illness is viewed in terms of a faulty mental apparatus caused not by biochemicals but by early life experiences, in particular, traumatic ones. The mental apparatus (or psyche or mind) is seen as performing a vital function for the person in much the same manner as any other organ in his body. Thus a malfunctioning psyche afflicts the person with an illness of the mind which is conceptually identical to an illness he may suffer in any other part of his body. Like these other illnesses, the person may be aware of the symptoms but not of the underlying disease process. For instance, a man with heart failure is aware of shortness of breath, dizziness, and so on, rather than the actual heart dysfunction. A person with mental illness may know that he is anxious, phobic or depressed, but he does not know why he experiences these symptoms.

This brings us to the central theme of the psychodynamic approach—namely, the unconscious. All mental disorders are a function of some unconscious process which can only be discovered by highly trained psychotherapists using sophisticated techniques (e.g. free association, dream analysis, projective tests, etc.) There are numerous hypotheses concerning the dynamics, structure and development of the unconscious, the most popular of which are psychoanalytic theories (Freudian and neo-Freudian). These theories have extended the meaning of unconscious to include not only ongoing mental processes but also a region of the mind. It is in this region where the primary causes of mental illness are deposited. The unconscious, therefore, becomes the central focus in the treatment of mental disorders as well as the basis for diagnosing the illness. The explanatory power of the psychodynamic approach can be illustrated as follows:

> When he was a child of 4, Mr. Jones was ridiculed and humiliated by his father at his birthday party. This traumatic event was unconsciously pushed into the unconscious region of Mr. Jones' mind, where it fermented like Thudichum's poisons until it destroyed his adult mental apparatus. Thus, Mr. Jones began abusing his own children, striking his wife, arguing with his bosses, spitting on the sidewalk, while he lavished his father with gifts and affection.

This rather dramatic aberrant behavior confused and befuddled everyone but Mr. Jones' psychoanalyst.

Depending upon the particular theory his analyst subscribed to, Mr. Jones might have been viewed as the victim of: (a) one or more conflicts between his id, ego and superego, (b) fixation at an early level of development, (c) an unsuccessful individuation process, (d) ignored archetypal predispositions, (e) a poorly developed self-system, and on and on. Furthermore, if his analyst were an eclectic, Mr. Jones might have been afflicted with any combination of these.

The treatment here, as elsewhere, is dictated by the assumed origins of causes of illness. If it is the unconscious, particularly a certain past or process, that is making a person mentally ill, to effect a cure one must somehow uncover or unmask that which is causing the disturbance by bringing the unconscious into the light of day. The devices used to bring about this insight include dream analysis, free association, imagery, any symbol analysis, hypnosis, role-playing, psychodrama, and a variety of confrontation techniques. In short, verbal surgery replaces psychosurgery.

Although seemingly disparate, both psychodynamic and biochemical approaches share the assumption that abnormal behaviors are symptoms of a mental illness which exists somewhere within the structure of the mind. In this sense, then, both approaches are organic, rooted in the medical tradition. Both, therefore, may claim credit for a large number of organically oriented treatments usually practiced on hospitalized mental patients. Prior to the massive chemotherapy programs that exist in most every mental hospital today, whereby patients are sedated, stimulated, tranquilized and anti-depressed, there were three popular treatment methods: insulin-coma therapy, electroconvulsive therapy, and neurosurgical procedures.

Insulin-coma therapy, developed in the 1930s, involved inducing a hypoglycemic coma by reducing the blood sugar level with large doses of insulin. Concurrently, electroconvulsive therapy was introduced into the mental health scene and has remained popular even today. The procedure here is to produce a gran mal convulsion by passing 100 volts of electrical current through the brain by means of electrodes attached to either side of the patient's head. Usually 10 to 20 treatments are given over a few weeks period (2 to 8 weeks). The neurosurgical procedure that was particularly popular in the 1940s and 1950s (and remains popular in some circles today) is the prefrontal lobotomy. In its most refined form, the lobotomy is performed by entering the skull cavity through the orbit of the eye and then proceeding to cut the nerve fibers between the prefrontal lobes and the lower parts of the brain.

In keeping with other traditional forms of medical treatment, psychiatrists concede that there are on occasion some undesirable side effects (iatrogenic symptoms) that accompany these treatment modalities. Nonetheless, they consider it their responsibility to drug, shock, or cut away the offending internal disease process. Surely, in terms of their complex theories and refined therapeutic techniques, these men of science have outdone their medieval counterparts. With respect to their logic, the validity of their theories and the success of their treatment, however, they remain on a.par with the inquisitors of old.

The Behaviorist Model

For decades clinical psychologists had lived in the shadow of the medical model, second-class citizens in a world dominated by psychiatrists. With the introduction of the behaviorist model in the 1960s, however, psychologists created a new and distinctive terrain for themselves. Borrowing theories developed by psychologists in academic laboratories rather than clinical settings, and research findings based upon animals rather than people, some clinical psychologists have fashioned a somewhat unique conception of mental illness as well as several unusual forms of treatment.

The theories that they have borrowed center on the idea that behaviors, even in their most complex forms, are learned through a series of stimulus-response connections. Moreover, any behavior can be learned, modified or shaped according to the use of positive and negative reinforcers, or the law of Reinforcement and Extinction. Armed in this manner, with all the trappings of academic behaviorism, these clinical psychologists enter the mental illness scene determined to be as scientific as their academic counterparts. In their earnestness, the behavioristic clinicians have devised the only therapy which can trace its beginnings to laboratory work in highly controlled situations with albino rats, pigeons and other creatures. In addition, they contend that to focus upon anything other than the behavior emitted by the patient (e.g. the unconscious, the conscious, feelings, thoughts, etc.) is not only unscientific but mistaken.

According to the behaviorist model, then, mental illness is a learned, maladaptive, unacceptable behavior pattern. That is, the abnormal behaviors are not the outcome or manifestation of some underlying disorder. Instead, the proponents of this model claim that the behavior itself is the disorder. Since the maladaptive behavior is learned, it can be "unlearned" or extinguished; it can be modified or reshaped into more acceptable behavior. The various forms of this treatment are called behavior modification. The removal of the symptom, the inappropriate behavior, is equivalent to "curing" the mental illness. For instance, the woman who refuses to fly in an airplane is cured when she boards a jet for Miami; the man who tells everyone that his wife is plotting to kill him is cured when he stops these accusations.

It is no simple task, however, to change sometimes long-standing, unacceptable behaviors to acceptable ones. This is where the skill of the behavior modification experts come into play. It is his or her task to determine what exactly will act as a positive or a negative reinforcer for a particular patient.

In keeping with their scientific concern, these clinical psychologists have compiled several therapeutically proven techniques: (1) positive reinforcement of acceptable behavior, e.g. taking charge of a mute patient's food and giving him a morsel every time he speaks a word; (2) positive reinforcement of unacceptable behavior, e.g. giving a patient a cigarette or two every time he uses foul language to the nurses; (3) token economy, e.g., paying a patient with tokens which he can exchange for meals, clothing, etc. whenever he does what you order him to do; (4) faradic aversive controls, e.g., applying an intense, though harmless, electric shock to the thighs of a young child whenever he bites his hands; (5) covert sensitization, e.g., having a patient imagine he is sick to his stomach and vomiting whenever he has a homosexual desire.

All of these techniques, in addition to several others, have been successful some of the time with some of the patients. When these therapeutic techniques cure patients of their undesirable behavior patterns, it comes as no surprise. The basis of the behavior modification techniques (deprivation, punishment, terror, exploitation, disgust, bribery) have been with us through the centuries. In civilized communities, however, most of these tactics have long been abandoned by fair-minded, humane individuals. Thus, the behaviorist model, under the cloak of scientific respectability, has not only reintroduced but has encouraged the use of these degrading, destructive, dehumanizing, totalitarian tactics not only in mental hospitals but in prisons, industrial settings and schoolrooms as well.

Behavior control or modification by fear, force and coercion is justified by those who use these techniques in terms of social adaptability. Specifically, they argue that society will be better off and the patient will be happier (since society will reward or at least stop punishing him) when the patient changes his undesirable, abnormal behavior; when the patient behaves the way he is supposed to. Moreover, if the clinical psychologist is not faint-hearted, he will acknowledge that a brief, painful experience (behavior therapy) is a small price to pay in exchange for the interminable pain of longstanding mental illness. In short, the behavior therapist rescues the patient from his bad habits by using whatever means available in order to resocialize him within a very special value system (the therapist's).

The primacy of the social order is peculiar to behavior therapy especially with respect to the explicitness in the treatment goals. As one leading behavior therapist has stated:

> No one owns his personality. Your ego, or individuality, was forced on you by your genetic constitution and by the society into which you were born. You had no say about what kind of personality you acquired, and there's no reason to believe you should have the right to refuse to acquire a new personality if your old one is antisocial. (McConnell, 1970).

The Imprisonment Model

Besides conducting epidemiological studies of the distribution, prevalence and incidence of mental disorders, sociologists in recent years have contributed a new approach to understanding the mentally deranged. Growing out of their work on deviancy, a number of sociologists (and others who have borrowed their concepts) have applied a social systems analysis to the area of mental illness. From this perspective mental illness is portrayed as an achieved social role rather than an individual form of psychopathology. That is, mental illness is little more than a label assigned to certain persons who occupy particular positions in the social system; a social role that carries with it specific expectancies. As with all role expectancies, the criteria here, too, reflect mainstream cultural values and norms.

To achieve the label and, therefore, the role, mentally ill, one first must act in a way that violates the rules of conduct and morality by which most people in the community abide. In this part of the analysis, the social system approach is similar to the behaviorists' viewpoint of abnormal behavior. Specifically, that mental illness is the outcome of a social definition of "normal" behavior or socially approved conduct. While the behaviorists act as society's apologists insisting that it has the right to eliminate or correct whatever behaviors it finds dysfunctional and disruptive, the social system advocates have taken a rather different approach.

The social system, social role perspective has, in fact, led to a variety of mental illness models each of which places emphasis upon different components of the social system, the individual and the interaction between the two. One of these models will be presented later on in the chapter. Here, however, we will examine one manifestation of this perspective, the *imprisonment model*.

Beginning with the landmark book by Goffman (1961), *Asylums*, the proponents of this model have taken the view that mental patients are victims, unfortunate eccentrics who, betrayed by their friends and family, are imprisoned against their will in monolithic, dehumanizing mental institutions. One of the consequences of this kind of imprisonment is the loss of self, of one's individuality by the oppressive, homogenizing institution. Thus, they see the mentally ill as prisoners in a jail (mental hospital), staffed by guards, wardens and other assorted jailers (psychiatrists, psychologists, social workers, nurses, aides). The crime for which they are being punished is exhibiting behaviors that are socially unacceptable. Indeed, the current interest in community mental health programs developed out of just these concerns. The mental hospital was seen as doing far more harm than good, overpowering and oppressing the individual, and leading to the phenomena of "institutionalization". That is, although there is little or nothing "wrong" initially with the person who is put away in a mental hospital, after a while the institution destroys his individuality, making him dependent upon and unable to function outside of the institutional context.

This model has been extended and popularized by the "antipsychiatrist", R. D. Laing, who contends that mental patients, schizophrenics in particular, are perhaps the only truly sane people in a society that has itself gone mad. He suggests that quite often schizophrenics represent an emotional elite, having travelled to regions of the mind where most fear to tread.

As one might expect, the treatment prescribed by the imprisonment model advocates is directed toward the "sick" society rather than the individuals who have been victimized by it. As such, the treatment involves diverse goals ranging from prohibiting involuntary or compulsory commitment to the abolition of mental institutions to a total revolutionary social upheaval.

Those who have taken the imprisonment model to its ideological extreme gather around the banner of "radical therapists". As they see it, mental illness is but another manifestation of an oppressive society, which can only be discovered and appreciated within a Marxist framework. They propose that a new radical psychology be formulated with a concommitant radical therapy; that is, radical psychology be a force for revolution. Thus, they view therapy as "political change . . . not peanut butter" (Agel, 1971). The movement proposes that radical therapy take the following forms:

> . . . organizing a community to seize control of the way it's run; . . . rooting out our own chauvinism and mercilessly exposing it in others; focusing on the social dimensions of oppression and not on "intrapsychic" depression, fear, anger, and so on; organizing against the war, against polluting industries, against racist practice; developing a political/therapy center for young people . . . (Agel, 1971, p. 290).

Just as the behaviorist model promises a brave, new world based on behavior modification, upon the establishment of social order by elimination or changing disruptive individual behavior patterns, the imprisonment model promises a new world based upon the modification of society by organizing society's victims to man the barricades and overthrow the established order. Once again, the poor, troubled and distressed of the world are presented with an exploitative alternative. Functionally there is little difference between emptying man of freedom, dignity, autonomy and intention (as the behaviorist model does), and filling him with oppression, hate and anger in order to empty institutions and society of freedom. Both exploit the persons whom they purport to help.

The Communality of the Models of Madness

The above conflict is, of course, more a battle between opposing political ideologies (e.g., Facists vs. Communists), each with their own clichés and slogans, rather than a scientific debate aimed at understanding and alleviating a complex human problem. Indeed, the conflict between all three of the dominant models of mental illness, the medical, behaviorist and imprisonment models can never be successfully resolved by the scientific evidence each might accrue, since their underlying (implicit or explicit) premises preclude an authentic search for truth.

The three models share in common a view of the "nature" of the mentally ill that from the outset of any inquiry makes it impossible to find little more than what they expect to. Specifically, they all present the mentally ill, regardless of etiology or causes, as being hapless, ineffectual *victims* (of a disease process, of a maladaptive learned behavior pattern, of a "sick" and oppressive society); as people *in whom and to whom* things happen. Not only are they never portrayed as anything other than passive, inept human beings but this portrait is never even questioned. It is a self-evident proposition, an unchallenged truth maintained without awareness that the mentally ill are pathetic dependent victims. This shared conception shapes the "reality" of what the proponents of each model see when they look at the mentally ill. The models only appear to be different when they attempt to explain the *why* of mental illness.

Thus, upon close inspection the apparent gulf between the medical, behaviorist and imprisonment models vanishes just as the centuries become minutes when we carefully and logically compare modern, scientific models with their ancient counterparts. It is no surprise, then, that the history of the study of mental illness is strewn with the debris of discarded theories and models as well as abandoned methods of treatment. But it must be emphasized that the earlier models and treatment modes were not abandoned because a new, more accurate, more scientific model appeared on the scene. Instead they were discarded because more fashionable, more politically compatible alternatives became available, models that were more in keeping with the temper of the times.

Now that we have come nearly full circle in psychiatry's, psychology's and sociology's failure to explain satisfactorily the phenomena of madness, is there any alternative conception available?

Alternatives to Madness

It was posited earlier that one major reason (if not *the* reason) for the gloomy history in this area of human concern is the self-evident truth concerning the "nature" of the mentally ill. What happens, however, if this unchallenged assumption is questioned? That is, what might we learn if we ask: Are the mentally ill ineffectual, hapless, dependent, acquiescent people? Are they, in fact, *victims* of their illness, their learning experiences, or their "sick" society?

This question was the basis of a large-scale systematic investigation by Braginsky, Braginsky and Ring (1969) with hospitalized mental patients most of whom were schizophrenics (one of the most severe mental disorders). Their research had its beginnings in what were initially informal observations of how mental patients conducted their daily lives. For instance, most patients reliably performed complex, demanding jobs within the hospital, lived peacefully and co-operatively with their fellow inmates, and participated as well as initiated hospital community activities. They were not, of course, the first to observe "normal" behavior among hospitalized mental patients. But rather than choosing to see this behavior as a perhaps temporary remission of symptoms or a disguise for some underlying madness, these authors assumed that mental patients were like most people, and that the concept of mental illness was a myth (Szasz, 1961). Their program of research, therefore, pitted this observation against the dominant models of madness. Let us turn first to what they found and then to the alternative their findings suggest.

Following a varied series of studies it was evident that long-term mental patients function as effective human beings and that they created lives for themselves within the institutions that satisfy their motivations, their needs, and their interests. For example, a major determinant of the patient's life in a mental hospital is the staff's assessment of his mental status or his psychopathology. Staff members evaluate a patient's psychopathology and decide how the patient is to live while he is in the hospital (to be put on an open or closed ward, or whether he is to be discharged).

These judgments are based on the patient's interactions with the nurses and aides, his performance on psychological tests and his behavior in formal psychiatric interviews. Several experiments demonstrated that mental patients used ingratiation strategies to stay on the "good side of the staff", selectively censored information on psychological tests to create symptoms of either mental illness or mental health (whichever served their best interest), and manipulated psychiatric interviews to avoid unpleasant outcomes or to gain desirable ones.

In one study (Braginsky & Braginsky, 1967) a staff psychologist interviewed chronic schizophrenics. On the way to the interview room, an assistant mentioned the purpose of the interview to the patient. He told some patients that the interview would determine whether they were well enough to be discharged (discharge condition), others that the interview would decide whether they should be transferred to closed wards (open-ward condition) and still others that the interview was to assess their mental status (mental status-condition). This last condition is typical of the periodic interview that is part of the standard hospital procedure. Its usual purpose is to determine whether the patient is ready for discharge; therefore, patients should perceive it as similar to the discharge condition.

All the patients in the study had lived on open wards for a minimum of 2 years and all were diagnosed as schizophrenics. The interviewer did not know which story the assistant had told the patients. After greeting each patient, he asked, "How are you feeling?" and proceeded to tape-record the patients' replies. Later three staff psychiatrists independently rated each of the thirty patients according to how severely ill the patient seemed, the degree of hospital control the patient needed, and how much anxiety he displayed. The psychiatrists who had no knowledge of the experiment and were unfamiliar with the patients, rated the ones in the discharge and mental status conditions as being the most disturbed and in greater need of hospital control. Almost half of these patients reported delusions, hallucinations, and other severely pathological symptoms. Patients threatened with locked wards (open-ward condition) never reported such symptoms; instead these patients emphasized how well they were functioning in the hospital and created a picture of well being. In no case, regardless of condition, did patients act in a bizarre manner or show undue anxiety. They merely reported, in a matter of fact way, how they felt. Clearly, when it served their purposes to remain in the hospital, the patients convinced the three psychiatrists that they were disturbed and in need of hospital care. When this same portrayal would lead to the locked wards, they avoided it, presenting instead images of "healthy" mental patients.

Obviously, the schizophrenics were able to behave effectively in an experimental situation, but could they be as effective at controlling their fates within the daily routine of institutional life? In order to answer this an 86-item attitude survey designed to elicit reliable and accurate information was given to 100 mental patients (mostly schizophrenic). Their responses indicated that patients want a comfortable, enjoyable, non-demanding milieu in the hospital. For instance, more than 70% of the patients believe that the best way to fit into hospital life is to try and have a good time, that it is foolish not to enjoy themselves, and what they need most is a period of relaxation, and that patients would feel better if the hospital made no demands upon them.

More specifically, they believe that they are not mentally ill or different from non-hospitalized persons, and they want to keep their civil and social rights. Most agree that many persons on the outside are more disturbed than old-timers in the hospital are. They feel that mental patients should be allowed to vote, that hospitalization should not be grounds for divorce, that they should not be denied a driver's license or re-employment at their former jobs. They believe that patients should have some formal voice in deciding how the hospital is run. In short, their desires and expectations are like those most of us have when we are on holiday weekends.

These patients see the mental hospital as a neighborhood. They feel that if they really wanted to leave, they could. Most old-timers are determined to subvert both the gate-keeping activities and the "therapeutic" efforts of the staff. For instance, they believe that a comfortable routine will help them "recover", that everything the patients do in the hospital is "therapeutic", including drinking coffee in the canteen, watching television, and relaxing.

The patients' wishes to enjoy themselves in the hospital and their lack of commitment to therapy and rehabilitation should make them professional about the pleasurable aspects of the institution (for example, where and when movies are shown) and selectively feeble-minded about "therapeutic" places and people. This was, in fact, what was found.

On the basis of a hospital-information test, patients showed greater knowledge about the recreational aspects of the hospital than about the places and people they wished to avoid. For example, 80% or more of the patients knew the location of the swimming pool, the gym, and the bowling alley; at least 70% knew where to find the post office, the garage, the theater building and the canteen. Two-thirds of the patients even knew the publication times of the hospital magazine, and half knew where it was printed.

On the other hand, only 26% knew the name of the psychologist or social worker in their building, only 22% knew where to find the social worker, and only a third knew the location of the nurse's office or the name of the nurse in their buildings. Almost as many patients (42%) knew where to buy used clothes and where to find the tailor as those who knew the name of their own psychiatrist (48%).

Therapy

The patients' participation in therapy reflected their selective avoidance of learning about the therapeutic aspects of the hospital. It should be noted that the hospital where this research was conducted had available many opportunities for therapy and often required the patients to partake in some form of therapy. A patient, if he chose, easily could spend 8 to 10 hours a day in the great variety of therapeutic programs offered by the hospital. Nonetheless, only 10 of the 100 patients interviewed were in either individual or group therapy at any time, and more than half of these spent only 4 weeks in psychotherapy. Every one of the 100 patients who had been in therapy managed to extricate himself from the therapy program within 8 weeks. It is reasonable to conclude that the patients' lack of therapeutic involvement reflects their attitudes, not the staff's.

From the perspective of the patient who desires to stay in the hospital, avoidance of therapeutic encounters is wise. Patients recognize the truth in the adage "out of sight, out of mind". In another study, psychiatrists were asked to recall the names of as many of their patients as they could. On the average, the therapists recalled 57% of their patients. When the patients who were remembered were compared with those who were not, it was found that remembered patients had initiated contact with their psychiatrists, while those who were forgotten had actively avoided their doctors. There were no differences in the amount of illness or disturbance the doctors attributed to each group.

A 5-month follow-up study turned up further proof of the patients' wisdom. Of those whom the physicians remembered, 42% were discharged, while only 8% of those the doctors had forgotten were discharged. By making himself "invisible", the patient maximizes his chances of remaining in the institution, where he can live the kind of "therapeutic" life he desires. (That some patients actively sought help suggests that these patients either were experiencing "mental distress" from which they wanted to escape, or were dissatisfied with the accommodations at that particular mental hospital).

If patients keep away from formal therapy programs, how do they spend most of their time? The typical patient spends more than 7 hours on the ward each day, about 3 hours in off-ward recreation areas, and about 2 hours working on jobs. Male patients spend their time on the ward watching TV, reading, sitting alone or playing cards; the women spend most of their time talking with each other.

When they leave the ward, patients congregate in the recreation rooms, canteen, gym, other wards and building lobbies. When they work, it is usually at unskilled though indispensable hospital jobs, such as cafeteria duty, laundry, and garbage collection. This menial work should not be seen as a sign of hospital control or demands. Seventy percent of the working patients volunteered for their assignments, which usually took them off their wards.

There was as much diversity among patients in how they spend their time as one might expect to find among visitors at Palm Beach, Aspen, or any other resort.

Weekends

In all of these studies, traditional psychiatric variables as diagnoses, severity of illness, premorbidity histories, and institutional demands were included. None of these factors was related to the behavior or attitudes of the patients. One could, however, predict accurately how a patient would behave in the hospital by discovering how he spent his weekends before he became a patient. The person who spent his weekends at home would, as a patient, spend most of his time on the wards. The person who visited and socialized with friends on the weekend would visit all week long in the hospital. In short, the hospital provided the patient with a long weekend, just as a resort does for the rest of us.

The picture that emerges from the study of long-term patients on open wards bears no resemblance to the sharply etched view that most mental-health professionals have of psychiatric patients and hospitals. The hospital and its formal functions are a fiction maintained by the staff and the outside world. In reality, the patients in the open wards live in a resort. On occasion, the imaginings of the staff become translated into such practices as lobotomies, electroshock treatment, and behavior therapy. For instance, a psychiatrist's belief in schizophrenia may lead to a lobotomy.

Resorts

Viewing the institution through the eyes of the patient immediately raises some new and interesting questions. For instance, do patients compare hospital resorts with one another? Is there an informal Baedeker's Guide to mental institutions? It does appear that former mental patients tell their friends and associates about the pleasant features of hospital life. As studies have shown, life in the hospital relieves many patients from worrying over where their next meals will come from, how they will keep warm in the winter, and where they will sleep. For others, free movies, swimming in a heated indoor pool, socializing with friends in the canteen, or just relaxing and reading in the library represent the luxuries not available to them outside. For all of them, worries over muggings, thefts, rape and murder all but disappear within the shelter of the hospital walls.

Friends

A study of new, first-admission patients showed that those who have ex-patients among their friends enter the hospital with attitudes similar to those of long-term patients. Within days of their entry, they adapt to styles of life that characterized their weekends at home. New patients who have no contacts with ex-patients enter the hospital with attitudes similar to those of the professional staff. Within a few months, however, they shed their preconceptions, begin to change their perspective and finally to enjoy their stay in the hospital.

Further evidence of the proselytizing or advertising activities of patients came to light when one study showed that a significant proportion of persons admitted to the hospital had homes or apartments close to each other on the outside (in the same or next building), were of the same sex and age, entered and left the hospital at nearly the same time, tended to get the same diagnosis upon entering, and paired or clustered so that one admission was always an ex-patient.

In short, these studies provide an empirical basis for those observers of the mental illness scene who have rejected current conceptions of psychological disorders (e.g. Haley, 1969; Leifer, 1969; Sarbin, 1967; Szasz, 1961, 1963, 1970). More specifically, the research demonstrates that the typical portrayal of the schizophrenic as an inept, helpless and passive person is, at best, a distortion, and more probably, a delusion. These studies also disclose the ineffectuality of both the mental institution and its "treatment" programs in intervening in the lives of its residents. Thus, the prison-like view of the mental hospital as an overpowering, dehumanizing institution that oppresses the patients is but another distortion.

The results of these studies are not surprising, if one merely views mental patients as persons and the mental hospital as a community or a resort. Indeed, these findings would appear trite were it not for the failure of the mental health professionals to *see* the patients and the hospital for what they are. Their perceptions are unfocused not only because of their conceptual biases and models of madness, but also because they, like most middle class people, are biased against certain segments of society, in particular, the marginal, lower class segment. It is this segment, in fact, that provides the bulk of persons diagnosed as schizophrenic (among other labels).

It was noted before that the relationship between social class and diagnoses was established as early as 1939 by Faris and Dunham. Hollingshead and Redlich (1958) also found that lower-class people were over-represented in the category of schizophrenia, while the middle-class mentally ill are labelled psychoneurotic. Only recently, however, have studies been conducted to directly investigate this relationship. Lee (1968) presented to diagnosticians a transcript of an interview between a doctor and a patient. The interview did not suggest that there was anything wrong with the patient, but the professionals were asked for a diagnosis and prognosis on this "patient". Lee varied the biographical data so that in one condition the patient was lower-class and in the other, upper-class. The "lower-class patient" was overwhelmingly rated as more mentally ill and had a worse prognosis than the "upper-class patient".

In a more complex study, Efron (1970) presented psychiatrists with one of three tape-recorded monologues. Each was performed by an actor who portrayed either very mild, moderate or severe psycho-pathology. In addition, the psychiatrists were given one of two accompanying biographical sketches, one of which depicted an upper-class man earning over $25,000 a year and the other, a lower-class man earning less than $5,000 a year. In total, Efron presented one of six combinations to each psychiatrist: Upper-class "patient" with (1) mild, (2) moderate, (3) severe psychopathology, or the Lower-class "patient" with (4) mild, (5) moderate, (6) severe psycho-pathology.

After reading the biography and listening to the tape, each psychiatrist evaluated the patient in terms of diagnosis, severity of disturbance, and prognosis. Just as in Lee's study, here the patient's social class strongly influenced the diagnosis and prognosis. Regardless of the symptoms the Lower-class "patient" exhibited (mild, moderate, or severe), he was judged to be extremely psychotic with a very poor prognosis. The ratings of the Upper-class "patient" varied according to the symptoms, but even the severe Upper-class "patient" (3) was judged as healthier than the best-off Lower-class "patient" (4).

Other presumably irrelevant factors also influence the diagnosis of people. For instance, Wenger and Fletcher (1969), after observing 81 commitment hearings, discovered a strikingly high and significant relationship between a lawyer's presence and the decision not to commit (p. 94). Even when they controlled for "sanity" to counter the possibility that those who brought lawyers were "saner" than those without legal counsel at the hearings, Wenger and Fletcher still found that the presence or absence of a lawyer very strongly influenced the outcomes of the proceedings.

Based upón two interrelated studies (Braginsky, Braginsky & Fitzgerald, in preparation; Braginsky, Braginsky & Edwards, in preparation), it was disclosed that the patient's political attitudes also affect what a psychiatrist or psychologist think of him. First a political attitudes questionnaire (Christie *et al.,* 1969) was administered to 100 hospitalized mental patients (50 men and 50 women) and to 50 mental health professionals at the same institution. The patients scored significantly higher on the New Left Philosophy and Radical Tactics scales than the staff. The patients, in fact, appeared to be more politically dissident that Columbia University students who had, prior to this study, received the highest scores of any group tested.

To more directly determine the relationship, if any, between political dissidence and diagnostic labels, two video-taped interviews between a doctor and a bogus patient were made. Both interviews had four segments: presenting complaints; expression of political philosophy; expression of political strategy; and evaluative comments about mental-health professionals.

The first segment of both interviews was identical, consisting of the patient's response to the question, "How are you feeling?" The patient complained of listlessness, fatigue, poor appetite, restless sleep patterns, irritability with friends, and other symptoms typical of mildly neurotic persons.

In the second segment, the patient expressed either a new left political philosophy or a middle-of-the-road political philosophy. In the third segment the patient with the new-left attitudes endorsed the use of radical tactics to bring about social change. The moderate patient decried the use of such tactics.

Both patients in the final segment criticized mental-health professionals, but did so from very different perspectives. The new-left radical accused mental-health professionals of being handmaidens of a repressive society, labeling, drugging and locking up anyone who disagreed with mainstream values. The middle-of-the-road patient charged that mental-health professionals had destroyed traditional values, encouraged permissiveness, and were in general too radical.

A different audience of mental-health professionals looked at each interview, then diagnosed the patient and rated the severity of his illness after each of the four segments. Thus, after segment one the videorecorder was stopped and the observers completed their ratings. Then the same was done after segment two and so on through segment four.

The results show that the more politically deviant the patient was, the more the diagnosticians said he was mentally disturbed. As the new-left radical patient's complaints shifted from himself to society, the diagnosticians saw him as increasingly deranged. When the patient suggested radical action to correct what is wrong with society, he was perceived as still more pathological. The moderate counterpart's mental illness rating stayed the same as he vocalized anti-new-left sentiments, and somewhat decreased when he criticized those who would radically change our social institutions. Both the new-left and middle-of-the-road patients dramatically increased their illness ratings when they criticized mental-health professionals. Even the politically "rational" young man (seen as moderately disturbed despite being presented as a hospitalized mental patient) became quite psychotic following his "irrational" attack on those who want to help him.

Indeed, the most spectacular change in the diagnosticians' perception of the patient occurred when the patient directed his insults at mental-health personnel. What would happen if a patient flattered mental-health personnel instead of attacking them? If diagnosticians judge a patient's insults as a function of his "paranoid" mind, could they conceivably view a patient's compliments as the function of a "normal" mind?

Returning to the videorecorder, a new fourth segment was constructed that accentuated the positive and eliminated the negative concerning mental-health professionals. This new segment four was used as a replacement on the new-left radical patient interview. A new hospital-staff audience was convened and the same procedure was followed.

The results for the first three segments of the interview paralleled those obtained before. On segment four, however, the very disturbed mental patient suddenly got well. Mysteriously, there was a complete remission of his symptoms, and a new found normality. Very simply, the cure consisted of telling the doctors, social workers, nurses and aides that they are kind, helpful, competent and, in general, wonderful human beings.

The research cited above all point to the socio-political nature of the diagnostic enterprise, and consequently of the entire mental health system including its institutions and treatment programs. An examination of diagnostic labels linguistically, historically and empirically (see Braginsky and Braginsky, 1974 for detailed analyses) makes it clear that these labels tell us nothing about the persons to whom they are assigned, but instead reveal a great deal about diagnosticians and the society they serve.

Rosenhan (1973) in his study "On Being Sane in Insane Places" vividly demonstrates the failure of these labels to be little more than stereotypes and prejudgments. Once he and his co-workers were admitted to psychiatric hospitals by telling the doctor they heard a voice say "hollow", "empty", "thud", there was nothing they could do to convince the staff that they were not schizophrenic. Despite the normalcy of their behavior, their daily comportment on the wards, and their life histories, the best they could do was be promoted to schizophrenic "in remission". That is, they were still schizophrenic but their symptoms were not showing.

Besides stigmatizing and potentially harming the persons who are labeled schizophrenic (or whatever), the use of diagnostic categories encourage professionals to *think* they understand, impeding them from looking further. As William James once stated, "The most immutable barrier in nature is between one man's thoughts and another's." If psychologists and psychiatrists were more humble, acknowledging what they do not know; if they faced the human condition without trying to classify it in terms of their own ideology, then they conceivably could dent this barrier and finally begin to understand the problems and suffering that beset many human beings.

References

Agel, J. (Prod.). *The Radical Therapist.* N.Y.: Ballantine, 1971.

Braginsky, B. and Braginsky, D. Schizophrenic Patients in the Psychiatric Interview: An Experimental Study of their Effectiveness at Manipulation. *Journal of Consulting Psych.,* 1967, 21, 543—7.

Braginsky, B. and Braginsky, D. *Mainstream Psychology: A Critique.* Holt, Rinehart and Winston, 1974.

Braginsky, B., Braginsky, D. and Edwards. The Political Attitudes of Mental Patients and Their "Keepers" in Braginsky, B. and Braginsky, D. *Mainstream Psychology: A Critique,* Holt, Rinehart and Winston, 1974.

Braginsky, B., Braginsky, D. and Ring, K. *Methods of Madness: The Mental Hospital as a Last Resort.* N.Y.: Holt, Rinehart and Winston, 1969.

Christie, R., Friedman, L. N. and Ross, A. The New Left and Its Ideology. *Proceedings of 77th Annual Convention of the American Psychological Association,* 1969, 229—30.

Efron, C. Psychiatric Bias: An Experimental Study of the Effects of Social Class Membership on Diagnostic Outcome. Unpublished Masters Thesis, Wesleyan University, 1970.

Faris, R. E. L. and Dunham, H. W. *Mental Disorders in Urban Areas: An Ecological Study of Schizophrenia and other Psychoses.* Chicago: University of Chicago Press, 1939.

Goffman, Erving. *Asylums.* Doubleday, 1961.

Haley, J. *The Power Tactics of Jesus Christ and Other Essays.* N.Y.: Grossman Publishers, 1969.

Hollingshead, A. B. and Redlich, F. C. *Social Class and Mental Illness: A Community Study.* N.Y.: Wiley, 1958.

Lee, S. Social Class Bias in the Diagnosis of Mental Illness. Ann Arbor, Michigan: University Microfilms, 1968.

Leifer, R. *In the Name of Mental Health: The Social Functions of Psychiatry.* N.Y.: Science House, 1969.

McConnell, J. W. Criminals Can Be Brainwashed—Now. *Psychology Today,* 1970, 3, 14.

Rosenhan, D. L. On Being Sane in Insane Places. *Science,* 1973, 179, 250—7.

Sarbin, T. On the Futility of the Proposition That Some People be Labled "Mentally Ill". *Journal of Consulting Psychology,* 1967, 31, 447—53.

Srole, L., Langer, T. S., Michael, S. T., Opler, M. K., and Rennie, T. A. C. Mental Health in the Metropolis: The Midtown Manhattan Study. N.Y.: McGraw-Hill, 1962.

Stearns, A. and Ullman, A. One Thousand Unsuccessful Careers. *American Journal of Psychiatry,* 1949, 11, 801—9.

Szasz, T. *The Myth of Mental Illness.* N.Y.: Hoeber, 1961.

Szasz, T. *Law, Liberty and Psychiatry: An Inquiry into the Social Uses of Mental Health Practices.* N.Y.: Crowell-Collier and MacMillan, 1963.

Szasz, T. *The Manufacture of Madness.* N.Y.: Harper and Row, 1970.

Williams, Ederyn. Models of Madness. *New Society,* Vol. 470, pp. 607—9, 30 Sept., 1971.

III

The Spiritual Context

CHAPTER 4

A Mystical-Occult Approach to Psychosis

The young man was foreign born but spoke English well. His family had travelled a bit, and he learned English during a period of time that they lived in Cyprus. He said that once during that time he stopped a cable car in midflight just by "willing it to happen". He described numerous other powers that he has; he can read other minds; he can transmit his own thought to others, and on occasion he can also bend metal objects with his mind. He describes how this developed; he says that the powers come from outside him, "from somewhere in our galaxy or universe or cosmos". He discovered these abilities at the age of 3, "My mother would come home from playing cards and I would tell her how much she won or lost—but exactly." His powers over matter became apparent to him at age 7. "I was sitting one day in school looking at my wristwatch, and I noticed that the hands were jumping ahead to a different hour. Then, later, when I looked at it, I could see that the hands were bending. At first I didn't connect any of this to myself. But, then I realized I could do things other people could not do. And it always seemed to happen in school or when there were other people around, so it seemed like I was drawing some kind of power from other people."

Now he is surrounded by many unexplainable events. Cameras stop; tape recorders malfunction; when he sat near the movie screen on a transcontinental airliner, the projector broke down. One time while in N.Y. he left his body and found himself walking along a beach in Rio de Janeiro. "It was scary", he said, "what if I couldn't get back?" This was so frightening to him that he decided to never do it again.

The above is a report drawn from an article in an American Medical Association periodical. It is a description of an obvious schizophrenic, right? Wrong. Or, at least, that is not the conclusion that is drawn in the article. This is from an article about the increasingly well known "psychic", Uri Geller. [1] How times are changing. A man who says things like this is no longer *a priori* presumed to be hopelessly deranged, even within a publication that falls within the sponsorship of the AMA.

The only question of doubt about Uri Geller is not whether he is delusional, but whether the things that he says happen really do happen. Uri Geller is becoming a national celebrity, performing his ESP feats on television, in the Houston Astrodome, and in New York's Town Hall. So the question that is asked is: Is he a conjurer, some kind of clever charlatan? From the medical viewpoint the only pathology that this brings into play about Geller is perhaps one of sociopathy. But attempting to explain Geller away or "diagnosing" him in this way is difficult, as his paranormal phenomena become increasingly verified by respected, or at least credentialed, men of science. Among these are Andrija Puharich, an MD who is well recognized in the area of psychical research, Dr. Edgar Mitchell, the astronaut, and a research team at the Stanford Research Institute who have investigated Geller under laboratory conditions and have found no alternative way than some kind of paranormal process to account for what he is able to do.[2] William Tiller, a physicist, who is chairman of the material sciences department at Stanford, has come to believe that "todays psychic phenomena is a manifestation of tomorrow's physics."[3]

My prime interest in presenting the above example is not so much to make a case for ESP, but to show an instance of a person who, presented to us in a way that implies a clinical setting, comes across to us a typical example of a flagrant schizophrenic, who in fact turns out to be someone whose statements about the nature of things, of reality if you will, are to be taken seriously. In this case, discovering who he is and what is the actual setting forces us to reconsider our initial and quite confident assessment of him. Had this same person actually come before a psychiatrist or psychologist and made those statements there is almost no way that he could have been judged to be sane. It was hard enough for Rosenhan, who did not say anything about unusual powers.[4]

The setting in which a person is presented to us is critical and decisive in forming the cognitive framework within which we judge his statements. Someone who comes before us in a clinical setting for the purpose of being evaluated or diagnosed is almost inevitably seen through a particular set of clinical "filters". One's whole training as a clinician, and one's legitimacy in being in that chair as an evaluator, is based on the precise fact that one has learned and absorbed those filters. The filters that are of particular concern to us here are the collections of structures that come under the heading of psychosis and schizophrenia (I will use these terms interchangeably).

I am quite convinced that a most certain way for a person to acquire a label of schizophrenia is to come before the clinician and talk about certain kinds of topics, these include the occult, ESP, religion, God, and the general range of metaphysical phenomena. I do not really think that *how* one talks about these things has much to do with whether or not he is given the diagnosis. He can be quite coherent and ordered in his speech, follow the rules of grammar and logic, and yet if he expresses serious concern with, or some kind of excitement in, these topics, he is on his way to winning the label. This contention is supported by research that shows that the *content* of written messages, not the *form,* largely determines whether someone is judged to be schizophrenic.[5]

I find this quite striking because it is in contradiction to the theoretical basis upon which Bleuler formulated the concept of schizophrenia in the first place. According to Bleuler, Schizophrenia was a breakdown in the *forms* of thought, a disruption in the normal associativity between thoughts — what we call loose associations, and not in any way related to what the "schizoprenic" talked about. Of course, throughout Bleuler's book, in his rich accumulation of case material, one finds example after example of his patients making reference to these metaphysical or cosmological themes, but this content is almost totally ignored by Bleuler as if he were blind and deaf. This precedent, of a formal analysis of schizophrenia, continued on, and deeply influenced a whole generation of later investigators. An example of this is illustrated by the classic *Language and Thought in Schizophrenia.* [6]

So there is the irony that for a long time we have been led to ignore the content of psychotic speech for the purposes of our theoretical understanding of what psychosis is, and at the same time have been subtly trained and conditioned to tune in on just this content for the sake of our clinical practice. In the course of this paper I intend to concentrate on the meaning of this content, which I find so intriguing, and which has bearing not only on our understanding of psychosis, but, if the thesis that I will present has any merit, on the whole question of what constitutes reality. It is another irony that the study of psychosis may bring us to this point, a new understanding of reality.

I would like to turn now to another example of the influence of the clinical setting in determining what we make of the things that a potential patient says to us. This is the experience of a friend of mine that occurred when he was a psychiatric resident.

He was at staff rounds where he was meeting patients who were newly admitted by the doctor who had handled the previous day's admissions. As a bright and eager student of psychiatry my friend was on the alert for "interesting" patients and symptoms. The first one or two of the several new patients he was introduced to were fairly ordinary. Neither of them were psychotic; perhaps one had taken an overdose of pills and the other was depressed. But the next one he met was striking, and clearly acutely psychotic. He rambled on in a fairly incomprehensible manner about electrons, physics, anti-matter, mind and matter, air, earth, fire and water, and so forth. "Well what do you think?" the admitting psychiatrist asked my friend as they walked away. "He sure is far out. What an incredible delusional system!" my friend answered (or something to that effect). Then he was informed that the patient he had just met was one of the world's leading physicists. My friend thought for sure that his leg was being pulled, but the fact that this was so was later proved to him. The patient was a physicist of international reputation. He had been brought to the hospital by some of his university colleagues who took great pains to inform the admitting doctor that this was the case, otherwise he himself would never have believed it.

As it turned out my friend was assigned to be in charge of this person's treatment. Despite the qualifying factor of the patient's profession the best diagnosis of his condition still turned out to be psychosis. It was also discovered that several years previously he also had a psychotic episode.

The fact that I do not necessarily disagree with this diagnosis may appear to muddy the waters in regard to my general purpose in bringing up this case. But these waters that we are sailing in are not easily cleared, and there are a number of subtle and intertwined issues that we are going to have to deal with. At this point let me distinctly state that I do not believe that the concept of psychosis is invalid (although I do believe that schizophrenia is).

The first point about this case that I would like to emphasize was that much of the content of the patient's discussion was the kind of stuff that we frequently hear from those we judge to be psychotic. When my friend was convincingly informed that this man was a physicist, he was positively jarred. His whole certain world of symptoms, signs, and classifications was instantaneously thrown topsy-turvy. The most immediate and obvious cues that he was using to judge this man delusional were completely thrown out of the window when he found that the man had a socially legitimate basis for saying what he did.

This brought home to him with full force the extent to which the clinical setting produces a certain kind of bias in the perceptions of the clinical worker. This kind of awareness can immediately raise the question of the validity of our clinical categories. Perhaps they are nothing more than a social labelling process that a person in one kind of psycho-social schema (the doctor) applies to a person in another kind of psycho-social schema (the patient), and furthermore this labelling has something to do with the ubiquitously occurring "politics" of deviance and conformity. There are a fair number of people in the field who tend to more or less take this point of view, and do so with reason and a good measure of clear-sightedness.[7]

But then another question raised itself for my friend. Isn't it possible for a physicist to become psychotic? Of course. As a matter of fact he was brought to the hospital by his colleagues who believed that he was psychotic, and they certainly did not do so because he was talking about physics. And I might add that it was clear that they were not conspiring behind his back to ruin his reputation and do him in by getting him labelled as insane. These happened to be his friends and obviously respected him, and who showed themselves over the course of time to be quite concerned about his condition.

But let us not take the concept of psychosis in a matter of fact way, as if there is such a definite thing, and that we really know what it is. As all the muddle and confusion about the concept of schizophrenia shows us, we really do not know what psychosis is. How can we when we have just begun to learn what consciousness is? It is precisely the purpose of this paper to present some new perspectives on psychosis, some of which are bound to be startling.

Our physicist patient in question was finally judged to be psychotic because he was confused and disoriented about many of the things that you do not have to be a physicist to know about, like who you are, where you are, and what is happening. So, in that sense, he was out of touch with reality. In fact, it was in the pursuit of Reality that he lost his way. As he recovered he said that before he became psychotic he had been practising a certain Eastern form of meditation, and in the course of this meditation too much "came up" and overwhelmed him. My friend judged him to be an emotionally constricted and rigid person, which is not too surprising in a highly developed scientific intellectual. From this it was fairly easy to see how his personality integration and balance could be upset by an intense experience.

His recovery proceeded rather quickly and before long he was out of the hospital. My friend feels that his therapeutic work with the person was definitely aided by his natural respect for what the man had to say. Even though my friend is philosophically egalitarian and in no way would intend to treat any of his patients with less than full respect, he was struck by the tangible increase in attentiveness and serious consideration that he had for even the wildest things that the patient said. He recognized that he never had accorded that measure of philosophical receptivity to what any of his other psychotic patients had had to say. Thus this man's status, rightly or wrongly, pulled from his therapist a special willingness to listen that few people who are labelled as psychotic or schizophrenic can command, and this treatment seemed to aid in his recovery. This is a point that anticipates some of the later things we will say about treatment.

Furthermore, the extent to which the patient was judged to be sick was considerably lessened by the knowledge of who he was. It soon became clear that his talking about physics was in some way related to what he had experienced that produced his psychotic disorientation. His physics and his psychosis were not separate entities. To further support this I was shown a series of notes that he began to make as he recovered in the hospital. To me they resembled just the kind of physical-mathematical notation that I have seen adorn many a university blackboard. But if I ignore who he is, and just think of him as a psychotic in hospital, his writing and diagrams bear a faint but striking relationship to the diagrams, charts, and mathematics that many psychotic people are prone to produce. Perry has shown that this kind of diagrammatic and highly symbolic communication is intrinsic to what is happening in the psychotic state.[8] Without making too much out of it at this point, let me just say that our physicist's experiences during the psychosis appeared to contribute in some way to the work he was doing in exploring the nature of the physical reality.

A Look Into History

Let us draw a bridge from physics to metaphysics, and in so doing we can prepare the way for the theory of psychosis that I wish to present. This bridge building will involve a little excursion into history.

It is the late 1890s. Roentgen had discovered X-rays and scientists were busily looking for other examples of invisible rays. Henri Becquerel in Paris had been experimenting with uranium and had discovered that it sent out rays which could fog a photographic plate even though the plate was covered by thin sheets of metal. And so the invisible, and its forces, started to make their presence felt in the halls of hard fact.

Also in the 1890s Frederick Myers was finishing the work on his book which was to be one of the two early cornerstones of the British Society for Psychical Research. His book, *The Human Personality and Its Survival of Bodily Death,* was published in 1903. It followed by a little over a decade the first major publication of The Society which was *Phantasms of the Living* (1886), largely the work of Edmund Gurney who was Myers' colleague in the founding of the Society.[9]

It is somewhat surprising that psychology has forgotten these two men, Gurney and Myers, since it is possibly to them that psychology owes the discovery and creation of the concept of the unconscious. Most of us, of course, think that it was Freud who had introduced this epochal idea to us. But the leading voice in American psychology at that time, and one of the outstanding psychologists of all time, William James, leaves us with this historical note,

> I cannot but think that the most important step forward that has occurred in psychology since I have been a student of that science is the discovery, first made in 1886, that, in certain subjects at least, there is not only the consciousness of the ordinary field, with its usual centre and margin, but an addition thereto in the shape of a set of memories, thoughts, and feelings which are extra-marginal and outside of the primary consciousness altogether, but yet must be classed as conscious facts of some sort, able to reveal their presence by unmistakable signs.[10]

Myers and Gurney did not use the actual term unconscious, which was a result of Freud's eventual influence, but another term which I find still preferable to Freud's.[11] Myers called this region of mental life the subliminal self, and sometimes the subliminal consciousness. We should note that Myers' first paper on the subliminal consciousness preceded Freud's earliest publications by a few years, and there is the delightful historical point that it was Myers in fact who was the first English-speaking scientist to notice Freud's early paper on hysteria and bring attention to it in England.[12]

If Myers' concept of the subliminal consciousness had taken hold in the world of science rather than Freud's, our outlook on the mind and on reality would be considerably different than it is today, for Myers conceived of the unconscious (to use the more well-known term) within the framework of the development of higher faculties, such as creativity, and what we today call ESP, rather than within the framework of pathology and the negative affects. Myers' concept of the unconscious is a lot closer to what Jung was to develop than it is to Freud's and Aldous Huxley has expressed the opinion that Myers' account of the unconscious is "superior to Jung's account in being more richly documented with concrete facts and less encumbered with those psycho-anthropologico-pseudo-genetic speculations which becloud the writings of the sage of Zurich".[13]

For Myers the subliminal consciousness included a higher consciousness in addition to Freud's notion of a lower consciousness. Myers envisioned the subliminal self as a series of mental regions that are not ordinarily manifested. The regions of the subliminal consciousness that were closest to ordinary consciousness resembled its modes and properties, but as more and more distant regions became manifested they displayed more and more unusual properties. The regions that were more or less just outside of the field of ordinary consciousness were those that Freud was to explore in *his* concept of the unconscious. But the regions that were furthest away from the ordinary threshold of consciousness were able to operate telepathically (a word that Myers coined), clairvoyantly, and eventually even to enter into communication with the consciousness of those that had physically died. Myers believed, and this is important for the thesis I will develop about psychosis, that many unusual manifestations of consciousness involved a mixture of several of these different regions. So that within what we might call an altered state of consciousness, or what Myers would call a deep trance, the person might express some long-forgotten memories, and perhaps in conjunction with that, some dissociated portion of the usually conscious self, as well as some information or knowledge that they could not have gotten in any ordinary or usual way, the paranormal in other words.

Why Myers' work never really caught on, even though it is considered by many a classic, and Freud's did, is probably due to a whole conglomerate of reasons, not the least of which is that Freud was, after all, a monumental and prolific genius who outlived Myers by some 40 years. But there are a couple of other reasons in particular that I would like to mention because they bear on the theme that we are presently pursuing in this essay.

The first is that despite the discovery of X-rays and other invisible phenomena, those days of the late Victorian era were still heavily and thoroughly steeped in both philosophical and ethical materialism. It was only the most open and free-minded persons then who began to realize the potential philosophical implications of the new physical discoveries. Therefore, Freud's early insistence on separating his conceptions from what he referred to as "the black mud of the occult", and basing it instead on material, non-spiritual, and sexual grounds, was much more in tune with the philosophical tenor of the times.[14]

The second reason for the limited influence of Myers' and Gurney's work is more important to me, because it bears on the whole question of the validity and truth of parapsychological findings, and in turn the validity of what I will shortly propose in regard to psychosis.

Gurney's and Myers' works are each impressive two-volume tomes of massive accumulations of material which support the existence of invisible occult realms, the areas that today are explored under the headings of ESP and parapsychology. (ESP is a catch-all term for the occult.) It was their hope that through their well-documented, and scientifically sound investigations, the iron-clad materialism of their age would be broken and the skeptical world would come to accept the reality of non-material, that is spiritual, human existence. In a way we can say that they were the first scientific explorers of the transpersonal.[15]

But it turned out to be the case that Gurney's and Myers' data was not nearly as solid as they had expected. A number of the people they had investigated, upon which they based considerable portions of their work, were later discovered to be practising fraud and deception. This applied to several mediums, telepathists, and even one of their own co-workers. Even those witnesses to unusual psychic phenomena who apparently had the most impeccable and respected credentials, were sometimes later found to be in shady and collusive relationships with the persons they had witnessed. There is even the suspicion that Myers, in his zeal to prove the existence of these occult phenomena, was sometimes less than the most critical or impartial researcher and observer. So all was not pristine in the Victorian land of the occult.[16] There was even a growing spate of interest in what was called "spiritualism", which for a time was somewhat of a Western fad, which rose in the late 1800s but began to decline around 1920 when various hoaxes and frauds in the field increasingly came to public attention.[17]

For the skeptic and the dyed-in-the-flesh philosophical materialist the existence of *some* frauds in the area of the occult is all he needs to condemn the whole field outright. He is pretty much convinced that all of these beliefs and theories are nonsense anyway, so all it takes is some proof of fraud and he is then able to dismiss any parapsychological or occult finding as false. But this kind of reasoning is only inferential, not deductive, and amounts to a practice of scientific guilt by association. More importantly, this kind of conclusion ignores the steadily accumulating mass of evidence, both experimentally and spontaneously gathered, that has stood up to challenge,

and careful scrutiny. People in all fields of scientific life are coming
to recognize this, one being Carl Rogers, the dean of American clinical psychologists, who says,

> Now with knowledge of many types of drug-induced states of expanded
> consciousness and changed reality, with all the years of careful study of ESP,
> with all the international study of psi phenomena, with serious theorists such
> as LeShan (1969), we will have a harder and harder time closing our eyes to
> the possibility of another reality (or realities), operating on rules quite dif-
> ferent from our well-known commonsense empirical reality, the only one
> known to most psychologists.[18]

Rogers is joined in these conclusions by Gardner Murphy, Arthur
Koestler, and a host of other scientists besides the aforementioned
William Tiller.[19] But name-dropping is certainly not the answer to
the problem, and in itself amounts to a practice of scientific truth by
association. All I would like to point out is that despite the fallacies
of some of the early work of the British Society for Psychical
Research, subsequent research has tended to support some of their
main conclusions, and I would say that Myers' conception of the
extent and reach of the subliminal self is still justified.

Admittedly, the reader is still within his limits of justification if he
decides to reject the reality of the paranormal. The case is hardly
closed. But I personally feel that there is enough basis to warrant the
theoretical speculation that I will put forth in regard to psychosis. I
would suggest to the reader that in the pursuit of things hidden, the
occult, the will *not* to believe can be just as deceptive as the will to
believe.

Physics and Metaphysics

The discoveries of Roentgen and the others that I previously
referred to make a very compatible parallel with the psychic investigators of that period, because there, within the realm of physics,
phenomena were discovered which provided a possible theoretical
rationale for what Gurney and Myers were talking about.

The physicists' discoveries opened the way for the atomic era and
the eventual establishment of Relativity and Quantum Theory. With
these theories the world of impenetrable matter became effaced, and
all that hard stuff was found to be nothing other than concentrations
of wave vibrations in a universe of wave vibrations. Quantum physics
has also showed us that there is a lower limit to our ability to
physically detect the operation of this vibrational energy. This is the

Uncertainty Principle. Thus we have discovered an inevitable gap in our knowledge of things. At the borders of this gap, the Quantum Gap as it is called, we find the wonderland of subatomic physics—entities have been found that defy our previous physical conceptions of the way things must be; Feynmann received the Nobel Prize in 1965 for describing the positron, an electron that moves backward in time; there is anti-matter and anti-gravity, and so forth.[20]

The upshot of all of this as far as I am concerned is that the world of physics no longer excludes the possible realities that have generally been described within the province of the occult. As it should be, there is no longer a hard and fast line between the natural and the supernatural; it all just seems to be a question of the usual and the unusual, and reality is no respecter of probability.

The physical world that we perceive and know with our everyday perception consists of just one portion of frequencies out of a much larger spectrum of energy, and the limits and possibilities of that energy are still unknown, even within the range of what is physically detectable. Thus it is reasonable to believe that as the faculties of perception undergo a shift, a new range of the energy spectrum may begin to disclose itself, at first on an intuitive, feel level of hunch and premonition, and then on an increasingly more "visible" level, how visible we will see shortly. This explanation can account for the possible abilities of someone like Uri Geller, but more importantly it can also account for a whole new world of phenomena that many occultists tell us exist. If this latter point turns out to be valid then we are provided for a whole new basis for understanding psychosis.

People who claim to be clairvoyant often refer to another "plane" of perception, a range of phenomena that is not visible through our usual channels of vision. They point out how difficult it is for a non-clairvoyant person to be convinced that there is such a "place" or range of phenomena. Here is the problem as put by one clairvoyant source. "It is like describing a rainbow to a man totally blind since birth—for all the blind man knows, the very idea of sight is a taunting myth. A hypothetical island wherein all the inhabitants have for untold ages been genetically sightless would very likely declare a visitor with normal sight insane were he to describe the beauties of the sunset and the starlit skies."[21]

What he says corresponds to reports that we get from a whole host of other mystics and occultists. Some of the better known among them constitute the saints and seers of religious history, and we do not have to go back to the hoary past to find them. Among them are St. Theresa, Emanuel Swedenborg, George Fox, and Joseph Smith.

In this connection it is interesting to note that Freud facetiously referred to St. Theresa as the "patron saint of hysteria".[22] This remark again puts the basic issue before the reader. Even more recently we have persons who report a similar kind of experience such as Max Heindel, Rudolph Steiner, Annie Bessant, and C. W. Leadbeater. In this category might also be included certain artists of "vision" such as William Blake, S. T. Coleridge, and W. B. Yeats. Most recently, we have Richard Bach who claims that his *Jonathan Livingston Seagull* was dictated to him on several separate occasions by a phantom "voice".[23]

Are all of these people's experience psychotic, or hysteric as Freud would put it? I seriously doubt it, at least not in any sense that is *independent* of the fact that they have had unusual experiences and perceptions. The problem with our analyses of these experiences, as scientists, is that heretofore we have had no other category in which to place them than the pathological. If someone perceived something other than our commonly known physical reality we would accept little other possibility than that he or she was, in some way, mad. This was certainly the case when Bleuler, and Kraeplin before him, were meeting people in a medical setting who had unusual experiences to report.

But now the situation is changing. The theories of modern physics, the increasing laboratory evidence for ESP, reports from people like Carlos Castenada, the experiences that are had with psychedelic chemicals, all make the existence of other realities more conceivable. Correspondingly, I think we ought to enlarge our concepts of what psychosis is about.

It seems likely to me that many experiences that we diagnose as psychotic involve real occult phenomena. Among those phenomena are what occultists and clairvoyants call the "astral plane". If the astral plane as described in the occult literature really exists, in the sense that it is not a hoax, then a whole new world of insight opens to us as to what hallucinations and delusions are all about, and why people that we believe are only psychotic, so tenaciously cling to the belief that their experiences are "real". A patient of Bleulor's put it to him very well about a voice he was hearing. "If that is not a real voice then I can just as well say that even you are not now really talking to me."[24]

The Astral plane and psychosis

Some of the most detailed description we get of the astral plane come from C. W. Leadbeater. He was born in 1847, died in 1934, and did most of his writing around the turn of the century. In all he wrote some twenty books describing various aspects of the occult panorama. This work forms part of the basic literature of the Theosophical Society, a fairly well known mystical-philosophical group that was founded about the same time as the British Society for Psychical Research, and like this group is still actively functioning today. Among its early membership were such known figures as Piet Mondrian, Yeats, George Russell (AE), and Maurice Maeterlinck. In 1916 Leadbeater was consecrated as Bishop of the Liberal Catholic Church of England.

I hope that we are now more or less prepared to read what Leadbeater has to say. Unless the reader is in agreement with much of the argument up to this point, he will either have difficulty in accepting the following material to be the statements of a sane man, or he will believe it to be a fictitious concoction. Now I think it is reasonable to hold either of these alternative hypotheses. If what I have said up to this point has not been comfortable, the challenge of the Leadbeater material to one's own sense of the way things are will be great. But I ask for whatever openness of mind the reader can muster. It will take this to give the occultists, and the present thesis, a fair hearing. Psychosis is a fantastic disorder. Its explanation may be equally fantastic. What Leadbeater has to say should at least be a challenge.

It will be worth presenting him at some length,

I know how difficult it is for the average mind to grasp the reality of that which we cannot see with our physical eyes. It is hard for us to realize how partial our sight is—to understand that we are all the time living in a vast world of which we see only a tiny part.

So when we speak of a man as rising from one plane or subplane to another, we do not think of him as necessarily moving in space at all, but rather as transferring his consciousness from one level to another—gradually becoming unresponsive to the vibrations of one order of matter, and beginning instead to answer to those of a higher and more refined order; so that one world with its scenery and inhabitants seems to fade slowly away from his view, while another world of a more elevated character dawns upon him in its stead.

The first conscious introduction to this remarkable region comes to people in various ways. Some only once in their whole lives under some unusual influence become sensitive enough to recognize the presence of one of its inhabitants, and perhaps, because the experience does not repeat itself, they may come in time to believe that on that occasion they must have been the victims of hallucination. Others find themselves with increasing frequency seeing and hearing something to which those around them are blind and deaf; others again—and perhaps this is the commonest experience of all—begin to recollect with greater and greater clearness that which they have seen or heard on that other plane during sleep.

We must note first that every material object, every particle even, has its astral counterpart; and this counterpart is itself not a simple body, but is usually extremely complex, being composed of various kinds of astral matter. In addition to this each living creature is surrounded with an atmosphere of its own, usually called its aura, and in the case of human beings this aura forms of itself a fascinating branch of study. It is seen as an oval mass of luminous mist of highly complex structure, and from its shape has sometimes been called the auric egg. . . .

In regarding his fellow-man he no longer sees only his outer appearance; almost exactly co-extensive with that physical body he clearly distinguishes the etheric double; while the vitality (called in Sanskrit prana) is also obvious as it is absorbed and specialized, as it circulates in rosy light throughout the body, and as it eventually radiates from the healthy person in its altered form.

Most brilliant and most easily seen of all, perhaps, though belonging to a more refined order of matter—the astral—is that part of the aura which expresses by its vivid and ever-changing flashes of colour the different desires which sweep across the man's mind from moment to moment. This is the true astral body.

One other point deserves mention in connection with the appearance of physical matter when looked at from the astral plane, and that is that the higher vision, when fully developed, possesses the power of magnifying at will the minutest physical particle to any desired size, as though by a microscope, though its magnifying power is enormously greater than that of any microscope ever made or ever likely to be made. The hypothetical molecules and atoms postulated by science are visible realities to the occult student, though the latter recognizes them as much more complex in their nature than the scientific man has yet discovered them to be. . . .

For example, one curious and beautiful novelty brought to his notice by the development of this vision would be the existence of other and entirely different colours beyond the limits of the ordinarily visible spectrum, the ultra-red and the ultra-violet rays which science has discovered by other means being plainly perceptible to astral sight. We must not, however, allow ourselves to follow these fascinating bye-paths, but must resume our endeavour to give a general idea of the appearance of the astral plane.

It will by this time be obvious that though, as above stated, the ordinary objects of the physical world form the background to life on certain levels of the astral plane, yet so much more is seen of their real appearance and characteristics that the general effect differs widely from that with which we are familiar. For the sake of illustration take a rock as an example of the simpler class of objects. When regarded with trained sight it is no mere inert mass of stone.

> First of all, the whole of the physical matter of the rock is seen, instead of a small part of it; secondly, the vibrations of its physical particles are perceptible; thirdly, it is seen to possess an astral counterpart composed of various grades of astral matter, whose particles are also in constant motion; fourthly, the Universal Divine Life is clearly to be seen working in it as it works in the whole creation, though naturally its manifestations differ greatly at successive stages of its descent into matter, and for the sake of convenience each stage has its own name. We recognize it first in the three elemental kingdoms; when it enters the mineral kingdom we call it the mineral monad; in the vegetable kingdom it is described as the vegetable monad, and so on. So far as we know, there is no such thing as "dead" matter. [25]

This material immediately presents us with its challenges and its possibilities. Is it delusional? If so, fine, no real problem in dealing with it, except perhaps to understand how Leadbeater managed to keep himself functioning and out of the mental hospital all those years. If he is not psychotic, then is he a fraud? Again, to this question each of us will have to pass our own judgment. As I have indicated, I think it is very worthwhile to keep open on this. It would be a shame to miss the dramatic and illuminating conclusions that would follow from Leadbeater's possible veracity.

These conclusions are at least two-fold:

(1) Our conception of "reality" must be altered. As I have pointed out, it looks like physics is already allowing for a very different view of reality than what we have inherited from nineteenth-century materialism and Newtonian physics. A new psychology could meet a new physics in a universe that only a rare mystic had previously been bold enough to envision.

(2) With a new conception of reality we are presented with a rich new basis for understanding what happens in psychosis, and what it is.

It is towards this latter point that I would like to direct the further quotations from Leadbeater, noting where correspondences occur between the two areas, the astral plane and psychosis. In doing so I will be moving towards the hypothesis that psychosis in some way involves an experience of the astral plane of perception.

To continue,

> It has often been called the realm of illusion—not that it is itself any more illusory than the physical world, but because of the extreme unreliability of the impressions brought back from it by the untrained seer.
>
> Why should this be so? We account for it mainly by two remarkable characteristics of the astral world—first, that many of its inhabitants have a marvellous power of changing their forms with Protean rapidity, and also of

casting practically unlimited glamour over those with whom they choose to sport; and secondly, that sight on that plane is a faculty different from and much more extended than physical vision. An object is seen, as it were, from all sides at once, the inside of a solid being as plainly open to the view as the outside; it is therefore obvious that an inexperienced visitor to this new world may well find considerable difficulty in understanding what he really does see, and still more in translating his vision into the inadequate language of ordinary speech. . . .

He has to learn not only to see correctly but to translate accurately, from one plane to the other the memory of what he has seen. To assist him in this he has eventually to learn to carry his consciousness without break from the physical plane to the astral or mental and back again, for until that can be done there is always a possibility that his recollections may be partially lost or distorted during the blank interval which separates his periods of consciousness on the various planes.

The scenery of these lower divisions, then, is that of the earth as we know it; but in reality it is also much more: for when we look at it from this different standpoint, with the assistance of the astral senses, even purely physical objects present quite a different appearance. As has already been mentioned, one whose eyes are fully opened sees them, not as usual from one point of view, but from all sides at once—an idea in itself sufficiently confusing.

When we add to this that every particle in the interior of a solid body is as fully and clearly visible as those on the outside, it will be comprehended that under such conditions even the most familiar objects may at first be totally unrecognizable.[26]

Here we see how the movement of consciousness through the planes can easily result in a confusion between them, and how "illusion" can become a problem in the physical plane for one new to the astral realms. From Leadbeater's descriptions it seems possible that the lower astral plane produces the experience that becomes the basis for hallucinations. If this is true we can certainly see how one can become confused and sound "crazy" to others who have no knowledge or experience of the astral plane.

According to Leadbeater there are several different classes of entities or beings that exist in the astral world. Several of these types seem to have precisely the devilish or impish qualities that are ascribed to hallucinations. Some of the entities that Leadbeater describes even come close to the usual psychological explanation of hallucinations as unconscious projections, but in a way that still gives them much more substance. To see this let us turn to Leadbeater's description of the "stuff" that astral objects are made of. He calls it the "elementals" in comparison to the physical world concept of elements.

I have explained that the elemental essence which surrounds us on every side is in all its numberless varieties singularly susceptible to the influence of human thought. The action of the mere casual wandering thought upon it, causing it to burst into a cloud of rapidly-moving, evanescent forms, has been described; we have now to note how it is affected when the human mind formulates a definite, purposeful thought or wish.

The effect produced is of the most striking nature. The thought seizes upon the plastic essence, and moulds it instantly into a living being of appropriate form—a being which when once thus created is in no way under the control of its creator, but lives out a life of its own, the length of which is proportionate to the intensity of the thought or wish which called it into existence. It lasts, in fact, just as long as the thought-force held it together. Most people's thoughts are so fleeting and indecisive that the elementals created by them last only a few minutes or a few hours, but an often-repeated thought or an earnest wish will form an elemental whose existence may extend to many days. [27—28]

In reading this let us keep in mind that this material comes from a book written in 1895 and was in no way directed to an audience of psychologists or psychiatrists, and was not written to shed light on the problems of psychosis. Therefore, the correspondences that arise are certainly remarkable. For some readers, the fact that I am taking Leadbeater seriously may be what they find remarkable.

Psychosis as a Confusion Between Occult and Ordinary Realities

If the astral plane descriptions are true then much of the phenomena of psychosis falls into place. A new light is cast on the content of the experience, the compelling reality of the experience, and the frequent unwillingness to abandon it, and finally, the sometimes positive change in the person that results from his being psychotic.

It may be asked: If the astral plane is really there then why has it been hidden to us for so long? It is my contention that it has not been so hidden, but has made up the bulk of those phenomena that we have called hallucinatory, delusional, and schizophrenic. The amount of "psychotic" experience in our society is well known to be no small number. Again, if these speculations are valid, then in the field of dealing with the "mentally ill" do we find our most direct and useable application of occult concepts.

Before going on it may help for me to summarize some of the points that have been made so far in order to put the concept of the astral in perspective.

With the example of Uri Geller I tried to show that if a clinical setting is suggested then many of the things that psychics or occultists say sound psychotic. I also have tried to show that many of the concepts of modern physics also sound like fragments of someone's delusional system. It was also pointed out that many occult concepts are gaining increasing scientific support, and that modern physics is seen as compatible with these phenomena. Then I said that occultists and clairvoyants may be those persons with an altered, or even evolved, perceptual system. People who claim to be such tell us about a whole different order of experience, and we can call it a reality, that has been referred to as the astral plane. From this it is not much to infer that many of the experiences that have been reported to us in our clinical settings may contain elements of valid occult experience.

Let me delineate what I think this means, and what it does not mean, for an understanding of psychosis. What I am saying is that many of the experiences that we have judged to be out of touch with reality, are in fact in touch with another reality, and that in itself does not imply psychosis. The other reality is really "there" in a definite sense, if by *there* we are not referring to a place in *physical* space.[29] It may only be our sensory boundedness that prevents us from experiencing it. Thus many people have been classified as psychotic on faulty grounds, although, given the state of our knowledge of these things, this uncomprehension is understandable. If anything, some of these "psychotics" are able to expand our spectrum of what is included in this grand thing we call the universe.

What I am *not* saying is that the concept of psychosis has no value and never describes a pathological condition. There are people whom we can legitimately conclude are out of touch with reality, on whatever plane of reality we refer to. Very often we will find that mental patients are those people who have made a transition from a valid mystical state into a psychotic state. We may be able to get a sense of the difference between these two states by looking at the following case descriptions. In them there is the suggestion that the person went through a process of change wherein a mystical state (to speak most generally) turns into a psychotic state.

The first one is from a 31-year-old woman who reports that she had the following experiences a week before she was hospitalized for an acute paranoid psychosis,

> Thoughts spun around in my head and everything—objects, sound, events —took on a special meaning for me. I felt like I was putting the pieces of a puzzle together. Childhood feelings began to come back, as symbols and bits from past conversations went through my head. The word *religious* and other

words from past conversations during the fall and summer months came back to me during this week and seemed to take on a new significance. I increasingly began to feel that I was experiencing something like mystical revelations. . . . at the gas station, the men smiled at me with twinkles in their eyes, and I felt very good, I saw smiling men's faces in the sky and the stars twinkling in their eyes. I felt better than I ever had in my life.[30]

Here is another such instance, a 21-year-old college student who felt that his life was completely changing,

He felt a sense of mission in the world which he now saw "as a completely wonderful place" and stated, "I began to experience goodness and love for the first time." Life for him took on an intense benevolent quality which he had never felt before. He talked with friends fervently about the "new life" and about the way he could now care for and understand people. The feelings progressed to frank delusions that he was a religious messiah and heralded an acute catatonic psychosis.[31]

I would say that psychosis is a *confusion* between two orders of reality, or in the specific terms we have been using, between the physical reality and an occult reality (perhaps the astral). I think this can stand as the beginning of a technical definition. In the second case above, at least from what we have in the description, the person becomes psychotic when he confuses his newly awakened occult energy and perception with his social role in the physical world, i.e., he comes to believe that he is the messiah. In both of these two cases the person was experiencing something that felt very fulfilling and meaningful to them, and each felt that they were beginning to operate on a new level. But this experience seemed to run amok and the person begins to lose all necessary orientation to the physical and social world.

The concept I am using here, outside of the occult implication, is not very different from what Carlson called the *acute confusional state.* Carlson reports the experiences of one of her patients who said, "I knew that either I was having hallucinations of unbelievable proportions, or that *the world was a much different place from what I had ever known.*"*[32] I see this as a very revealing, and in itself, non-psychotic statement that perhaps describes an opening up to occult experience. All too often it is the person's first alternative that our clinical practices reinforce.

I don't wish to pretend that the distinction between valid occult experience and the confusion that I am calling psychotic is easy to

*my italics.

make. But I am saying that this distinction is crucial if we are to separate, and help our patients separate, the potentially luminous and valid new vision from the remainder that *is* a distortion, and thus truly pathological. This statement also implies that both kinds of elements can exist simultaneously in the same person, which is what is stated in Myers' theory of the subliminal consciousness. This is really the crux of the matter, and in my opinion is what we are mostly dealing with in those whom we encounter as psychotic patients. The disentanglement of mystical and psychotic elements is what is necessary if the most meaningful and positive therapeutic work is to be done.

Let me again use some illustrations from the clinical literature to show the kinds of experiences we are dealing with. I would like to show a range of possibilities, from what is almost purely mystical, to a case that shows a typical combination of occult and pathological elements, and then finally a case that is at an-end-point of total psychosis.

Here is the first one, which is an excerpt from a longer statement given by a businessman in his forties,

> Things became less and less real. My surroundings were fading away, I found myself on a different floor in a locked room. I had no recall of being moved. There was a male voice, very distinct, that talked to me. Made remarks about Freudian psychology and about the physical phenomena governing the earth. It told me I was going to see the interior of an atom. I know I lost all consciousness of my surroundings. I was within an atom. I saw the neutrons and electrons, all the parts revolving. Then there was a gap and I awoke in a different room. This was when I had a very wonderful experience. There was a woman, dressed in a kind of robe, white, I think. She was not young or old. She had a strong spiritual quality. She was not beautiful as women are usually considered beautiful. It was a kind of moral beauty. There was a strong impression that she was timeless, or ageless. She gestured with her hands as she talked.
>
> She talked in the same sort of "cosmic" vein as the voice. She told me the world would not be at peace, that there would be strife and dissension. She said there had been a great mistake in giving the atomic secret to mankind. The gift had been intended to be useful but had been used destructively.
>
> This woman's presence was absolutely no less real than yours is right now. There was also the experience of leaving my body, being off in space. I was completely conscious, but not of my hospital surroundings. [33]

I find this particularly interesting because in it we witness a person describing a transition through the physical world, through its atomic structure, and then into another reality. Now this could merely be a fantasy, as in a dream, and have nothing to do with an occult reality. Against this we have the person's own statement as to the vivid and real quality of the experience, and parenthetically we may note that some occultists look on certain kinds of dreams as occult experiences (on p. 106 I quoted Leadbeater to that effect).

For the moment this issue is not the point. The point is that within itself I would say this statement displays little or no psychotic elements; there is no inference that these things are happening in the physical world, the appearance of the woman in white seems to be well confined to another plane of phenomena, another world, and the descriptions are clear and rational. (This is not to say believable, just rational.) Of course, the best place to find a non-psychotic occult experience is outside of the context of the mental hospital. But I use this excerpt from a book titled, *This is Mental Illness* to show that such experiences may be found in that context as well.

The next material is a clinician's third-person description of a patient, and is taken from Kolb's well-known text,

> As the patient's mental disorder progressed, he developed a great wealth of delusions. He stated that he was "the link between the living and the dead", that he was a "universal medium", that a certain physician called on him by mental telepathy for added strength and skill in surgical operations. He believed that someone was hiding in a trunk in his house and so he fired several bullets into the trunk. He accused his brother of spraying him with chloral hydrate from the third floor of his house. He therefore sat behind a closed door waiting for his brother, and upon hearing a noise, shot through the door. He grew a beard because his face, he said, was being changed in subtle ways by outside influences, adding that if he wore a beard, his true identity would be known. Following his admission to the hospital, he often spent long hours in his room where he could be heard pacing the floor, moaning, or making a noise like a dog, striking his head with his fist, or pounding the wall. When asked the reason for his behavior, he explained that he was suffering tortures because people abused their powers of mental telepathy and were directing those powers toward him. He spent nearly all the day in his room where, during the fourth and fifth years of his hospital residence, he would frequently be heard shouting, screaming, and uttering noises that the attendants described as resembling the howling of a wolf. In explanation of these noises, the patient stated that there was a woman spiritualist who, in some way through persons in the hospital, was exerting a peculiar spell on him, and that by making these noises, he could drive the spirits away. His thought processes became progressively disorganized.[34]

From the usual, non-mystical clinical perspective this person appears to be totally crazy. There are hardly any redeeming features here. But from the perspective I am suggesting there are numerous indications that the person, at least at some time in his history, had been having occult experiences. At the time of this case description the person is quite disoriented, so it seems to be the case that whatever occult experiences he had are well diffused into his physical world experience, and thus we more or less have a jumble—but even here the threads of a possible occult reality may be discerned.

Here is the third sample,

> Now to eat if one cannot the other can—and if we can't the girseau Q.C. Washpots prizebloom capacities—turning out—replaced by the head patterns of my own capacities—I was not very kind to them. Q.C. Washpots under-patterned against—[35]

I am presenting this as a case of "word salad", or even delirium. There is almost no coherence here. Through total confusion the person is reduced to the pathetic state of what Laing calls a "chaotic nonentity". The tragedy has been that it is mostly chronic hospitalization that has produced this kind of condition, so that this stage of psychosis can be seen as an almost exclusively iatrogenic condition.

The Longitudinal View

Phase I: The development of the ego

We have seen some instances of how a possible occult perception may become intermixed with distorted perception to produce the compound experience that we refer to as psychosis. Our next step is to see where occult experience fits into the longitudinal sequence of events that make up the history of someone who becomes a mental patient. This will involve an imaginative reconstruction of what I see as a typical case, and as such is based on some degree of guess-work. As clinicians we generally only meet our patients during a psychosis and afterwards, and much more rarely *before* they become psychotic, so an explanation of the development of a psychosis always involves some degree of speculation.

Myers' concept of the multi-faceted or multi-potential subliminal self comes into play again here, as well as the general notion of a multi-faceted self, regardless of whether it is subliminal or not; for the self, as ego, is always multi-faceted and is never completely unified and integrated. From the mystical viewpoint this is so because the ego is ultimately a false creation, a social fiction, and as such it can never be whole. Inayat Kahn calls it the prime delusion.[36] Imagine that, the part of us that we hold so dear, he calls it the prime delusion! For real integration and wholeness, from the mystical standpoint, this ego-fiction must be surrendered to a higher, because real, self. In modern parlance this higher self has come to be called the transpersonal self.

Reaching this mystical realization is a high point of developmental maturity, and is certainly not equivalent to being psychotic. Maslow has elucidated some of this.[37] The psychotic state happens much earlier along the line, and I think is particularly a result of the person trying to build up and establish as real this ultimately false and delusional self, the ego. One way to understand the difference between the mature mystic and the psychotic is to see the former as having given up his ego, and the latter as still trying to get his.

One gets oneself in this potentially psychotic position when one's emotional and spiritual existence has been threatened and crushed, perhaps from the cradle.[38] Before the delusion of separate egoic existence can be given up (as an act of choice), it must first be established. Before a fruit can drop from the tree it must be allowed to ripen. The one who becomes psychotic has never had the chance to ripen. This is what is meant when it is said that he is ontologically insecure. This person grows up fighting for survival, for self-survival, for soul survival, and before he has won that fight his ego delusion is tenuous or porous.

The ego is that mechanism which ordinarily relates perception to a certain portion of the available energy spectrum. This is like a tuning in. Socialization is the process of learning to tune in, to receive that portion of the energy spectrum which the culture calls reality. This can also be seen as the process of drawing boundaries—this is in, this is out. This part of the energy spectrum is in, this part is out. This part is you, this part is not you. And so on. I see this as a cooperative effort between the person and his close others. It is natural and necessary. For some people it does not work so well as those boundaries are tenuously and precariously established, and the person never feels reasonably established as a self.

Some theories of psychosis tend to concentrate on this phase of the process and view psychosis strictly as a poorly integrated ego, and as a severe sense of inadequacy and insecurity. Those derived from a social learning, or ego psychology, point of view tend to be in this category. While I think these theories throw much light on the problems of personality development and the social dynamic roots of psychosis, and are certainly very valuable, they do not deal with what I see as the core experience that ought to strictly define psychosis, which is something that occurs in the next phase of the process. These theories equate what I see as a schizoid existence, with psychosis, and this blurs what may be a critical difference between these two states of being. In this schizoid stage I think there are little or no occult elements present. I think this is precisely what marks out the next stage.

I also have not been persuaded that there is a discontinuity between schizoid existence and neurosis. I am very much in favor of a concept that is put forth by modern therapists such as Alexander Lowen, that the schizoid condition is the necessary factor underlying all of the more traditional clinical disorders such as hysteria, neurosis, character disorders, and so forth, each of them being only a particular manifestation, a coloring, of this basic problem in being. [39] So I do not think it is the case that only one kind of person can become psychotic and a different kind of person can become neurotic. The "normal" condition of man is a schizoid condition, in the sense that we are divided selves, some more so and some less so, and from this it follows that anyone can become psychotic. Just what this is we now turn to.

Phase II: The mystical-occult breakthrough experience.

If one who is already in a fairly tenuous ego state is pushed past the breaking point then he may become psychotic. I see psychosis as a distinctly different condition from all previous existence. The paradigm form of psychosis is acute or reactive psychosis—the psychotic break. The sharp difference between, before and after the event is caught by the word "break". I am going to posit here, at least for the sake of theoretical precision, although the world of phenomena is never as precise as our theories, that the event of the acute psychosis most always involves some form of mystical or occult experience. What I mean by this was suggested in some of the examples that I quoted on page 111. These cases were drawn from Bowers and Freedman's paper *"Psychedelic" Experiences in Acute Psychoses,* which I think begins to put its finger on the heart of the matter. These authors summarize their impressions of the acute phase of the psychosis in the following way,

> In brief it seems these patients are describing a state, early in their illness, in which they recognize an altered way of experiencing themselves, others, and the world. They report having stepped beyond the restrictions of their usual state of awareness. Perceptual modes seem heightened and the emotional response evoked is singularly intense. Such experiences are frequently felt to be a kind of breakthrough, words and phrases such as *release* or *new creativity* being used to characterize them. Individuals experience feelings of getting to the essence of things—of the external world, of others, and of themselves. On the other hand, there is usually a vague disquieting, progressive sense of dread which may eventually dominate the entire experience. [40]

Well before Laing wrote a book called *The Divided Self,* William James used that same term in a chapter heading in his book, *The Varieties of Religious Experience.* Here he talked about the conflicts, uncertainties, and depression that often mark the lives of persons before they become integrated and set at ease through a religious experience. James discussed these experiences in his next chapter which he called *Conversion.* Let me present an excerpt from one of the examples of conversion experiences that James presents. This occurred to a man when he was 23,

> I will now relate my experience of the power of the Holy Spirit which took place on the same night. Had any person told me previous to this that I could have experienced the power of the Holy Spirit in the manner which I did, I could not have believed it, and should have thought the person deluded that told me so. . . . At first, I began to feel my heart beat very quick all on a sudden, which made me at first think that perhaps something is going to ail me, though I was not alarmed, for I felt no pain. My heart increased in its beating, which soon convinced me that it was the Holy Spirit from the effect it had on me. I began to feel exceedingly happy and humble, and such a sense of unworthiness as I never felt before. I could not very well help speaking out, which I did, and said, Lord, I do not deserve this happiness, or words to that effect, while there was a stream (resembling air in feeling) came into my mouth and heart in a more sensible manner than that of drinking anything, which continued, as near as I could judge, five minutes or more, which appeared to be the cause of such a palpitation of my heart. . . .[41]

If our psychology does not have any mystical categories there is almost no other way to judge this experience than from a pathological perspective, viz. the man begins by having what we would call an anxiety attack. He follows this by compulsively speaking out, though no one is present. Then he has what we could only describe as tactile, and perhaps gustatory hallucinations.

But what this points to is the parallel between the early stages of what we know of as mystical and religious development, and the early stages of psychosis—the parallel in terms of the divided self stage, and then the breakthrough experience, which may include a contact with the unseen. Bowers and Freedman's position, which I am in agreement with, is that the breakthrough experience is multi-potential; it can have different outcomes ranging from a healthy mysticism through an out-and-out psychosis. The factors that pre-dispose the outcome one way or the other, I do not believe lie in the essential breakthrough experience itself, but in terms of the variables that surround the experience, variables that make up both the values, beliefs, and personality state of the person himself, even his moral strength if you will, and those of the environment of persons that surround and have contact with that person. This environment also includes the mental health professionals that he may come in contact with.

The position towards psychosis that I am taking is this—the heart of what *becomes* a psychosis is a mystical-occult experience, but this experience is not in itself psychotic. As a matter of fact, the experiencing is an opening to a broader glimpse of reality, the breadth of the possible. The permeability of those boundaries that define a person's ego may allow for this experience of other dimensions of reality, such as the astral plane. Porous ego boundaries allow these experiences to break in, thus there may in fact be some kind of relationship between the extent of schizoid existence and the propensity towards this other-world experience. But once this experience occurs it is not intrinsically pathological, as we have already indicated; it may in fact be redemptive.

The issue becomes, how is one able to cope with this new and overwhelming experience, one that reveals unimagined possibilities, new awareness, and possibly psychic powers? It is quite possible that the person himself may be convinced by the experience that he is crazy—or that he may even prefer craziness, with its unambiguity, than to deal with the awesome possibilities, both epistemologically and morally, that the mystical experience reveals. (Witness in this context the statement of Carlson's patient that I quoted on p. 111.) This is to say that the state of himself as ego, is not adequate to cope with the challenges that the mystical-occult experience presents.

A related, and quite likely possibility, is that the person is very confused and uncertain about what is happening to him, and seeks some kind of answers from those around him. Given the general state of our cultural beliefs towards mysticism and the possibility of other realities, it is very likely that the person's environment will support a pathological interpretation of the person's experience. And if the person comes to an expert in such matters, the psychologist or psychiatrist, for a clarification, the pathological interpretation is likely to get even further reinforced.

While I am drawing this kind of picture I must also acknowledge that the concept of being crazy also exists in cultures that have a much larger scope for mystical and occult experiences, and that the phenomenon of psychosis is not purely a phenomenon of social misunderstanding and hostility. But these factors enter strongly into the picture and I want to delineate them here. Ultimately psychosis must be defined without regard to a particular social environment, but "topologically", or intra-psychicaly, and this is what I will ultimately do, if but briefly.

Phase III: Ego usurpation of the mystical-occult experience.

The failing attempt to integrate and adequately deal with the mystical experience marks the third phase of the psychotic process, which I might describe as the stage of social defensiveness. It is here that symptoms like paranoia and delusions enter the picture. These tendencies become increasingly pernicious the further in time the person moves from his initial mystical experience. That is why acute psychosis has a much better "prognosis" than chronic or process psychosis. The mystical-occult experience is fresh in the acute phase, and the ego's response to it is still fluid and open. Healthy and even spiritual resolution of the experience is still possible. And here I would like to emphasize that the contrast provided in an acute experience between the physical realm, and another realm, such as the astral, is very helpful in discriminating between these two separate realities. As the fundamental alteration in ego functioning gets prolonged in time the likelihood of a possible resolution diminishes, and the contrast between the occult and the physical realities becomes much harder to make. This condition was demonstrated in the second case of the three that I presented starting on p. 110.

In the mystical experience the ego is shown something greater than, and beyond itself. How the person reacts to his experience at this critical time is very much a moral one, and also one of personality integration. Notice here that the word "integrity" can be used in both senses, as moral strength, and as a unification of parts. In regard to a phenomenological description of the ego both of these usages come down to the same thing. Being moral is being "together", being integrated. So ultimately, whether a person becomes psychotic or not is as much a moral one, as it is psychological or scientific.

Paranoia is the ego's distorted attempt to substantiate and maintain itself against a force that is potentially greater than it. It is the fear of submission and surrender. From a spiritual standpoint it is well known that this submission and surrender is what is finally required. The experience of being pursued by an outside force, the combative ego may express as paranoia; the ego who chooses a spiritual destiny expresses it as "the hound of heaven".[42] For the incipient psychotic this fearful and threatened feeling can attach itself to strange and mysterious forces such as "secret radar stations", or sinister social organizations like the communists or the fascists, or individual persons such as a neighbor or one's relatives. The point is that in the mystical-occult experience the person is in touch, I believe, with a very real and tangible force, a heretofore hidden source of power, and in a desperate and defensive attempt to explain this force the person contrives the paranoid explanation. (Indian Yoga has always had the concept of hidden and occult forces that can be tapped through various practices, and has given this force various names, such as "kundalini" or "prana", which they see as an out-flowing of the power of God.[43] Recent work in what is called Kirlian photography has lent some modern scientific support to this concept. [44])

My explanation for delusions follows closely this explanation for paranoia, as the two phenomena often go hand in hand. Roger Brown, the distinguished social psychologist, after having some contact with "schizophrenics", following his years of only academic knowledge of the phenomenon, could find only one feature of their behavior that distinguished them from anyone else, and that is the presence of delusions. He was struck that he could be talking to someone who seemed perfectly sunny and cheerful, and quite normal, when the person would mention some clearly false or outlandish belief, such as when he left the hospital he would go to Scotland to try out for the lead in "Fiddler on the Roof."[45] Some delusions are just rather odd, like this one, others are more flagrantly grandiose, such as one's proclamation of messiahship, and still others are paranoid.

There is a class of theory about schizophrenia that seems to me to concentrate on this third phase of the process, and view psychosis as a certain kind of communication strategy (or non-communication strategy), or as a social game with weird pay-offs. As with the theories that concentrate on the schizoid side of the process, I think there is much value to these theories, but I also think that they overlook the core element in psychosis, which is a particular kind of strange experience. The theories of Jay Haley, and perhaps Thomas Szasz I would locate here.[46] It seems to me that Laing has been one of the few people to have covered the full developmental range of the process of psychosis, through all three of these phases that I have demarcated, and has properly put the emphasis on the altered nature of the psychotic's experiencing.[47] For Laing, the defensive and elusive social game-playing of the schizophrenic is for the purpose of protecting his unique experience from social annihilation.

Along with his paranoia the psychotic's delusions are also his attempts to explain and account for the strange experiences that are threatening to overturn his ego's precarious existence. This attempt to explain derives from the needs of the self, its own requirements for intelligibility and comprehension, and in the demands of dealing with others.

But this need to account for the very strange things that one is experiencing in itself does not explain delusions. The mystic, too, must have made some attempt to understand what was happening to him. The difference that makes for psychosis, I believe, lies in the ego's attempt to use the very experiences that are overcoming it, to enhance and sustain its existence. The mystic's ego surrenders to the hound of heaven, the psychotic's ego attempts to enlist the hound in its own service.[48] Thus we find that the stuff of psychotic delusions are very "egotistical" statements that generally have the proportions that we describe as grandiosity. This ranges from the mild, "I am going to get a part in 'Fiddler on the Roof' ", to the insufferable, "I am the god that controls the universe".

In order to fully appreciate the public behavior and assertions of a delusional individual we have to understand the double causality of his state. In his delusional proclamations he is both defending the reality of a very profound experience against an often hostile and non-receptive environment, and also bolstering the existence of a struggling ego. The sensitive therapist has to be able to make the delineation between these two factors and respond differently to each. He should respect the former while trying to contain and re-orient the latter.

The further the psychotic person gets from the acute process, the more the delusions become rigidly locked into the system of ego defensiveness, and the less vitality and expanded reality they indicate. At this point the optimum therapeutic goal may be to undermine the delusion and thus set the person back again into an active and acute psychotic state. As shocking and radical as this may sound this is precisely the approach that Sullivan used in dealing with well-systematized delusional states. viz:

> It is by disturbing such paranoid elaborations that one opens the way to recovery. Before such a patient can recover, I believe that one has to return him to the unhappy, boundless sort of cosmic existence which makes up severe schizophrenic stress—which in some cases, where I have succeeded at this maneuver, meant that the patient became stuperous.[49]

For Sullivan the state of acute psychosis was not something to be gotten away from, but a possible place from which a real ego development could begin. The classic and perennial mistake in our field has been to overlook the revitalizing value that may lie in these experiences. There is the telling remark of mental patient Lara Jefferson, "I cannot escape from the madness by the door I came in, that is certain—nor do I want to."[50]

The Topological View

We have just taken a longitudinal view of psychosis, the way it develops over time, but that does not completely present a picture of the model of psychosis that I am advocating. To do this we will need a topological, or cross-sectional, view, one that gives us a picture of psychosis as an "intrapsychic" condition. This is a picture of psychosis that is essentially presented to us by the occultists themselves. Here is a statement of it by Max Heindel,

> The vital body [astral body]* plays an important part in health and in sickness. It is affected by amputation, accidents, anaesthetics, drowning, shock, regret and remorse. When it is not in a concentric position, in regard to the Ego's other vehicles, insanity and idiocy may result.[51]

A few points of clarification about this statement. Heindel uses the term "vital body" which is his word for what some other occultists might call the astral body or the etheric body. For our present purposes it is not important whether these terms refer to exactly the same structure. What matters is that they are all references to the inner, occult "bodies". Secondly, Heindel is using the term ego in a different way than I have. He uses it to mean the whole person, or what I prefer to call the Self; notice that he capitalizes "Ego".

The conception that Heindel presents, which I have basically already suggested, involves the idea that the physical body is just one of the bodies that make up the person. Each of these bodies corresponds to another world of phenomena, and exist within the physical body and its physical world, in the sense of interpenetrating it. These inner worlds.and bodies are what is meant by the terms occult realities. Our usual sense of having an emotional and mental existence, as well as a physical, is the common way in which these inner bodies are experienced. They are experienced as feelings or thoughts whereas for the clairvoyant they begin to take on the quality of perceptions.

Normally, these several bodies are "concentric", or in an alignment that prevents an infringement between them, so that one body and its world, say the astral, does not interfere and overlap the

---

*My insertion.

physical body and its corresponding world. Occasionally, for a variety of reasons, there is an overlapping of these ordinarily separate bodies, and then we have the basis for psychosis. If the cause of the collision between the bodies is a trauma or shock to the person, then the probability of a psychotic outcome increases. Emotional shocks arising out of intense negative emotions, such as anger or grief, tend to precipitously drive consciousness inward, and in so doing produce the disalignment. When the occult world comes to consciousness in this way, then the person finds himself in a very poor emotional position to deal with this new experience objectively and rationally, and to truly assess its nature and worth. The ego, already hurt and defensive, then tends to adopt this occult experience for its own aggrandizement, in the way that we have already discussed.

Therapeutic Implications

The nature of psychosis most often requires that an institution be involved in the care and treatment of one in that condition. Therefore, it is misleading to talk about psychotherapy with psychotic people as if it were another instance of one to one, and perhaps contractual, psychotherapy. If we would hope that progress be made in the humanistic and therapeutic treatment of psychosis we must really expect that the whole treatment setting, from top to bottom, undergo the necessary transformations. Contrary to our cherished picture of individual psychotherapy, the treatment of someone who is acutely psychotic is a milieu effort, and it is the milieu that must be seen as the change agent, at least at certain critical phases.

The difficulty in changing whole environments represents the difficulty that we have had in recognizing or demonstrating that human interaction can be beneficial for someone who is psychotic. I say "human interaction" rather than psychotherapy, because to me psychotherapy in its essense is that. I do not see it as a specially technical or esoteric procedure (and I am certainly inclined towards the esoteric). While I believe it is true that training and experience in this interaction can make one better at it, I want to assert that it is something we all do, all the time. In a hospital all who have contact with the patients "do it", for better or worse, and not just the one whom the hospital labels as therapist, or doctor.

These observations are nothing new, and have become trite by now, but to me they have bearing on the conclusion that a number of people in our field have reached, namely, that *psychotherapy* with schizophrenics is ineffective. Although the people who hold this belief may disagree, I cannot help but see it, at rock bottom, as the belief that human interaction with schizophrenia has no effect on ameliorating the person's condition. The following remark is common, "We have tried psychotherapy and it doesn't work, so now we have to try something else." References are made to the May study, and some others, for support.[52]

But I have never been able to see psychotherapy as other than a development, or refinement (hopefully) in the ways in which we, as humans, meet and share our time together. Therefore, I do not see psychotherapy as a thing, an object with finite boundaries and definition, as a pill is a thing, or even a shock treatment is a thing. In contrast to what Gertrude Stein said about roses, psychotherapy is not psychotherapy. That is to say that each of us is different, we meet others differently, and interact with them in our own unique ways.

I am appalled by the bald conclusion that psychotherapy does not work with psychotics. All I believe that can ever be drawn from a study such as May's is that psychotherapy (human interaction) as practiced by *those* persons with *that* philosophy was not shown to be ameliorative, within the confines of the study. And if the impact upon a psychotic person is a function of a milieu of persons, rather than a single one of those persons meeting the patient 2 or 3 hours a week, it is not surprising that the human element does not come through as being significant.

The studies demonstrating the ineffectiveness of psychotherapy never tell me anything about "psychotherapy", but only tell me that we must try still harder, and formulate our concepts still further, in a word we must continue to evolve in our learning how to be good for one another. The concepts that I have advanced in this paper are part of a continuing step in this direction. The general theoretical framework that I have advocated here was hardly conceivable in psychology at large, or with psychosis in particular, until the early sixties, when it surfaced in the writings of Laing, Perry, and a few others.[53] If the mystical point of view proves to be valid and relevant for understanding psychosis then it is also not a surprise that psychotherapy based on the standard psychodynamic principles would, in general, fall short of the mark.

Transpersonal concepts and practices will never be fully tested until they are adopted on a milieu basis, but they hardly will be so adopted until they show promise on an individual basis. So let me address the remainder of my remarks towards a few of the general therapeutic implications that come from this point of view, at least some of the ones that I have been able to see, and hope that they will encourage other sympathetic efforts wherever the opportunity arises.

We must undergo a very fundamental shift in how we view what is happening in psychosis. We must see the "illness" as not necessarily a breakdown, but as a possible breakthrough. In it the miserable, double-bound, and spiritually bereft egoic existence is dramatically brought to an end, and in this moment the person has the opportunity for what has been traditionally known as rebirth.[54] Therefore, the purpose of therapy is not to cure an illness, but to bring to a proper fruition and completion the transformation process that the breakthrough experience has already begun. The therapist must view his role as that of an obstetrician who has to bring a new being into the world, in what is turning out to be a very difficult and critical delivery, and not the role of a surgeon who is trying to repair a ruptured appendix.

Bert Kaplan catches this point of view perfectly in his preface to his book, *The Inner World of Mental Illness.*

> It seems to us that the change process is much more inclusive than this and that it usually encompasses both illness and cure. In this view change starts with the illness itself which has the meaning of negating a form of existence that the person has decided not to live with any longer. The illness establishes a new kind of psychic reality, which however can generally not be considered successful because it is tied to being the negative of something else. The cure, or solution, must be neither a return to the so-called normality that preceded the illness nor a negation of the illness. The new state must rather involve a genuine moving to a new solution, a movement which we can see would have been impossible without the illness.[55]

Sensitive therapists in the past have carried out this direction almost intuitively, even if they were operating out of the psychoanalytic framework which is not generally supportive of a mystical point of view. This was the case with Sechehaye, Freida Fromm-Reichmann, Sullivan, and some others.

But we face something today that these therapeutic pioneers did not have to contend with, and that is the oppressive reliance on, and almost automatic administration of psychoactive drugs. While the use of these substances may have made the management of large numbers of psychotic patients easier, and diminished the obviousness of psychotic behavior, I see them as one of the greatest obstacles today to a thoroughgoing and wholehearted psychotherapy of the psychoses.

I am not condemning drugs altogether. They may have their place. But they clearly today mitigate against understanding of psychotic experience, and the use of that understanding for positive interaction with psychotic people.

Most psychotic people who are on phenothiazine drugs do not feel that they are really "better" until they are off the drugs, and in the earlier stages of their condition, until they have surrendered to the allopathic system, are constantly pressing to get off the drugs. They seem to be reacting to an inner sense that all is really not well with them while they are on the drugs, and they will really not be "cured" until they stop taking the drugs. I am inclined to agree with their perception.

Advocates of extensive and indefinite drug use point to the fact of the high "relapse" rate when a patient stops taking his medications or is taken off them. I think that this is more or less true, but I see a quite different meaning in the fact. Laing has acknowledged Bateson's view that what we call schizophrenia is a frustrated form of a natural organismic healing process.[56] My basic accord with this position is indicated by the theory that I have put forth in this paper. From this position we may view the "relapse" as the continuation of a healing (whole-ing) process that was stifled by the administration of drugs. If the so-called relapse is a return to the more acute stage of the psychosis I would see it as a return to the mystical-occult breakthrough experience—which is the starting point of a new life for the self. The reliance of drug therapy I see as essentially preventing this development.

The drugs appear to arrest the processes which we label as psychotic, and hold them in check. When the drugs are removed the process often renews again and continues on its course. From an illness standpoint the phenothiazines function very much like insulin does for diabetes. Insulin does not cure diabetes but just serves to dampen it. When the insulin is removed the diabetes again becomes active. For those who view psychosis as solely an illness, like diabetes is an illness, it makes perfect sense to want to maintain someone for long periods of time, and even indefinitely, on phenothiazines, or some other such drug. But if psychosis is much more like I have described it here, then the dangers of adhering to the traditional medical model become apparent, in that they prevent a natural self-restorative process from running its course. This new restored ego, born out of the ashes of psychotic dismemberment, may be, in Laing's words, "the servant of the divine, no longer its betrayer."[57] The old ego was the betrayer of the divine.

The divine, which can be seen as the numinous truth within, can be betrayed in at least two ways. One way is the way of "normality", the assertion that the ego is the dominant existence, and is completely independent and sufficient unto itself. This ego, through its hubris, has brought us on a world-wide scale to the brink of suffocation, destruction, and collapse. The other betrayal is the "abnormal" betrayal, the psychotic's betrayal, which I have previously outlined. Whereas the normal ego does not recognize and acknowledge the existence of a higher self, the psychotic ego does so but identifies itself with that presense, e.g., "I, John Jones, am god." Whether this is a worse or better error than the more usual one is open to some debate.

However, the issue for therapy is the double stance that the therapist must take. He must respect the potential truth elements in the person's breakthrough experience, but he must oppose the appropriation of this experience by the psychotic ego. That is to say, he must acknowledge the person's intrinsic worth as possibly revealed to him in the core experience of his psychosis, while not accepting or humoring the grandiose egotism that has in fact made for the psychotic resolution of the experience. This is a tricky posture, and errors are easily made on two sides—the therapist either accepts too much of what the psychotic presents, or he rejects most of it. The first we might characterize as the liberal's error, the second is the conservative's. The mystical path, thinner than a razor's edge, avoids foundering on both of these shoals.

In the midst of a psychosis a person's inner life, his internal system of energies, has gone topsy-turvy. He is perhaps in contact with a new plane of experience; hidden forces have been sprung loose within him, what the Indians call "kundalini". He does not know what is happening to him and he is confused. The transpersonal therapist at this juncture is prepared to offer some explanation to the person about what may be happening to him. I call this kundalini counseling, although the use of these specific terms with the patient is not necessarily called for. But let him know that he is not just sick, or only going crazy. You may tell him that new energies are opening up within him and he can turn them into something positive. You will try to help him. Along with this it is generally a good rule to encourage the person not to fight what he is experiencing, but to "go with it", to be open to it. You may have to assure him that he is not going to die, even though he may feel like he is. His "death" may be his new birth.

If only he could allow himself to "die". The irony of psychosis appears to be that it is an incomplete ego death. The psychosis is the undying remaining fragments of an ego that is resisting its annihilation. But we, as therapists, generally help the ego resist, and it is no wonder. We are afraid of death, in any of its forms. The whole medical system conspires with all its technological forces to prevent anyone's death, no matter how called for that even seems to be.[58] We live with a great disequilibrium. We call birth a blessed event but we shrink from so doing to its equal and complementary member. And yet from a mystical point of view these are the two great mutualities. To be whole we must understand both, and live with equanimity in the space that lies between both these mighty poles.

The psychotic appears to have seen something of death, of becoming separated from the physical, and quite often has been a witness to "death's" value and, paradoxically, its life-renewing qualities. But being embedded within the exigencies of our present culture, the value of his vision is denied to him, in the same way and for many of the same reasons that the sweet release is denied to many of his fellow sufferers on other floors and wards of our institutions of healing, our hospitals. And here again we see why the transformation of our ways of dealing with psychosis must be a transformation that touches all levels of The System.

And so at this point of death, which may signal new life, it comes time to draw this essay to a close. The therapeutic suggestions offered here have been all too few and too vague, but more would be premature. Hopefully, they are yet to come.

In this paper I have speculated about a reality that may possibly underlie unreality. In trying to understand psychosis we may find that we come to understand much more than that.

References

1. Kiester, Jr., Edwin, Behind Science's Growing Fascination with Psychic Phenomena, *Today's Health*, 1973, **51**, 11.
2. As of this writing the information, opinions, and controversy about Geller's authenticity continue to accumulate. Harold Puthhoff and Russell Targ's work with Geller at The Stanford Research Institute have been published in *Nature*, Oct., 1974. Follow-up articles by other researchers also tending to support Geller's ESP abilities appeared in the 10 April, 1975 issue of *Nature*. Meanwhile *New Scientist*, another British scientific weekly presented parallel critical analysis of the research with Geller. Uri Geller's own mind-boggling account of his experiences is presented in his autobiography, *My Story*, Praeger, 1975. Andrew Weil presents a first-hand account of his visits with Uri Geller, and The Amazing Randi, a magician who is critical of Geller, in *Psychology Today*, June, July, 1974.

   I found the Weil pieces most pertinent as well as profound. After thoughtfully analyzing his experiences with Geller and Randi, Weil comes to the conclusion that the question of whether Geller is real or not is "essentially unanswerable". He then goes on to say, "It might be possible to take more conscious control over the process by which reality is shaped and made to seem objective. 'Wishful thinking', though it has a negative connotation, is an appropriate term to describe this process. We all engage in it, often unconsciously to bring things into reality to our needs, and to make them leave reality according to our needs." (July, p. 82.)
3. Ref. 1. Also see Ferguson, Marilyn, *The Brain Revolution*, Taplinger, 1973, pp. 316—20.
4. This refers to David Rosenhan, a psychologist, who incognito, got himself admitted to a mental hospital, and describes the great difficulty he had in obtaining a diagnosis that he was sane. Rosenhan, D., On Being sane in insane places, *Science*, January 1973.
5. Brown, Roger, Schizophrenia, Language and Reality, *American Psychologist*, 1973, **28**, 5, 395—403.
6. Kasanin, J. S. (Ed.), *Language and Thought in Schizophrenia*. New York: Norton, 1944.
7. The better known among these are Szasz, Goffman, and some of Laing's work, particularly *Sanity, Madness and the Family*. England: Penguin, 1970; Szasz, T. S., *The Myth of Mental Illness*. New York: Harper & Row, 1961; Goffman, Erving, *Asylums*. New York: Doubleday Anchor, 1961.
8. Perry, John W. Reconstitutive processes in the psychotherapy of the self, *Annals of the New York Academy of Sciences*, 1962, **96**, 853—76.
9. Myers, F. W. H. *Human Personality: and its Survival of Bodily Death*. 2 Vol., London, 1903. (New 1 Vol. edition, New Hyde Park, New York: University Books, 1961); Gurney, E., Myers, F. W. H., and F. Podmore, *Phantasms of the Living*. London, 1886. (Reprint edition available, Society for Psychical Research.)

10. James, William, *The Varieties of Religious Experience.* Publ. 1903. (New York: New American Library, Mentor Books, 1958, p. 188.)
11. My arguments against the Freudian use of the concept of the unconscious are given in a book I have in preparation. The present essay is based upon the themes that are presented in that book in a fuller treatment.
12. As noted by James Strachey in his edition of Breuer, J. and Sigmund Freud, *Studies on Hysteria.* New York: Basic Books, 1957, p. xv.
13. Ref. 9, 1961 Ed., p. 7.
14. As noted by Carl Jung, *Memories, Dreams, Reflections.* New York: Pantheon, 1963, p. 150.
15. This term, "transpersonal", is currently used in place of "mystical", in order to avoid some of the connotations that are evidently ascribed to the latter term. See, for instance, *Journal of Transpersonal Psychology,* P.O. Box 4437, Stanford Calif.
16. The problems with Gurney and Myers' work are described from a sceptic's point of view in Trevor H. Hall, *The Strange Case of Edmund Gurney.* Gerald Duckworth & Co., 3 Henrietta Street, London, W.C. 2, 1964.
17. See Georgess McHargue, *Facts, Frauds, and Phantasms—a survey of the Spiritualist Movement.* New York: Doubleday, 1972.
18. Rogers, Carl, Some new challenges, *American Psychologist,* 1973, 28, 5, p. 385; LeShan, L. *Towards a General Theory of the Paranormal.* New York: Parapsychology Foundation, 1969.
19. Murphy, Gardner, *The Challenge of Psychical Research: A Primer of Parapsychology.* New York: Harper & Bros., 1961; Koestler, Arthur, *The Roots of Coincidence.* New York: Random House, 1972.
20. Ibid., Chapter II.
21. Kueshana, Eklal, *The Ultimate Frontier.* The Stelle Group, P.O. Box 5900, Chi., Ill., 1963, p. 216.
22. Ref. 12, p. 232.
23. One reference to this is in *Publishers' Weekly,* 1971, 200, 16, p. 34. Bach refers to his experience as a "visionesque spooky thing".
24. Bleuler, Eugen, *Dementia Praecox or the group of schizophrenias.* Publ. 1911. (New York: International Universities Press, 1950, p. 94.)
25. Leadbeater, C. W. *The Astral Plane.* Publ. 1895. (The Theosophical Publishing House, Wheaton, Ill., 1963.) Quotations are from pp. 4, 16, 10, 20–1, 21–2, 25–7.
26. Ibid., pp. 6–8, 19.
27–8. Ibid., pp. 125–6.
29. Let me refer again to my forthcoming book, ref. 11, which expands considerably on this point.
30. From Bowers, M. B., and Daniel X. Freedman, "Psychedelic" Experiences in Acute Psychoses. *Archives of General Psychiatry,* 1966, 15, Sept., 240–8. Also in Charles R. Tart (Ed.), *Altered States of Consciousness.* New York: John Wiley & Sons, 1969.
31. Ibid., p. 241.
32. Carlson, Helen B., The Relationship of the Acute Confusional State to Ego Development. *International Journal of Psychoanalysis,* 1961, 42, p. 533.
33. Grant, Vernon W., *This is Mental Illness.* Boston: Beacon Press, 1963, pp. 123–4.

34. Kolb, Lawrence C. *Noyes' Modern Clinical Psychiatry.* Philadelphia: Saunders, 1968, p. 382.
35. Maher, Brendan, The Shattered Language of Schizophrenia. In *Readings in Clinical Psychology Today.* Del Mar, California: CRM Books, 1970, p. 47.
36. Kahn, Inayat, *Metaphysics.* New York: The Sufi Movement, 1939.
37. Maslow, Abraham, Theory Z. *Journal of Transpersonal Psychology,* 1969, 1, 2.
38. The work of the social anthropologist Jules Henry, who has done *in vivo* studies of psychoto-genic families, demonstrates this very vividly. See his *Culture Against Man,* New York: Random House 1963, and *Pathways Into Madness.*
39. Lowen, Alexander, *The Betrayal of the Body.* New York: Macmillan, 1967. (New York: Collier Books, 1969, pp. 19—20.)
40. Ref. 30, pp. 243—4.
41. Ref. 10, p. 158.
42. This is a reference to Francis Thompson's well-known poem, which can be found in most anthologies of English poetry. The poem begins with these lines:
    I fled Him, down the night and down the days;
    I fled Him, down the labyrinthe ways of my own mind. . . .
43. For instance see Gopi Krishna's *Kundalini,* Berkeley: Shambala, 1970, or his, *The Biological Basis of Religion and Genius,* New York: Harper and Row, 1971—2.
44. Referred to by Stanley R. Dean in Metapsychiatry: The Interface Between Psychiatry and Mysticism, *American Journal of Psychiatry,* 1973, 130, 9, 1036—8.
45. Ref. 5.
46. For Szasz see *The Myth of Mental Illness,* Ref. 7. One sparkling expression of Jay Haley's position is in The Art of Being Schizophrenic, *Voices,* 1965, 1, 133—47.
47. Laing's complete position is most clearly evident in *The Politics of Experience,* New York: Ballentine Books, 1967.
48. An account of this "contest", with a reference to some of the pitfalls on the way is available in C. S. Lewis' autobiography, *Surprised By Joy,* New York: Harcourt, Brace & Co., 1955.
49. Sullivan, Harry S. Schizophrenia, Paranoid States, and Related Conditions, in Zax, M., and George Stricker (Eds.), *The Study of Abnormal Behavior, selected readings,* New York: Macmillan Co., 1964, p. 242. This is taken from chapter 14 of Sullivan's book, *Clinical Studies in Psychiatry,* New York: W. W. Norton & Co., 1956.
50. A large excerpt of her experiences are available in Bert Kaplan's edited volume, *The Inner World of Mental Illness: A Series of First-Person Accounts of What it Was Like.* New York: Harper & Row, 1964. I also understand that her long unavailable book, *These are my sisters,* will soon be reprinted.
51. Heindel, Max. *The Vital Body.* Oceanside, Calif.: The Rosicrucian Fellowship, 1950, p. 57.
52. May, Philip R. *The Treatment of Schizophrenia: A comparative study of five treatment methods.* New York: Science House, 1968.
53. See Ref. 8, as well as Perry's Image, Complex and Transference in

Schizophrenia, in Burton (Ed.), *Psychotherapy of the Psychoses.* New York: Basic Books, 1961.

54. The different byways of the "death and rebirth" process has been described in Joseph L. Henderson and Maud Oakes, *The Wisdom of the Serpent: The Myths of death, rebirth and resurrection.* New York: Macmillan Co., 1963 (Collier Books, 1971). Chapter IV specifically deals with psychotherapy.

55. Ref. 50, pp. xi—xii.

56. Ref. 47, pp. 117—18.

57. Ibid., p. 145.

58. This has been very effectively explicated by Elisabeth Kubler-Ross in *On Death and Dying,* New York: Macmillan Co., 1969. Also, as this is going to press various tragic cases have been given prominence in the news.

CHAPTER 5

The Christian Approach to Schizophrenia

The Problem Today

Last year, in the midst of growing dissatisfaction and confusion, it happened. The report that appeared in *Medical World News,* and subsequently as a national news release, generated a tidal wave of comment that not only engulfed the professional world, but spilled over on the general public as well. And why not? After all, had not twelve persons as sane as you or I erroneously been admitted to twelve of the nation's leading mental institutions? And more to our immediate concern, of the twelve, eleven falsely had been declared to be schizophrenics. Serious questions that usually had been asked softly prior to this report now hardened. Clearly, it seemed, we do not know how to diagnose schizophrenia. Indeed, old questions, now revived, began to be aimed at the very concept of schizophrenia. It is not surprising, for instance, that Karl Menninger, long-time critic of current labeling practices, in commenting about this fiasco should remark: "Schizophrenia to me is just a nice Greek word."

The truth of the matter seems to be that the word "schizophrenia" in many quarters has become a non-specific wastebasket term covering a multitude of problems (and often covering up a vast amount of ignorance), all of which appear to have but one common denominator: the inability of the counselee to function meaningfully in society because of bizarre behavior. Yet, to add to the confusion, counselors with as diverse orientations as R. D. Laing and Hoffer/Osmond wish to define the term narrowly in their own new ways.

Personally, with Menninger, it seems to me that we must abandon the word as misleading and confusing, particularly when its use provides such a convenient temptation for diagnostic abuse. Add to all of the other possible factors that might be mentioned the hopelessness generated by labels, the tendency of many counselees to play the role they think the label implies, the irreparable damage that cavalier use of this label by careless, irresponsible, overworked or

even malicious parties can have upon a client's future,[1] and you have
an almost airtight case for rejection of the term. The word has been a
source of trouble ever since Bleuler introduced it in 1911. I shall,
therefore, use the word "schizophrenia" throughout the remainder
of this article merely for the sake of present convenience—I cannot
argue here for the use of different nomenclature. But I do so reluctantly and with great reservation. The sooner we can adopt new
terminology, the better. Whenever the word "schizophrenia" appears
I shall be referring not to any definable, diagnostic category representing a specific illness or behavior. Rather, I shall view it solely as a
broad collective term having no one clearcut referent, but rather
pointing to bizarre behavior that is the result of any cause—contrived
or otherwise—or any complex of causes that may lead to severe
inability to function in society. I, therefore, consider the words "red
nose" to be on precisely the same communicational level with the
word "schizophrenia." To observe that one has a red nose is to say
nothing more than that; the statement carries no necessary causal
implications. The words refer to an observable effect, not to etiology. That is to say (whatever its cause), the observation refers to an
effect that may have any number of different and widely diverse
causes. Thus, the statement, "You have a red nose", does not necessarily carry with it the insinuation (for instance) that the person
addressed has been boozing. It would be wrong to infer that from the
simple statement itself. Indeed, he may have fallen asleep under a sun
lamp, his wife may have punched him in it, he may be growing a
pimple on it, etc. Similarly, to say that one is schizophrenic is merely
to observe that his behavior has become so bizarre that he is unable
to function (or is not allowed by others to function) in society.

And, as an additional complication, it must be remembered that
the line between the abnormal and the normal is not always clearly
definable in a society whose values are in flux. What is tolerated (or
even prized) in certain communities or cultures may be rejected by
others.[2]

Forty years ago in a standard textbook, these words appeared:
"Schizophrenia, the mystery of psychiatry, constitutes a challenge to
investigators in every field of medical research." The situation has
not changed materially in the intervening period.

To summarize, then, it may be noted that all of the problem

[1] Instance Senator Eagleton's plight.

[2] This is the same sort of basis upon which R. D. Laing and Timothy O'Leary
have argued for the schizophrenic state as preferable.

behaviors generally identified as schizophrenia stem from two sources: (1) forces distorting one's ability to perceive or evaluate the world as it is in reality, or (2) self-induced forces that cause one to misread or mislead one's self or others. But within each of these two very broad categories, the varieties of situations and types are manifold. For instance, poor perceptual intake may lead to proper brain functioning that turns out badly because it is based on faulty data; on the other hand, the behavior may stem from malfunctioning of the brain because of a tumor, while the perceptions are intact. Therefore, to speak of schizophrenia as if the term denoted any clearly definable condition, distinguishable from all others, is to misunderstand entirely.

For convenience sake, we may classify (roughly) the causes of schizophrenia as organic/inorganic (or from a telic perspective as misreading/misleading activities), always keeping in mind the fact that even the boundaries between these categories are not fixed and impassable. What may have begun largely as misleading activity (i.e., deception) may at length turn into a misreading activity (self-deception), or a bit of both.

> "Narcotics agents are after me," John insisted. The charge—as his "evidence" proved—was ludicrous. Yet the reality construct by which he justified the claim was perfectly reasonable to him. It was so because the construct of reality into which he pigeonholed data had gradually emerged over a period of time as the result of a long history of flight. John's problem originated within a reality construct that was true to life. There was a time when he was a drug pusher. At that time it was realistic for him to be suspicious and wary. But the life patterns developed then, continued long after he had abandoned drugs. The pattern of looking over his shoulder, however, persisted. The guilt of the past, the patterns of life, etc., all continued until he came to forgiveness and put on a new and Christian reality construct. As Proverbs put it, "The wicked flee when no man pursues" (Proverbs 28:1).

Or, conversely, what began as a misreading activity (dysperception) in time may develop into a life of misleading (deception of others or self). Visual perceptual distortion may lead one (for instance) to dysperceive the shapes of the faces of loved ones who appear (to the person whose chemical processes are malfunctioning) to be scowling at him when in fact they are not. Visual cues that do not fit auditory communication may lead him to suspect the motives of others and to respond with caution, etc., that is appropriate to the faulty data but not to the reality situation. Such action will be interpreted as bizarre. He may develop a suspicious attitude toward others that at length may become a reality construct for falsely interpreting all of life.

The Christian Perspective

Given the situation described above, how does a counselor in the Christian tradition begin to handle the many problems of schizophrenic behavior? To answer that question, I shall have to describe something of the fundamental assumptions underlying Christian thought and activity that must govern his approach. Otherwise, the following may seem too bizarre or even schizophrenic to some! Every counselor, of course, brings a wealth of assumptions to his life choices, whether he recognizes this or not. He cannot help but do so. There is no such thing as neutral thought or action. As Neal Miller puts it, "Pure empiricism is a delusion." We all work, think, choose, write, speak within a chosen context, from which we can never emerge without radical changes in belief. At the bottom of our attitudes and expectations is a faith commitment, not based upon empirical evidence (even those who try to base all thought and activity upon empirical data do so *because* of a basic faith in such data. No one can escape the presuppositional issue), that opens and closes doors for us. Even the selectivity of areas, data, etc., to a large extent depends upon one's commitment. Thus, to postulate the existence or non-existence of the God of the Scriptures makes a tremendous difference in one's approach to counseling. If the Scriptures are true, and if they tell us about man's condition and the basic solution to his problems, as they purport to (and as the Christian indeed believes that they do), then the Christian counselor comes to counseling with a set of assumptions that will govern all that he does.[1] How could he do otherwise? To reject these data — so pertinent to the conditions with which he is dealing — would be pernicious. The same could be said to be true of the one who rejects the Scriptures as revelational; he could not for a moment entertain biblical data in his counseling theory.

That man may be subject to (or may subject himself to) internal and external forces that may impair his ability to function, that he is capable of intentionally and unintentionally stimulating and simulating such impairment in order to mislead, and that over a period of time (or suddenly) he can develop such faulty responses to stress situations that he loses a grip on reality (i.e., he may misread it) is to picture him at once as a frail, a conniving, a self-deceptive and a foolish being. That is to say, as Christians look at it, man is a sinner,

---

[1] For a fuller discussion of these assumptions, cf. Jay Adams, *The Christian Counselor's Manual* (Presbyterian and Reformed Publishing Company: Nutley, 1973), esp. pp. 21–30.

who, according to the Bible, has been subjected by God to vanity because of his rebellion against his Creator.[1]

Sin, the violation of God's laws, has both direct and indirect consequences that together account for all of the bizarre behavior of schizophrenics. That is why Christians must refuse to ignore the biblical data. From the perspective of these Scriptural data *all* faulty behavior (which for the Christian is behavior that does not conform to the law of God. Notice how when one thinks from a revelational position he adopts a set of biblical criteria as his standard.) stems ultimately from the fundamental impairment of each man at birth in consequence of the corruption of mankind resulting from the fall. No perfect men are born by ordinary generation. They all inherit the fallen nature of Adam together with its organic and moral defects that lead to all faulty (including all bizarre) behavior. Every aspect of man has been marred by sin and consequently, to state it in theological language, men (including those who counsel others) may be described as "totally depraved". Total depravity does not mean that each man is as bad as he could be (the common grace of God restrains sin from fully manifesting itself), but rather that every man is affected by sin in all of his being. No aspect of a human being, no function has escaped the distorting effects of sin. To some extent, therefore, the same problems seen in schizophrenics are common to all. The differences lie in (1) what bodily functions are impaired, (2) how severely, and (3) what sinful life responses have been developed by the counselee. It is also vital to ask whether the individual is redeemed by the grace of God, since redemption involves a gradual renewal of human nature (cf. Ephesians 4:22–24; Colossians 3:10).

You may think such language to be ludicrous, horrendous, irrelevant, or whatever. But from the Christian's viewpoint, it is important to use accurate theological labels where they are appropriate, since the identification of a problem more than anything else points toward its solution. The identification of the problem of schizophrenia as a theological difficulty points toward a theological solution. In the same way, a non-theological diagnosis ("mental illness", etc.) leads to a non-theological solution. This is important for many reasons, not the least of which is the Christian counselor's concern not merely about the presenting problem of the counselee, but also for his basic

---

[1] Romans 8:20. "Vanity" (ματαιοτητι) in this passage refers (among other things) to the consequences of the corruption of the world and of human nature due to sin. The New International Version interestingly translates ματαιοτητι "frustration".

relationship to God. A problem involving one's relationship to God cannot be solved by medicine, by alteration of one's relationship to others, by introspection, or by the manipulation of the environment. It can be solved only by a direct confrontation with that God, *and* on His terms. Those terms (again) are spelled out in only one place: in the Scriptures.

Wrong labels point in wrong directions which, in turn, end only in more frustration. *Schizophrenia* is a psychological or psychiatric label which leads toward psychological or psychiatric solutions. If, on the other hand, investigation shows that a particular kind of bizarre behavior should be labelled as a chemical malfunction (stemming not from personal sin such as sleep loss; but is rather solely the result of the fall), that conclusion leads toward a medical solution; or if it indicates that the problem comes from sinful living, the term "sin" points in the direction of a theological solution. It is a serious fault thus to suggest that anything less than God himself can solve a problem that fundamentally has to do with one's relationship to Him.

The Christian counselor's approach, therefore, will begin with an attempt to discover whether the behavior of any given counselee stems fundamentally from organic defects or from sinful behavior on his part. In the case of bizarre behavior, whenever indicated, he will insist upon careful medical examinations that will be calculated to detect any glandular or other chemical malfunction, brain damage, toxic problems, etc. But when he is reasonably assured that (at base) the problem is not organic (or that it is not only organic), he will counsel on the supposition that such behavior must stem from sinful life patterns. He will be aware, of course, of the vital fact that the counselee is a whole person whose problems cannot always be divided neatly into the categories *organic* and *inorganic* (or into categories of misreading or misleading). There are often (if not always) elements of both. And most assuredly the organic affects the non-organic and vice versa.

When Philip smashed a chair on the floor, attacked his counselor, wept uncontrollably, whined in self-pity and spoke of hearing voices and taking trips on a flying saucer, not only one problem lay behind these difficulties. Sleep loss, possible chemical malfunction, twelve years of frustration with an inexplicable problem, resentments (and suspicion) toward physicians, psychiatrists and ministers, bitterness over scores of shock treatments, a severely distorted reality construct, sinful patterns of living and institutionalization (and a number of other problems), all influenced and motivated by a sinful nature, combined to produce the bizarre behavior.

The Christian has always been aware of the psychosomatic (or, as he might prefer to call it, *hamartiagenic*[1]) nature of much illness, because the fact is taught throughout the Bible.

Recent studies in biofeedback by Miller, Green *et al.*, have extended our awareness of the great extent to which man controls his physical condition. They appear to show: (1) that we have much more control over our bodily functions (blood pressure, heartbeat, muscletone, galvanic responses, etc.) than heretofore was realized; (2) that we are, therefore, more responsible for our organic condition than we had suspected; (3) that we can control and are responsible for many (if not all) of the glandular and neurological responses that occur in some forms of bizarre behavior. It is altogether possible that the chemical/electrical processes that govern perception may be controlled by attitude, etc., in a manner that makes man more responsible for these functions than most have thought. That is to say, beliefs and attitudes (in addition to other factors) also may be at the root of perceptual dysfunctioning (misreading of reality). Studies of attention related to the recticular formation demonstrate how data may be selected for rerouting past awareness. We are only on the threshold of much new information in this area, but already the early returns clearly seem to indicate that man has a greater degree of moral involvement in and, therefore, responsibility for the organic processes of his body than previously was thought. The "involuntary" nervous system seems to be quite a bit more subject to voluntary control than was suspected when this apparently inappropriate name was attached to it.

The Christian, in harmony with biblical promises (e.g., Psalm 32:1, 2; Proverbs 3:1, 2, 8, 16; 4:10, 20–2; Berkeley Translation), has affirmed that the fundamental biofeedback that he has needed for *hamartiagenic* problems is the Scriptural criteria themselves. Conformity to biblical patterns of life, with the emotional states and attitudes that grow from them, enables one to regulate his bodily functions (albeit unconsciously) in ways that promote good health. Conversely, failure to do so produces malfunctioning. The biblical principle to care for the body as "the temple of the Holy Spirit" means that he must not ingest hallucinagenic drugs that will distort perception; it means also that he will not push his body beyond its capacity through subjecting it to significant sleep loss that could cause similar dysperception. The principle "Do not let the sun go down on your anger" (Ephesians (4:26) is filled with implications

[1] *Hamartiagenic* means "sin-engendered".

concerning the healthy functioning of the glandular processes and their effects. Moreover, the principle "He who conceals his transgressions will not prosper; but he who confesses and forsakes them will obtain mercy" (Proverbs 28:13), implies the fundamental benefits of a clear conscience plainly enough so that there is no need to expand upon it. These, and a large number of similar exhortations and promises, when followed, promoted healthy living because the body was properly regulated by the attitudes that were created, growing from self-evaluation of one's behavior. The Christian may have known little or nothing of the functioning of the human body. But he (nevertheless) benefited from living in ways that promoted proper functioning. S. I. McMillen, in his book, *None of These Diseases,* has set forth popularly (but convincingly) many of the positive psychosomatic effects of living according to Scriptural injunctions. From the Christian's perspective, then, it is fair to say that Christian living will, itself, preserve (reclaim) one from those harmful bodily functions which are autogenically controlled and that may lead to bizarre behavior. Christian living, or course, will not prevent or counter such behavior when it is produced indirectly as the result of bodily defects or breakdown due to purely somatic factors.

Roughly, then we may break down *schizophrenia* into several categories as Fig. 5.1 visualizes.

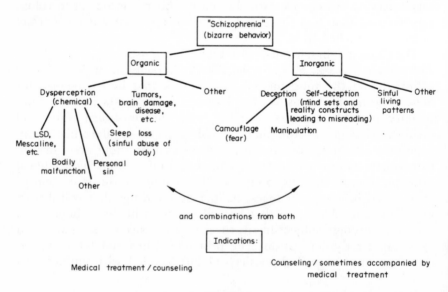

Fig. 5.1

All of which leads to the Christian conviction that man is largely (or in many instances totally) responsible for his behavior, even when it is, of a bizarre nature. Passages such as I Peter 3:14 ("Be neither terrified nor troubled by their threat") more fully come alive under such considerations. It is not impossible to *command* the control of one's emotions. By proper attitudes and actions the Christian *without biofeedback* controls his bodily functions and states as God intended him to. Except in those relatively infrequent cases (such as brain damage) that are validly organic at base, the Christian counselor seeks to deal with schizophrenia in the same manner as he would in confronting those who have other problems occasioned by sinful living patterns. In this large measure of responsibility lies hope. What is due in sin can be changed; there is no such certainty if, as some think, schizophrenia is largely due to other factors.

Biblical counseling is best described, perhaps, by a study of one of the biblical words for counseling: *nouthesia*.[1] This Greek term, which may be transliterated in English as *nouthetic confrontation*, occurs frequently in the New Testament and in the Septuagint version of the Old Testament. It involves three elements which presuppose three qualifications in the counselor:

Nouthetic Confrontation	*Qualifications of the Counselor*
1. Discernment of wrong-doing in another that God says must be changed.	1. Scriptural knowledge of the will of God (Romans 15:14; Colossians 3:16).
2. Verbal confrontation of another with the teaching of the Word of God in order to change his values, attitudes and behavior.	2. Ability to use biblical wisdom in one's relationships to others (Colossians 3:16).
3. Confrontation of another for his individual benefit.	3. Good will and concern for other members of the body of Christ (Romans 15:14).

Interestingly, these three elements contrast sharply with fundamental premises of the three major schools of psychotherapy: Freudianism, Rogerianism, Behaviorism. While Freud thinks that man cannot be held responsible for what he does (and thereby removes all hope), nouthetic confrontation maintains that there is hope precisely because God holds him responsible and has provided instruction and help for the changes that He requires of His redeemed children. Whereas Rogers thinks that man has all of the

---

[1] For a fuller description of nouthetic confrontation cf. *Competent to Counsel, op. cit.,* pp. 41–64, and *The Christian Counselor's Manual, op. cit.,* pp. 13, 14.

resources potentially prepackaged within (thereby ultimately ensuring discouragement and failure to already confused persons), nouthetic confrontation provides an authoritative word directly from God to slice through the dense confusion. Though Skinner thinks that man is only an animal and that the one and only value is the preservation of the human herd — there is no value to the individual (thereby reducing the worth of human life to a merely utilitarian level which would allow for manipulative breeding practices, etc.) — nouthetic confrontation involves individual concern for each counselee as a human being of worth because he was created in the image of God. This contrast allows for no compromise that may lead to eclectic borrowing.

To put it succinctly, the three elements may be summarized as (1) godly *change* effected by (2) Scriptural *confrontation* that (3) grows out of Christian *concern*. In these elements responsibility and hope predominate.

Since I have written elsewhere at length of the biblical principles of counseling that are essential to meeting needs of persons whose patterns of sinful living lead to great difficulty, I shall not repeat what I have said there. Let me turn, therefore to the discussion of a case in point.

When Barbara received the unpleasant news that her son, George, had gotten his girlfriend pregnant, she was unprepared for it. This news came in the wake of other unsolved problems that had been piling up in the family, some of which were due to Barbara's own sin. John, Barbara's husband, phoned the office of a nouthetic counselor and described the scene: upon hearing the bad news, Barbara had gone to their bedroom, sat down on the bed, and had frozen — stiff as a stone. This would classically be called a catatonic state. She had been in that position, staring ahead at the wall, totally uncommunicative, acting as if she were "out of touch with reality", for 7 hours. "Out of touch with reality" may be a presuppositional phrase that gets counselors into trouble in handling many bizarre behavior problems because they feel obligated to act in accordance with it. Too often the words better describe the counseling method than the state of the counselee. In our case, however, the counselor arrived and did three things:

1. From the account (much more fully given) which he elicited through directive data gathering from others in the home, he surmised that there was no organic cause for this behavior.

2. He assumed that Barbara was *not* out of touch with reality and (therefore) could hear, understand, and act upon what he was about to say.

3. He then spoke to Barbara in a firm, loving manner, stressing hope and issuing a warning. Greatly summarized, here is what he said:

> Barbara, I know that you can understand everything that I am saying, and I want you to listen carefully. First, you are running away from your problems this way. That is wrong; it is not God's way of handling life's disappointments and dilemmas and will create only larger difficulties for you and your loved ones if you persist in it. Not to respond is sin. I recognize that your problems are serious and that you don't know what to do about them. I do not want you to think that I minimize them one bit. They are probably worse than I now could realize. Yet, your Lord Jesus Christ is greater, and if you will let me I shall help you to work out the answers to them from His Word. The sooner that you begin to talk, the sooner we can begin to lay out a biblical plan to solve these problems. But apart from your willingness to face the situation God's way, there is no hope.

Barbara stirred a bit, but did not respond. The counselor went on to describe the alternatives:

> If you will not face your problems, you will force John to take the only other and far more unpleasant course of action that lies before him. First, it will be necessary for him to let you sit here for a day as you are. You will find that lack of food and toilet needs will make the situation exceedingly uncomfortable. If, even under those circumstances you still do not budge, John can do only one more thing — he must send you to a mental institution. Do you have any idea of what it is like to live in a mental institution? Let me describe . . .

It was not too far into that description that Barbara broke down. She wept in relief, then poured out the story of her disappointments, anger and fears. The counselor, as a result, was able to help her meet these God's way.

As one can see in this abbreviated account, much of the seemingly bizarre behavior (if not most) is not bizarre to the person himself. That is, the behavior makes sense to him *from his viewpoint.* Even original schizophrenic concepts of a split between affect and behavior (and/or speech) are explainable on this basis. There is no split for the counselee; the affect and behavior seem out of sync *only for the counselor.* Thus, to speak of the schizophrenic's evasions, suspicions, silly grins and giggles is to speak as one who is evaluating another's behavior from the point of view of what, at times, can be entirely different data. Here Barbara did not know what to do, so she did nothing. She was afraid that any action that she might take would worsen rather than help the situation, so she took no action. She was angry, her pride was hurt, but rather than reveal this in the outbursts that she was afraid these emotions would occasion, she restrained her feelings to the point of immobility. It was wrong behavior, but not irrational; the rationale behind it is clear.

To a person with perceptual difficulty resulting from chemical malfunction, the world may seem all askew. Chairs may appear to fly off the ground toward one's head, lights may pulsate strangely, faces may seem grotesquely distorted, etc. Given such dysperception, one's actions, although strange or bizarre from the point of view of an onlooker, to the counselee are not strange but explainable. To protect one's self from a flying chair by leaping from its path is rational behavior, but it seems outlandish and irrational to one who does not perceive the chair as moving at all. Indeed, in time, his rationality may be questioned by the counselee himself. After all, the chair never arrived!

Of course, all such bizarre behavior may be simulated for various purposes *in order to appear* insane.[1] There is a mounting conviction that much bizarre behavior must be interpreted as camouflage intended to divert attention from one's otherwise deviate behavior.[2] The explanation of much behavior as coverup or camouflage runs something like this: bizarre behavior some time in the past (perhaps far back in the past) was rewarded positively when it succeeded in deflecting attention from one's deviant behavior. Bizarre behavior of this sort must be viewed (like all other sinful behavior) as the product of a "deceitful heart" (cf. Jeremiah 17:9). Therefore, on succeeding occasions the client again attempted to hide behind bizarre actions and discovered that frequently this ruse worked. If this occurred frequently enough a pattern of such action was established. Bizarre behavior then became the natural (habitual) means to which he resorted whenever he sinned.

However, such behavior, though often successful at the outset (frequently enough to become a deeply etched pattern and thus the first resort when one does wrong) does not continue to work as successfully as it did in the past. As one grows out of childhood and into adolescence, for instance, he finds it more difficult to hide. Now he is expected to give rational explanations for his behavior. Rather than change, the habit-dominated person will endeavor to continue

---

[1] Cf the case of David cited in I Samuel 21:13.

[2] Cf. O. Hobart Mowrer, *Crisis*, pp. 81–102 (esp. pp. 83–91) where Mowrer sets forth Tim Wilkins' "Dick Tracy Theory of Schizophrenia". In this view, the counselor is thought of as Dick Tracy rather than Ben Casey. A recent illustration of this viewpoint is found in Walter C. Stolov's work at the University of Washington's hospital in the rehabilitation of patients with severe ambulatory problems. Cf. *Medical News*, Vol. 209, No. 10, 8 September 1969, p. 1442.

to resort to bizarre behavior as his solution. But repeated failures of recent attempts at length force him to make some change. Yet, even then, he changes not the nature of his response but its intensity. So in order to continue to cover up his behavior, his actions become more and more bizarre. If the pattern is not broken, his behavior eventually will become so deviant that in the end society will institutionalize him. In this way behavior can become totally unacceptable in a very short time.

In the long run the counselee finds that such behavior, even when it hides him from detection, is not really successful. Increasingly as his actions become more bizarre he finds that his behavior tends to isolate him. His social contacts are broken off, and the society which he needs so desperately drifts away from him as he hides from it. He knows he is living a lie, and his conscience triggers painful psychosomatic responses. So at last he becomes a very miserable person, externally isolated and alienated from others, and internally torn apart.

Steve was a young man of college age whom the writer met in a mental institution in Illinois. Steve had been diagnosed by psychiatrists as a catatonic schizophrenic. He did not talk, except minimally, and he shuffled about as though he were in a stupor. Upon sitting down, he became frozen in one or two positions. At first, communication with Steve seemed impossible. He simply refused to respond to questions or to any kind of verbal overtures. However, the counselors told Steve that they knew he understood fully what was going on, that though he might have fooled others—the psychiatrist, his parents, the school authorities—he was not going to fool them. They assured Steve that the sooner he began to communicate the sooner he'd be able to get out of the institution. Steve remained silent, but was allowed to continue as a part of the group observing the counseling of others. The next week the guns were turned on Steve, and for more than an hour the counselors worked with him. Steve began to break down. His hesitant replies gave evidence that he clearly understood everything. There was no reason to believe that he had withdrawn from reality.

As Steve began to respond, the rough outlines of his problem emerged. But the third week he broke down entirely. Steve had no mental disorders. Steven had no emotional problems. Nothing was wrong with his mind or his emotions. His problem was autogenic. Steve's problem was difficult but simple. He told us that because he had been spending all his time as prop man for a play rather than working at his college studies, he was about to receive a raft of pink slips at the mid-semester marking period. This meant that Steve was going to fail. Rather than face his parents and his friends as a failure, Steve camouflaged the real problem. He had begun acting bizarrely, and discovered that this threw everyone off track. He was thought to be in a mental stupor, out of touch with reality — mentally ill.

The truth was that Steve was hiding behind the guise of illness in much the same way that a grammar school child will feign illness when he doesn't want to take a test for which he has not prepared adequately. Steve had done this sort of thing many times before, but never quite so radically. At times he would go off by himself and grow quiet and still and become hard to communicate with, and at other times he would walk off down the road and wouldn't return for hours. Over the years Steve gradually had developed an avoidance pattern to which he resorted in unpleasant and stressful situations. When the college crisis arose he naturally (habitually) resorted to this pattern. Steve's problem was not mental illness, but guilt, shame, and fear.

As he spoke with the counselors, Steve recognized that they were asking him now to make the basic decision he had previously sought to avoid. Steve knew that now he must decide whether he was going to tell the truth to his parents and his friends and leave the mental institution, or whether he was going to continue the bluff. When we left, on the fifth week, Steve was still working on that decision. He was actually posing the question himself in these words: "Would it be better to continue the rest of my life this way, or to go home and face the music?"

In the process of working with Steve, it became clear that the more others treated Steve as if he were ill, the more guilty he felt. This was so because Steve knew that he was lying. It is important for counselors to remember that whenever clients camouflage, whenever they hide to avoid detection, whenever they purport to be ill when they are not, sick treatment only makes them worse. To act as if they may be excused for their condition is the most unkind thing one can do. Such an approach only compounds the problem.

When Steve was approached by those who held him responsible, he responded. For the first time since his commitment, he gained some self-respect. Under those circumstances he began to talk about his condition. Contrary to much contemporary thought, it is not merciful to be nonjudgmental. To consider such counselees victims rather than violators of their behavior as neutral, or as not blame-worthy only enlarges their lie and increases the load of guilt. Such treatment, Steve explained, had been for him sheer cruelty because of the compounded mental anguish and distress it engendered. Nothing hurt more, he said, than when his parents visited him and treated him kindly, like an innocent victim of circumstances.

Mary, during the first interview, tried to camouflage herself in order to avoid detection, just as Steve had done. But the techniques that Mary had developed over the years were quite different. Mary had been diagnosed by psychiatrists as a manic-depressive. Instead of shutting up, withdrawing, rearing a wall and challenging the world to batter it down as Steve did, Mary's ploy was "I'll drown you out so that you'll stop bothering me." As soon as the counselors began to put their finger on the real issue in Mary's life (which in the end turned out to be adultery with her next-door neighbor), Mary began to howl and cry and scream at the top of her lungs. Besides inarticulate sobbing, she cried, "Leave me alone; leave me alone!" In the past Mary had successfully warded off all attempts by her parents and others to discover the reasons for her distress by driving them away. Mary was now using her tried-and-true ruse with the counselors, but they were not abashed at such responses. Instead, they looked Mary squarely in the eye and said:

> O be quiet! Unless you stop this kind of nonsense and get down to business, we simply can't help you, Mary. Surely a young girl like you doesn't want to spend the rest of her life in this institution. We know that you have real problems, and we know that there is something wrong in your life. Now let's start talking turkey.

Instead of showing her sympathy, instead of responding to her tears, instead of being taken in by Mary's tactics, the counselors brushed aside the camouflage and pursued a straight course directly to the heart of the matter. At this, Mary turned off her antics almost automatically as if she had pushed a button. She told the story, a miserable story, which had been so hard to tell she had never told it to another person before.

Mary was helped only because her counselors were not shaken by Mary's screams and tears. They dealt appropriately with her feelings and demanded more content. They insisted on working with data. They called a spade a spade. Mary needed to learn that her habitual response pattern was faulty and that she would have to abandon it if she really wanted help. Agreeing, Mary found help in confession and change.

Often persons come for counseling prepared to perform their little acts, to go through their patterns. Women come with their purses stuffed full of Kleenexes. Men come with their tempers on edge ready to flare out. But the Christian counselor considers such acting out behavior an opportunity to help. He calls attention to the present behavior and confronts the counselee not only about the other problems, but also about the very way in which he is handling the counseling situation itself.

When confronting someone concerning such avoidance patterns, counselors must seek to correct such behavior for his benefit. They must point out the principles involved, give instruction in biblical responses, and help him to understand how these very patterns of avoidance played a part in getting him into trouble.

One factor that must be kept in mind is that many persons with problems serious enough to be labelled schizophrenic are persons who (if their behavior is autogenic) are desperate and who already have reached a point where they are willing to take radical measures to solve their problems. Their behavior itself is evidence of this fact. Herein lies hope for the counselor. A person in despair may be ideally suited for dramatic change. The seemingly most difficult cases often afford the most unique opportunities. Sweeping life changes frequently are recorded. This should not be thought strange: a person with a scratch will settle for a band aid; someone with cancer will submit to radical surgery. In the providence of God, often persons who have reached the end of *their* rope are ready at last to take hold of *His*. The diagram below shows the dynamic:

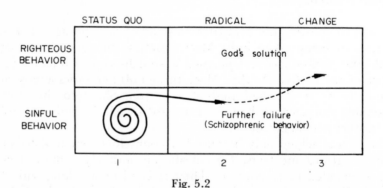

Fig. 5.2

If the counselee is confronted in time, the "set" (column #1) may be directed toward the upper box in column #2. He is "wound up" (set) for radical action (column #1); there is often opportunity to divert this action from the contemplated behavior that results in the schizophrenic label. But even if he is contacted only after he has arrived in the lower box (column #2), often there is still much momentum, or a new "set" (rewinding) for change that can be diverted into the upper box, column #3.

Finally, then, in recognizing the rationality of all such behavior, the Christian seeks to penetrate to the factors involved in each case taken individually. To these he brings Scriptural solutions. He refuses to lump all cases in one symplistic category. In doing so, he tries at every point to begin with the good news of salvation (through faith in the death of Christ for sinners and His resurrection from the dead), and then moves to the specific implications and applications of this basic solution that are appropriate to the circumstances of each case. The presupposition that salvation provides the basic solution for human problems also will lead him to combine evangelism and counseling whenever indicated and always will require second level solutions that grow out of and are in every way consistent with biblical principles.

Schizophrenia, for the distinctively Christian counselor, provides no more or no less of a challenge than any other problem involving original sin, personal sin and the consequences of both. He believes that the resources provided in the Scriptures, coupled with the power of God through His Spirit are more than adequate. As the Scriptures themselves put it: "Where sin increased, grace abounded all the more" (Romans 5:20b, NASV).

References

Adams, J. *Competent to Counsel.* Nutley: Presbyterian and Reformed Publishing Company, 1970, pp. 31, 114—23.

Adams, J. *The Big Umbrella.* Nutley: Presbyterian and Reformed Publishing Company, 1972.

Adams, J. *The Christian Counselor's Manual.* Nutley: Presbyterian and Reformed Publishing Company, 1973.

12 Admissions of Mental Error, *Medical World News,* 9 February, 1973, p. 18. Ibid.

Jonas, G. *Visceral Learning.* New York: Viking Press, 1973, p. 28. For further comments on the role of presuppositions, see J. Adams, The Use of the Scriptures in Counseling, *Bibliotheca Sacra,* January—March, 1974, Vol. 131, No. 521, pp. 14—25.

Karlins, M. and Andrews, L. M. *Biofeedback.* New York: Warner Publishing Company, 1973.

Lawrence, J. *Alpha Brain Waves.* New York: Avon Books, 1972.

McMillen, S. I. *None of These Diseases.* Westwood: Spire Books, Fleming H. Revell Company, 1963.

Rosenhan, D. On being sane in insane places. *Science,* 1973.

Strecker, A. and Ebaugh, F. G. (Eds.), *Practical Clinical Psychiatry,* 14th ed. Philadelphia: P. Blakiston's Sons & Co., 1935, p. 355.

IV

The Behavioral Change

CHAPTER 6

The Modification of "Schizophrenic" Behavior[1]

Behavior modification has been employed successfully to alter the behavior of diverse treatment populations including schizophrenics. Prior to reviewing research on the modification of psychotic behavior, some preliminary comments are in order. The comments outline the model which "underlies" the approach implicit in behavior modification strategies. The model, sometimes referred to as the sociopsychological model of behavior, has been lucidly described in several sources (Bandura, 1969; Kanfer and Phillips, 1970; Krasner and Ullmann, 1973; Ullmann and Krasner, 1969). The present comments will provide only a conspectus of the model and its assumptions.

Initially, the sociopsychological model assumes that the principles or laws which govern behavior do not differ across "normal" or "abnormal" behaviors. Indeed, as Skinner noted (1956), ". . . the behavior of the psychotic [is assumed to be] simply part and parcel of human behavior. . . ." Abnormal behavior is not regarded as distinct from normal behavior in terms of how it develops or is maintained and altered. Abnormal behavior is not assumed to represent a dysfunction or disease process which has overtaken normal personality or psychological development. Rather, certain learning experiences or a failure to receive or profit from learning experiences can account for behavior (Bandura, 1968).

Whether behavior is referred to as abnormal is based upon a social designation rather than qualities which inhere in the behavior itself. There is no evidence of qualitative differences inherent in abnormal behavior. The ascription of various labels to behavior is understood in a large measure by examining the normative standards of those who make the subjective judgments (Becker, 1963; Sarbin, 1967; Szasz, 1960). Abnormal behavior is inferred from the degree to which behavior deviates from social norms and thus is a function of

[1] Preparation of this chapter was facilitated by a grant (MH 23399) from the National Institute of Mental Health.

both the individuals who make the normative judgment and the context which defines the particular norm invoked. (For discussions of social contingencies, labeling, and values and their role in a socio-psychological formulation of psychotic behavior, see Braginsky, Braginsky, and Ring [1969], Scheff [1966], Ullmann and Krasner [1969].)

The behavioral approach does not make assumptions about the "nature of schizophrenia". Behaviors labeled schizophrenic are assumed to be learned (as are nonschizophrenic behaviors) and amenable to principles of learning. Specific statements, couched in the terminology of "learning theory", made about the behavior of schizophrenics typically describe the current behavior of the patients rather than necessarily reflect etiological insights. For example, Ullmann and Krasner (1969) suggest that among other features, "schizophrenics" fail to respond to cues in the environment to which most individuals respond (Ullmann and Krasner, 1969; p. 383). Such a description suggests current areas where behavior is deficient and offers no specific information about etiology. Since the assumptions apply to behavior in general independently of classifications made upon social valuations, the behavioral view, in a sense, adheres to the "nonnature of schizophrenia" as a unique or qualitatively distinct category. Specific assumptions about the nature of a "disease" process or inherent psychological impairment, if adopted, might delimit application of experimental findings from psychology in general (Davison, 1966), an approach most behavior modifiers would eschew.

Viewing schizophrenic behavior as behavior *per se* has the appeal of parsimony. Learning processes are assumed to account for deviant and nondeviant behavior. It appears as if extremely deviant behavior (including "psychotic" behavior) can be developed in the home through straightforward learning processes (Lidz, Fleck, and Corneli-son, 1965). However, there is no firm evidence which reveals that individuals labeled as schizophrenic have such a unique history or particular learning experiences which inexorably result in schizophre-nic behavior.

To many individuals, the maleability of certain behaviors assumed to be characteristic of psychotic patients via learning techniques attests to the plausibility that these behaviors result from particular learning experiences. However, the efficacy of a given treatment technique does not necessarily advance any substantive etiological approach. For example, the use of antipsychotic drugs to suppress delusions or hallucinations may tempt one to assume that a chemical imbalance is solely responsible for the onset of such behavior. Similarly, the successful elimination of delusional statements with behavioral techniques may tempt one to conclude that the onset of such behavior was due to faulty learning. In fact, the leap from treatment efficacy to etiology is not warranted, although in any given instance it may have heuristic value. However, the main issue is whether the assumption of faulty learning in deviant behavior is useful in generating techniques of behavior change. Much of the evidence reviewed in subsequent sections suggests the viability of behavioral treatment techniques, although strictly they do not support an etiological position.

Behavioral interventions with hospitalized psychiatric patients and other "treatment" populations have relied heavily upon operant conditioning. Several early investigations revealed the efficacy of the operant approach with diverse populations (cf. Ullmann and Kranser, 1965). Many of these early investigations with treatment populations focused upon only one or a few individuals at one time, employed one or a few reinforcers, and altered behavior within restricted experimental sessions rather than on the ward. Indeed, such investigations served primarily demonstrational rather than therapeutic purposes.

Certainly, the most notable applications of operant techniques to psychiatric patients were reported by Ayllon and his colleagues (see Davison, 1969 for a review of this work). In several reports, operant techniques were applied to develop adaptive and prosocial behavior and to eliminate bizarre behaviors. Ayllon's work, of course, has had substantial impact in illustrating the therapeutic viability of operant procedures with institutionalized populations.

Currently, operant programs represent rather elaborate extensions of early research. Routinely, procedures are applied in a variety of settings, employ groups of individuals, focus on relatively complex responses in situations where control over behavior is limited, utilize a variety of reinforcers, and attempt to effect therapeutic change across diverse behaviors (Kazdin, 1975 a, b). The present paper reviews behavior modification programs with psychotic patients, particularly those patients diagnosed as "schizophrenic". Token economies represent a widely utilized technique allowing the large-scale application of reinforcement contingencies in facilities such as institutions and will constitute the major emphasis in the paper. Aside from reviewing the relevant behavior change research, some issues and problems associated with behavioral interventions will be entertained.

As noted earlier, behavior modifiers are not apt to view

schizophrenia as a distinct "entity". Thus, there are no studies in the behavior modification literature, at least to the knowledge of this author, which have claimed to provide a "treatment" of something referred to as "schizophrenia". Nevertheless, there are two kinds of treatment-relevant studies which will be reviewed. First, there are a number of investigations in which patients diagnosed as schizophrenic (or in some cases are merely referred to as "psychotic") are placed into a behavioral program such as a token economy. The specific behaviors focused upon in these programs would not be regarded traditionally as crucial to schizophrenic processes, deficits, or other attributes commonly considered to typify psychotic impairment. Second, another group of studies has focused on behavior considered, at least traditionally, to be symptomatic of or generally associated with schizophrenia. Each of these areas of research will be reviewed.

Investigations of Operant Programs with Schizophrenic Patients

A large number of token economies in psychiatric hospitals focus upon routine ward behaviors including self-care skills, grooming, taking medication, attending and participating in activities on the ward, engaging in jobs in the hospital, and other behaviors considered adaptive in the hospital. There is little question, in view of extensive and consistent evidence, that these behaviors can be altered markedly (cf. Kazdin and Bootzin, 1972 for review).

From the standpoint of "treating schizophrenia", it is important to note a criticism of focusing on routine behaviors in the hospital. Initial work, and even most of the research currently conducted, has utilized performance of patients *in the hospital* as the criterion for success of the program. An early defense of this approach was that the purpose was to determine whether the behavior of chronic patients on the ward could be altered on a large scale. Further, reinforcement for performing a variety of behaviors in the hospital was employed to combat behavioral deterioration associated with institutionalization. To many, such considerations are not germane to the point. What value do operant programs have for altering those behaviors which have contributed to hospitalization?

Research often indicates that the development of adaptive behaviors in the hospital, i.e., overcoming problems which are not necessarily peculiar to schizophrenic patients, *does* lead to changes in behaviors which are bizarre or "symptomatic". Thus, developing adaptive behavior on the ward can eliminate bizarre behaviors which might interfere with community adjustment. For example, O'Brien and Azrin (1972) altered a high rate of screaming in a female schizophrenic patient by providing tokens for "functional behaviors" such as social skills, housekeeping, and grooming (which were not necessarily incompatible with screaming). An increase in desirable behaviors was associated with a decrease in screaming. The authors suggested that positive behaviors "functionally displaced" the screaming.

In another program with hospitalized psychotics (mostly diagnosed as schizophrenic), verbal reinforcement was delivered during therapy group sessions for personal appearance (DiScipio and Trudeau, 1972). Patients who were reinforced made fewer negative statements about themselves on a self-esteem scale (evaluating their appearance and attractiveness) and were lower in psychotic belligerence on the Psychotic Reaction Profile relative to controls who did not receive reinforcing consequences.

In a project with hospitalized neurotically depressed males (Hersen, Eisler, Alford, and Agras, 1973), tokens were delivered for engaging in occupational therapy and personal hygiene. An increase in token-earning behaviors was associated with a reduction in depression, as measured by behavioral ratings. In a reversal design, depression varied inversely with the performance of the target behaviors.

Shean and Zeidberg (1971) used token reinforcement to develop self-care and role behaviors, and to increase extra hospital visits. Token reinforcement led to greater patient cooperativeness on the ward, communication skills, social interaction, participation in hospital activities, time out of the hospital, and a reduction in the use of medication. The majority of these improvements were not directly shaped with reinforcement.

Maley, Feldman, and Ruskin (1973) compared psychiatric patients reinforced with tokens for a variety of behaviors on the ward with controls who received custodial treatment. Behaviors during a standardized interview and ratings of video-taped behavior served as dependent measures. Patients in the token economy ward were better oriented, more able to perform a discrimination task, and more likely to follow complex commands and to handle money in making business purchases than control patients. Additionally, behavior ratings revealed that token economy patients showed more appropriate mood states, were more cooperative, and displayed better communication skills than control patients. Importantly, token economy patients were rated in less need of hospitalization and more likeable. Since patients received tokens for specific behaviors on the ward (e.g., grooming), the beneficial effects obtained for behaviors not included in the contingencies represent generalized effects. Similarly, Bennett and Maley (1973) noted changes in mood, communication, and social skills in two psychotic patients who received tokens for conversing with each other. These patients showed greater token earnings on the ward and greater participation in activities than did controls. Since the behaviors specifically reinforced in the experimental sessions were restricted verbal interactions, the effect of the contingencies generalized considerably.

Gripp and Magaro (1971) reported a program with psychiatric patients who received tokens for job performance and other "pre-selected desirable behaviors". After 6 months of the program, patients on the token economy ward showed significant reductions in withdrawal, thought disorder, and depression on the Psychotic Reaction Profile. Nurses rated patients as improved in social competence, neatness, irritability, and manifest psychosis. Improvement in these areas either was markedly less or not apparent on control wards which did not receive token reinforcement.

The above research shows that there are beneficial effects of reinforcement programs which transcend single response targets. It might be for this reason that increased discharge and decreased readmission rates are frequently documented with patients who participate in operant programs (e.g., Birky, Chambliss, and Wasden, 1971; Heap, Boblitt, Moore, and Hord, 1970). Of course, changes in discharge and readmission rates are not always clearly related to therapeutic efficacy and patient behavior change. In any case, ward programs which focus on adaptive behaviors within the hospital do result in broad changes. Often criteria traditionally used to evaluate treatment efficacy (e.g., measures of "psychoticism" and discharge) as well as target behavioral measures reflect patient change.

Focus on Specific "Symptomatic" Behaviors

Target "symptoms" have been focused upon directly rather than displaced indirectly by reinforcing other adaptive behaviors. Three areas have been investigated including bizarre verbalizations, social behavior, and attentiveness to external stimuli.

Bizarre Verbalizations. One area of behavior focused upon is the bizarre verbalizations emitted by schizophrenics. Liberman, Teigen, Patterson, and Baker (1973) evaluated the effect of social reinforcement in altering the behavior of four schizophrenics (mean hospitalization of 17 years) with "paranoid and grandiose" delusions. To eliminate delusional speech, two procedures were applied. First, daily interviews conducted individually with the patients were terminated at the onset of delusional talk. Second, patients could earn time to chat informally with a nurse during the evenings by speaking rationally in the daily interviews. The contingencies, evaluated carefully in a multiple-baseline design across patients, effected substantial behavior change although some delusional talk remained. Interestingly, reductions in delusional speech generalized to a situation in which performance was not consequated.

In another report (Patterson and Tiegen, 1973), one patient who participated in the previous study increased in rational talk but continued to answer questions incorrectly when queried about her personal history. With token reinforcement (exchangeable for a variety of privileges on the ward), correct answers to questions were developed. There was some evidence that responsiveness was partially maintained several weeks after discharge.

Also employing token reinforcement, Wincze, Leitenberg, and Agras (1972) altered delusional talk in therapy sessions with paranoid schizophrenics. Evaluation of verbal behaviors on the ward showed less dramatic change even though tokens were delivered for nondelusional talk with the staff. In another investigation (Kazdin, 1971), psychotic speech was suppressed in an adult prepsychotic retardate. Delusional statements decreased dramatically and did not recover over a 6-month follow-up period.

Social Behaviors. A significant response class for psychiatric patients is social behaviors. Of course, a precondition for social interaction may be elimination of certain bizarre behaviors. However, elimination of deviant behaviors alone does not ensure the appearance of social behaviors. An increasing number of investigations have focused directly upon social behaviors.

Kale, Kaye, Whelan, and Hopkins (1968) developed social responses in three chronic schizophrenic patients (mean hospitalization of approximately 16 years). The patients rarely interacted with staff or other patients. Using cigarettes as a reinforcer, greeting responses ("Hi!" or "Hello, Mr. ———".) were reinforced on the ward when made spontaneously or in response to greetings from staff. Over the training sessions, cigarettes were administered on an increasingly intermittent schedule. When greeting responses had been well established, new experimenters were introduced into the situation to ensure generalization of responses across staff. At the end of the investigation, greeting response remained at a high level although reinforcement had been eliminated.

Milby (1970) developed social interaction in two patients diagnosed as chronic undifferentiated schizophrenics. Social behavior was defined as talking to, and working or playing with another patient or staff member. When staff provided contingent attention (going in close proximity to, looking at, nodding, and talking approvingly) to the patients, social interaction increased.

Liberman (1972) trained four withdrawn and verbally inactive patients to engage in conversation with a group. Conversation increased substantially with token reinforcement contingencies based either upon individual or group performance. Similarly, Bennett and Maley (1973) provided two schizophrenic patients with tokens (exchangeable for a variety of items at a store) for conversing with each other in experimental sessions. Social interaction increased in the sessions and on the ward as well.

Horn and Black (1974) provided tokens to chronic patients for responding orally in a group situation. Group participation increased substantially. Regrettably, albeit predictably, when tokens and back-up reinforcers (candy and cigarettes) were withdrawn, participation immediately returned to baseline levels.

Leitenberg, Wincze, Butz, Callahan, and Agras (1970) treated a patient who avoided social interaction with staff by providing contingent token reinforcement for conversation. Neither instruction nor contingent reinforcement had increased social behavior.

Attentiveness to External Stimuli. An attentional deficit or inability to respond appropriately to external stimuli is often considered to be "symptomatically" significant with schizophrenic patients (cf. Maher, 1966). There have been few attempts to directly alter attentional sets using behavioral techniques. However, two investigations recently reported quite promising results (Meichenbaum and Cameron, 1973). The investigators developed attentional control of schizophrenic patients by training them to administer instructions to themselves to guide behavior. During training, subjects observed the therapist perform a variety of sensorimotor tasks. While performing the tasks, the therapist "talked to himself out loud". The verbalizations modeled by the therapist included: questions about the nature of the task, answers to these questions by mentally rehearsing and planning his actions, self-instructions in the form of self-guidance, and self-reinforcement. Essentially, the experimenter modeled "thinking out loud". Eventually, the patients themselves were trained to perform the tasks while instructing themselves aloud and then saying them covertly (privately). The purpose of self-instructional training is to develop a general learning set of talking to oneself, pausing, and thinking before responding.

Self-instructional training subjects (relative to controls exposed to the same training materials with the omission of self-instruction training) evinced substantial changes on a variety of dependent measures including proverb interpretation, "sick talk", recall tests under conditions of planned distractions, and perceptual integration as measured by inkblot responses. Importantly, the improvements in behavior were maintained at a 3-week follow-up assessment.

Treatment: Summary

Behaviors focused upon in operant programs for hospitalized patients have progressed well beyond basic skills fundamental to hospital living such as grooming and self-care. Routine ward behaviors are still important, particularly since reinforcement of these behaviors in many cases are associated with generalized effects. Of course, development of social skills, appropriate interaction patterns, and elimination of bizarre behaviors are crucial for extrahospital adjustment (cf. Freeman and Simmons, 1963). The significance of current research in the behavior change of schizophrenic patients is that behavior change in diverse areas is readily achieved. The behavioral technology applied is still in a relatively primitive state. Although refinements are made with well-studied behavioral interventions, gross manipulations still are conducted and entirely new independent variables (e.g., economic variables) are continually being introduced (cf. Winkler, 1972). The thrust of the present research is in beginning to focus on aberrant behaviors which supposedly reflect specific "psychiatric disorders". The mutability of relatively complex behaviors is increasingly apparent.

Operant Procedures Compared with Other Treatment Strategies

Typically, operant procedures are evaluated using any of a variety of within-subject designs in the absence of between-group comparisons. The rationale for such comparisons have been reviewed elsewhere (Baer, Wolf, and Risley, 1968; Kazdin, 1973d; Risley, 1970; Sidman, 1960). Recently, a number of questions have arisen which can be easily answered by between-group comparisons such as the relative effectiveness of different treatment strategies including no treatment and traditional custodial control procedures and the magnitude of change which can be attributed to parametric manipulations of specific variables. An increasing number of investigations has examined the relative efficacy of operant procedures with other treatments with hospitalized psychiatric patients using between-group comparisons.

In one of the first comparative investigations (Marks, Sonoda, and Schalock, 1968), reinforcement and relationship (individual) psychotherapy were compared with chronic schizophrenics. Each of two groups received each treatment but in a counterbalanced order. During the reinforcement condition, staff delivered tokens at their own discretion (rather than for well defined performance criteria) for improvement in individualized problem areas such as personal appearance and expressing oneself. On a variety of dependent measures the treatments were *not* different. The authors alluded to the difficulties in maintaining differences in the two forms of treatment (e.g., avoiding reinforcement in the individual therapy).

Hartlage (1970) also compared individual (insight) therapy with reinforcement (social reinforcement, privileges, and consumables) for "adaptive" responses. Pre- and post-treatment comparisons showed greater adjustment resulting from reinforcement therapy. Yet, on self-concept data, treatments were not significantly different. Therapists' ratings of improvement favored reinforcement therapy.

Gripp and Magaro (1971) compared token reinforcement with routine hospital care on a number of dimensions. Schizophrenic patients on a token economy ward made several changes on scales reflecting cognitive and affective concomitants of psychoses whereas fewer gains (and some instances of regression) were noted for patients on control wards. As mentioned earlier, other investigations have found reinforcement procedures to be superior to traditional ward care on a variety of dependent measures (Maley *et al.,* 1973; Shean and Zeidberg, 1971).

A few investigations have evaluated the effect of different procedures on release from or time spent out of the hospital. In an investigation by Olson and Greenberg (1972), psychiatric patients received one of three treatments, milieu therapy, interaction (milieu plus 2 hours of weekly group therapy), or token reinforcement, for a 4-month period. The reinforcement group earned tokens for group decision-making related to ward administration and for attendance to activities. The token reinforcement condition resulted in a greater number of patients spending days on town passes, having days out of the program, and attending activities. Although not all measures favored the token system (e.g., ratings of social adjustment), the program tended to be more effective than other procedures.

Heap *et al.* (1970) compared behavior-milieu therapy consisting of token reinforcement, ward government, and other adjunctive procedures, with traditional ward care in developing self-care skills. The reinforcement group showed greater performance of self-care skills and rate of discharge than the control ward. In contrast, Birky *et al.* (1971) found no differences in the *number* of patients discharged from the token economy and two traditional care control wards (i.e., patients who remained out of hospital for at least 6 months). However, the patients discharged on a token economy ward had a significantly greater length of previous hospitalization. Thus, the reinforcement procedure had greater effect in discharging patients who were more chronic.

As a general statement, the results of comparative studies indicate that greater therapeutic effects accrue to operant procedures than to other techniques used in psychiatric hospitals. However, the conclusion must be tentatively made. Comparative studies in hospital settings require careful research methodology. Often the essential ingredients for unambiguous results do not obtain. A variety of confounding influences compete as rival interpretations of the results (cf. Campbell and Stanley, 1963; Kazdin, 1973d). For example, the efficacy of operant procedures relative to other procedures has been confounded with a change in the setting employed across treatment modalities (Heap *et al.,* 1970), differences in the patients prior to treatment (Shean and Zeidberg, 1971), and selection of special staff on the ward administering operant procedures (Gripp and Magaro, 1971). Presently, the benefits derived from comparing operant procedures with other techniques have been slight. Such comparisons often focus on group behavior (as reflected in mean scores on a performance measure). However, to many investigators the main advantage of the operant approach is the focus on individuals and the single-subject (patient) experimental designs which are employed to evaluate change.

Restructuring Patient Social Contingencies

As typically practiced, behavioral programs (as well as many other treatment strategies) are designed and implemented by the staff with little input or participation of the patients. A system which is externally imposed on a patient may be counterproductive in a number of ways (Kazdin, 1973c). Initially, patient behavior may come under control of a system which bears little resemblance to the contingencies which normally control behavior in everyday life. Relatedly, the staff may become associated with the performance of desirable behavior. The staff may exert stimulus control over behavior because of their association with reinforcement (cf. Redd, 1969). Recently, peers have been incorporated directly into the contingencies and patients themselves have been utilized in the development or execution of the program. Thus, attempts are made to restructure the social contingencies of the setting to foster adaptive behavior. Rather than developing responsiveness to contingencies dictated completely from external sources (the staff), an individual's peers, and the patients themselves are employed as a source of control (Kazdin, 1975a).

A major use of patients on the ward is developing group peer social structure which supports and actively contributes to the appropriate behavior of individual patients. The contingencies are devised so that each individual's performance dictates the consequences delivered to his peers. For example, in one psychiatric hospital (Pomerleau *et al.,* 1972), patients were grouped into dyads. The dyads formed larger groups. Consequences in the program (e.g., fines) ordinarily imposed upon a single individual were shared by other members of the dyad or by other dyads. By making patients accountable to others for their behavior, it is hoped that the group will exert influence on behavior. Such an influence may well be adaptive once the program is withdrawn.

Olson and Greenberg (1972) also have employed sharing of consequences with peers on a psychiatric ward. To exert group pressure, patients were allowed access to their funds (or coupons negotiable at a local canteen) on the basis of their own performance and the performance of the group to which they belonged. Group performance was evaluated on attendance to scheduled activities and making group decisions regarding ward administration. The contribution of the group contingency to overall program efficacy was not determined.

Feingold and Migler (1972) employed token reinforcement with one chronic schizophrenic to increase activity on the ward, attendance to work, and social interaction. To augment the effect of the contingencies, two other patients were chosen to benefit from the target patient's daily token earnings. The number of tokens earned by the target patient were also allotted to the other two patients. (To spend these, the other patients had to earn tokens for their own performance.) The target patient's performance during the contingency in which the patient earned tokens for herself and others was markedly superior to her performance when she earned tokens for herself alone. Anecdotally, the authors noted that the other patients initially complained about the contingency arrangement. However, after the first few days, one of the other patients began to help the target patient (e.g., with self-care) by providing verbal prompts and criticism to encourage "appropriate" behavior. Prior to the project these patients did not interact socially. However, during the special contingency, a variety of interactions increased (e.g., going on trips and dancing together).

Patient and peer group influences have been employed in other ways in behavioral programs in psychiatric hospitals. Increasingly, patients participate actively in the design of the program of which they are a part. Instead of having treatment imposed upon them, patients actually design contingencies, decide policy in the program, and, in some cases, administer the programs of others (Pomerleau *et al.*, 1972; Kazdin, 1975b). Attempts are made to place control of the program into the hands of the patients. For example, O'Brien, Azrin, and Henson (1969) increased the frequency that chronic schizophrenic patients suggested improvements in their treatment. Interestingly, the number of suggestions made was a function of whether the suggestions were followed (i.e., reinforced), as carefully demonstrated in a reversal design. As noted earlier, Olson and Greenberg (1972) reinforced patients for making group decisions related to treatment recommendations. The group received tokens on the basis of their decisions.

The beneficial effects of contingencies involving peers remain to be explored empirically. However, preliminary information is intriguing and suggests viable ways to restructure social relationships in the hospital. The development of social interaction might be readily enhanced if programs routinely incorporated peers into the administration or design of the contingencies in addition to reinforcing social interaction directly. A possible benefit is that the behaviors developed by the patients may come under stimulus control of their peers and the social contingencies derived therefrom rather than from the staff and the administration of tokens *per se* (Kazdin, 1973c). In addition, the frequency and opportunities for reinforcement (planned and inadvertent) for performance of the target behaviors are likely to increase. Finally, increased reliance upon peers in the hospital can free staff for supervision of other programs (Kazdin, 1972).

Problems and Outstanding Issues

There is little question that the results for treatment of psychotic patients have been quite promising. Yet, there are some limitations relevant to evaluating treatment efficacy which are apparent and warrant discussion. Two major issues include the extent to which behaviors altered with behavioral interventions are maintained and transfer to nonprogrammed settings and the ability of the interventions to change seemingly intractable patients. Since these issues have been detailed elsewhere (Kazdin and Bootzin, 1972; Kazdin, 1973b; Kazdin, 1975a), they will only be highlighted.

Maintenance of Treatment Effects

The promising effects of reinforcement contingencies on behavior of hospitalized patients suggest that within a highly structured environment patient behavior can readily be altered. Yet, the obvious question is the degree to which changes can be maintained once the program is withdrawn and the patient leaves the setting. The extensive use of reversal designs in operant work contributes to this concern. In the reversal design, of course, the effect of the experimental intervention is demonstrated by withdrawing (or altering) and reinstating the contingency to show that behavior repeatedly improves when the contingency is in effect and deteriorates when the contingency is withdrawn (Kazdin, 1973d). Of course, performance during a phase in which the program is withdrawn provides a preview of what will probably happen when the program is withdrawn entirely. A major issue is whether behavior will be maintained.

A few preliminary comments are warranted. First, in some cases the withdrawal of the intervention has not resulted in a deterioration of behavior (e.g., Kazdin, 1973a; Kazdin and Polster, 1973; Surratt, Ulrich and Hawkins, 1969). However, these are exceptions. Second, the maintenance of behavior, as an area of experimental inquiry, has only recently been explored with the attention merited. As the priority for repeated demonstration of reinforcement with different sorts of patients has diminished, the research issues have changed. Now that behavior change seems readily feasible, the issue of maintenance has increased in significance.

Various techniques seem to be useful in ensuring response maintenance and transfer to extratreatment settings. In some instances, the efficacy of the technique as a maintenance strategy has been empirically supported. The techniques which can be used include:

1. *Substituting reinforcers normally present in the environment for extrinsic reinforcers employed in the program.* If tokens are used, as they often are in hospital programs, social reinforcement (praise) may be substituted without a deterioration in behavior (e.g., Reisinger, 1972).

2. *Gradually fading the contingencies.* Initially, highly structured contingencies may be employed to alter patient behavior. However, after performance has become consistent for a protracted period, reliance upon the contingencies can be decreased without losses in performance (e.g., Atthowe and Krasner, 1968; Jones and Kazdin, 1975).

3. *Training individuals in the client's environment.* The continued execution of treatment contingencies, at least in some form, increases the likelihood that performance will be maintained (cf. Lovaas, Koegel, Simmons, and Long, 1973). Individuals in the patient's environment (relatives, spouses, peers) can be trained in basic contingency management.

4. *Scheduling reinforcement.* Initially, reinforcement can be delivered on a "rich" schedule, although continuous reinforcement is rarely feasible in a ward setting. Increasingly intermittent reinforcement can be employed until little (Phillips, Fixsen, and Wolf, 1971) or no reinforcement (Kazdin and Polster, 1973) is actually delivered without losses in performance.

5. *Varying the conditions of training.* The degree of response maintenance is partially a function of the stimulus conditions which control performance. It is desirable to develop responses in the presence of a variety of cues to ensure broad stimulus control over behavior. Ideally, behaviors will develop in those situations in which the patient will be expected to perform.

6. *Self-control training.* Presumably, patients might be able to control their own contingencies and consequate their own behavior. One self-control technique, self-instructional training, appears to have particular promise (Meichenbaum and Cameron, 1973). At present, it is premature to evaluate self-control strategies in terms of maintaining patient behavior (cf. Kazdin, 1975a).

7. *Manipulating reinforcement delay.* At the initial stages of a reinforcement program, patients are usually reinforced at frequent and regular intervals. The delay of reinforcement (either tokens or

back-up reinforcers) is not great. To enhance maintenance, it may be useful to have patients receive increasingly delayed consequences for their performance (Jones and Kazdin, 1975).

The techniques briefly outlined above represent tentative solutions to the maintenance and transfer of training problem. Albeit maintenance has been achieved in various studies (e.g., Kale *et al.,* 1968; Jones and Kazdin, 1975), this area of inquiry requires a great deal of attention. Even so, preliminary evidence suggests that response maintenance is not at all elusive.

Unresponsiveness of Some Patients

In spite of the success of token reinforcement programs, a number of investigations report a small number of patients who appear to be unresponsive to the contingencies (Kazdin, 1973b). A recent investigation highlighted this problem by carefully showing different subgroups which may participate in operant programs. Allen and Magaro (1971) categorized psychiatric patients in a token economy ward according to when they performed the target response or whether they responded at all in response to the reinforcement contingencies. Three groups were distinguished: patients who performed the target response (attending occupational therapy) without reinforcement, those who performed the response only when tokens were delivered, and those who did not respond at all even when tokens were delivered. This last group is particularly interesting since patients did not respond to contingencies as initially programmed even though strong incentives were provided.

When patients fail to respond to the program, a number of interpretations may be advanced such as the lack of appropriate or sufficiently powerful incentives to change behavior (i.e., which back up the value of the tokens), severe response deficits, a failure to individuals to comprehend the relationship between performance and reinforcement, or particular problems with the administration of the contingencies (e.g., reinforcement is too intermittent for some patients).

It is important to note that when investigators claim unresponsiveness on the part of some patients, this signifies a failure to respond to a particular program rather than necessarily a characteristic of a given individual across several programs. Individuals who do not respond to an initial program may respond when alterations are made in the procedures. For example, Winkler (1971) reported individualized contingencies in a program for schizophrenic and retarded patients.

Innovative individualized contingencies were invoked with patients who had not responded to the "routine" token economy procedures. For example, in the case of one patient who would not attend occupational therapy, the exchange rate between tokens and back-up reinforcers was manipulated. The patient was told that until she attended the activity, she would have to pay double the usual prices whenever she spent tokens. When she missed occupational therapy, she paid double until the next time she attended. The patient increased attendance dramatically. Moreover, attendance was maintained up to a 10-month follow-up period after the schedule had been discontinued. This example suggests that the initial unresponsiveness of a patient to a program must be interpreted cautiously. A failure to respond may in part be a function of the persistence on the part of the investigator and the innovativeness of the program.

As with response maintenance, there are currently a number of techniques of potential value in resolving initial unresponsiveness of patients (Kazdin, 1973b). One solution is to increase the value of reinforcers available in the setting. Using a technique referred to as *reinforcer sampling,* the reinforcing value of available events in the setting can be increased (e.g., Ayllon and Azrin, 1968). The procedure entails providing a small sample of the event (e.g., a few minutes of a movie) which increases the likelihood that the entire event will serve as a reinforcer. Once the reinforcing value of the event is firmly developed, patients will continue to work for the event (i.e., perform those behaviors which will be reinforced) even though the sample is no longer provided.

Another technique is to alter the back-up value of the tokens. In some cases, the range of reinforcers may not be sufficiently varied to include those events which will effectively reinforce everyone. For example, Mitchell and Stoffelmayer (1973) selected two schizophrenic patients who did not respond to tangible reinforcers (candy, cigarettes, fruit, biscuits). The investigators altered the reinforcers to determine whether behavior change could be achieved. While the patients engaged in a work task, sitting in a chair for 90 seconds (a high probability behavior) rather than standing up while working was made contingent upon completion of a unit of work. This contingency was extremely effective in increasing work. The removal and reinstatement of the contingency showed a clear relationship of the high probability behavior and work output. The results are particularly demonstrative given that the patients were initially selected for the lack of responsiveness to the usual events employed in the setting.

Another procedure to increase responsiveness to reinforcement contingencies is alteration of various economic variables in a token system. As Winkler (1972) has noted, when the token savings of patients are reduced, token earnings increase. A number of basic economic principles dictate performance in token economy systems (Kazdin, 1975b).

Although operant programs have been successful, often a few individuals in the program do not respond to the contingencies. Preliminary evidence suggests that the nonresponsiveness is a function of the particular program. Once an innovation is made or the contingency is altered, behavior may change. Thus, the general approach of manipulating environmental events appears viable even with the individuals who appear to be "unresponsive". A number of specific procedures briefly outlined above can be employed when initial contingencies do not affect behavior.

Token Economies: Innovative Change or Complicity

There is a great deal of enthusiasm of individuals participating in operant programs in various facilities—and perhaps with just cause. Dramatic behavior change has been achieved in a number of instances. The careful control of behavioral interventions has been well demonstrated in hospitals and a variety of other settings (Kazdin and Bootzin, 1972). Moreover, preliminary investigations of behavioral interventions are underway to effect significant areas of social concern ranging from racial integration, unemployment, pollution, energy conservation, and others (cf. Kazdin, 1975a). Yet there are general issues and reservations which require reflection.

A major reservation relevant to psychiatric patients is the stance that behavior modification has taken, at least implicitly, in institutional programs. Programs ordinarily are established and function well within the existing system of institutional life. The behavioral approach has adapted to the hospital system and consequently may include or support some inherently counterproductive features. It is beyond the scope of this paper to decry the actual and potential undesirable features and consequences of institutional life (cf. Paul, 1969; Goffman, 1961). The debilitating effects of institutionalization may delimit the potential of any treatment strategy which has as a goal long-term social adaptation of the patient in the community. Some argue that hospital behavior modification programs effectively counteract the delimiting effects of institutionalization (e.g., Kazdin and Bootzin, 1972). However, this view may be naïve. A great deal of effort in behavioral programs is required to overcome limitations of the pre-existing situation rather than achieving positive advances in patient behavior.

Behavior modification in hospitals (or other institutional settings) in many instances stands in contrast to the mainstream of behavioral interventions. Probably, the greatest impact of behavioral programs is in changing behavior in those situations in which behavior is problematic (e.g., the home, classrooms). Indeed, the literature refers frequently to behavior change in the "natural environment" (Tharp and Wetzel, 1969) and training those individuals who exist in the "natural environment" to effect change (Ayllon and Wright, 1972; Guerney, 1969).

There are several reasons for focusing on behavior in the "natural environment". First, those individuals in everyday life with the clients have access to the problematic behavior and the consequences which can be used to alter behavior. Moreover, it is possible that the individuals who are living with the client engage in various behaviors which sustain deviant performance. Thus, it is likely that changes in the behavior of agents in the natural environment can have a major impact on problematic behavior (Guerney, 1969). Second, bringing patients into an artificial situation does not guarantee alteration of conditions which maintain deviant behavior. Individuals who come into contact with patients in the institution may operate under contingencies of their own which exacerbate existing behaviors or develop new bizarre behaviors (cf. Ullmann, 1967). For example, early applications of operant techniques with psychiatric patients (e.g., Ayllon and Michael, 1959) firmly demonstrated that the behavior of attendants in contact with patients was responsible for at least some of the deviant behavior evinced on the ward. Thus, it is quite possible that bringing clients into settings with new agents of change can further create patient problems.

Third, bringing clients into institutional settings can and may pose various limitations related to the notion of stimulus control. Initially, much of an individual's behavior is situation specific. Alteration of the situation (with its contingencies) results in variations of behavior (cf. Mischel, 1968). Removing a patient from everyday life, when avoidable, can alter the behavior that supposedly resulted in hospitalization. It may be that in hospitals much of the problematic behavior that supposedly led to hospitalization does not appear or is somewhat different in the hospital from what it was in everyday life.

A related problem is achieving generalization of behavior to nontreatment settings after behavior change within the hospital has been

achieved. The problem of achieving maintenance and transfer of behavior results in a large part from focusing on behavior *in* the hospital. If behavior is to be performed in a given situation (e.g., at home,
in the community), it should be developed in that situation or settings which simulate the actual situation.

From the above arguments it is difficult to justify, at least on the
basis of effecting significant treatment change, the existence of
psychiatric hospitals *qua* treatment facilities of behavioral (non-
medical) problems. Behavior change programs probably are best
conducted in a natural environment rather than in institutions. Conducting a program in a hospital setting improves the patients'
behavior relative to custodial care, as noted earlier. But this should
not be a criterion of success. Perhaps, institutional life contributes to
the problems that treatment techniques ordinarily are employed to
change. Considering permanent (i.e., "chronic") placement of patients in the community as a criterion for evaluation, advances made
by current treatment approaches seem equivocal. Moreover, it is
unclear whether this end could be achieved by conducting programs
as part of traditional hospital routine.

Actually, conducting a program in a traditional mental health
facility may be innovative *within* the hospital system, but also
reflects complicity with the system. It cannot be assumed that the
vast majority of patients must be institutionalized for the purpose of
protecting themselves or others (Scheff, 1966). In special cases, of
course, programs in "nonnatural environments" might well be required where no one else could conduct treatment in a natural
setting (e.g., Phillips, 1968). However, the structure of such facilities
may have relatively little resemblance to the majority of psychiatric
institutions with their possibly inherent deleterious contingencies. Of
course, these comments do not consider recent innovations in the
treatment of psychiatric patients as reflected in halfway houses
(Raush and Raush, 1968), community mental health (Denner and
Price, 1973), and treatment facilities enmeshed with community
existence (Henderson and Scoles, 1970). Yet these latter innovations
remain exceptions.

Conclusion

The application of behavior change techniques with individuals
labelled schizophrenic has already yielded significant effects. The
results are promising, especially considering the recency with which
techniques have been widely applied on a large scale with

hospitalized populations. Although programs have been employed for less than a decade, changes occur in areas ordinarily considered to reflect "success" of hospital treatment programs including changes in bizarre behavior, "apathy", adaptive skills, and discharge and re-admission. Of course, the criteria for success might well be disputed. However, most behavioral programs have automatically taken as goals those ends toward which the institution are administratively committed.

Although the changes made have been substantial, some features of traditional "treatment" have remained, viz., institutions. Yet, some of the problems of current behavioral programs stem, at least in part, from traditional assumptions about treatment and the facilities to be employed. As discussed earlier, response maintenance, and un-responsiveness of some patients to the treatment program are signifi-cant issues for future research. Present work shows the therapeutic effects of restructuring the contingencies in existing traditional treat-ment facilities. Future work is likely to add to this technology and focus more on behavior change interventions enmeshed with community life.

References

Allen, D. J. and Magaro, P. A. Measures of change in token-economy programs. *Behaviour Research and Therapy*, 1971, 9, 311–18.

Atthowe, J. M. and Krasner, L. Preliminary report on the application of contingent reinforcement procedures (token economy) on a "chronic" psychiatric ward. *Journal of Abnormal Psychology*, 1968, 73, 37–43.

Ayllon, T. and Azrin, N. H. *The token economy: A motivational system for therapy and rehabilitation.* New York: Appleton-Century-Crofts, 1968.

Ayllon, T. and Michael, J. The psychiatric nurse as a behavioral engineer. *Journal of the Experimental Analysis of Behavior*, 1959, 3, 323–34.

Ayllon, T. and Wright, P. New roles for the paraprofessional. In S. W. Bijou and E. Ribes-Inesta (Ed.), *Behavior modification: Issues and extensions.* New York: Academic press, 1972, pp. 115–25.

Baer, D. M., Wolf, M. M., and Risley, T. R. Some current dimensions of applied Behavior analysis. *Journal of Applied Behavior Analysis*, 1968, 1, 91–7.

Bandura, A. A social learning interpretation of psychological dysfunctions. In P. London and D. Rosenhan (Eds.), *Foundations of abnormal psychology.* New York: Holt, Rinehart and Winston, 1963, pp. 293–344.

Bandura, A. *Principles of behavior modification.* Holt, Rinehart and Winston, 1969.

Becker, H. S. *Outsiders: Studies in the sociology of deviance.* New York: Free Press, 1963.

Bennett, P. A., and Maley R. F. Modification of interactive behaviors in chronic mental patients. *Journal of Applied Behavior Analysis*, 1973, 6, 609–20.

Birky, H. J., Chambliss, J. E., and Wasden, R. A comparison of residents discharged from a token economy and two traditional psychiatric programs. *Behavior Therapy*, 1971, 2, 46–51.

Braginsky, B. M., Braginsky, D. D., and Ring, K. *Methods of madness: The mental hospital as a last resort.* New York: Holt, Rinehart, and Winston, 1969.

Campbell, D. T. and Stanley, J. C. Experimental and quasi-experimental designs for research and teaching. In N. L. Gage (Ed.), *Handbook of research on teaching.* Chicago: Rand McNally, 1963, pp. 171–246.

Davison, G. C. Differential relaxation and cognitive restructuring in therapy with a "paranoid schizophrenic" or "paranoid state". *Proceedings of the 74th Annual Convention of the American Psychological Association*, 1966, 2, 177–8.

Davison, G. C. Appraisal of behavior modification techniques with adults in institutional settings. In C. M. Franks (Ed.), *Behavior therapy: Appraisal and status.* New York: McGraw-Hill, 1969, pp. 220–78.

Denner, B. and Price, R. H. (Eds.), *Community mental health: Social action and reaction.* New York: Holt, Rinehart and Winston, 1973.

DiScipio, W. J. and Trudeau, P. F. Symptom changes and self-esteem as correlates of positive conditioning of grooming in hospitalized psychotics. *Journal of Abnormal Psychology*, 1972, 80, 244–8.

Feingold, L. and Migler, B. The use of experimental dependency relationships as a motivating procedure on a token economy ward. In R. D. Rubin, H. Fensterheim, J. D. Henderson, and L. P. Ullmann (Eds.), *Advances in behavior therapy.* New York: Academic Press, 1972, pp. 121–7.

Freeman, E. H. and Simmons, O. G. *The mental patient comes home.* New York: Wiley, 1963.

Goffman, E. *Asylums.* New York: Anchor, 1961.

Gripp, R. F., and Magaro, P. A. A token economy program evaluation with untreated control ward comparisons. *Behaviour Research and Therapy,* 1971, 9, 137–49.

Guerney, B. G., Jr. (Ed.), *Psychotherapeutic agents: New Roles for nonprofessionals, parents, and teachers.* New York: Holt, Rinehart and Winston, 1969.

Hartlage, L. C. Subprofessional therapists' use of reinforcement versus traditional psychotherapeutic techniques with schizophrenics. *Journal of Consulting and Clinical Psychology,* 1970, 34, 181–3.

Heap, R. F., Boblitt, W. E., Moore, C. H., and Hord, J. E. Behavior-milieu therapy with chronic neuropsychiatric patients. *Journal of Abnormal Psychology,* 1970, 76, 349–54.

Henderson, J. D., and Scoles, P. E. A community-based behavioral operant environment for psychotic men. *Behavior Therapy,* 1970, 1, 245–51.

Hersen, M., Eisler, R. M., Alford, G. S., and Agras, W. S. Effects of token economy on neurotic depression: An experimental analysis. *Behavior Therapy,* 1973, 4, 392–7.

Horn, J. and Black, W. A. M. The effect of token reinforcement on verbal participation in a social activity with long stay psychiatric patients. *Australian and New Zealand Journal of Psychiatry,* 1974.

Jones, R. and Kazdin, A. E. Programming response maintenance after withdrawing token reinforcement. *Behavior Therapy,* 1975, 6, 153–64.

Kale, R. J., Kaye, J. H., Whelan, P. A., and Hopkins, B. L. The effects of reinforcement on the modification, maintenance, and generalization of social responses of mental patients. *Journal of Applied Behavior Analysis,* 1968, 1, 307–14.

Kanfer, R. H. and Phillips, J. S. *Learning foundations of behavior therapy.* New York: Wiley and Sons, 1970.

Kazdin, A. E. The effect of response cost in suppressing behavior in a prepsychotic retardate. *Journal of Behavior Therapy and Experimental Psychiatry,* 1971, 2, 137–40.

Kazdin, A. E. Implementing token programs: The use of staff, patients, and the institution of maximizing change. Paper presented at Sixth Annual Meeting of the Association for Advancement of Behavior Therapy, New York, October, 1972.

Kazdin, A. E. The effect of response cost and aversive stimulation in suppression punished and nonpunished speech disfluencies. *Behavior Therapy,* 1973a, 4, 73–82.

Kazdin, A. E. The failure of some patients to respond to token programs. *Journal of Behavior Therapy and Experimental Psychiatry,* 1973b, 4, 7–14.

Kazdin, A. E. Issues in behavior modification with mentally retarded persons. *American Journal of Mental Deficiency,* 1973c, 78, 134–40.

Kazdin, A. E. Methodological and assessment considerations in evaluating reinforcement programs in applied settings. *Journal of Applied Behavior Analysis*, 1973d, 6, 517—31.

Kazdin, A. E. *Behavior modification in applied settings*. Homewood, Illinois: Dorsey Press, 1975a.

Kazdin, A. E. Recent advances in token economy research. In M. Hersen, R. M. Eisler, and P. M. Miller (Eds.), *Progress in behavior modification*. New York: Academic Press, 1975b.

Kazdin, A. E. and Bootzin, R. R. The token economy: An evaluative review. *Journal of Applied Behavior Analysis*, 1972, 5, 343—72.

Kazdin, A. E. and Polster, R. Intermittent token reinforcement and response maintenance in extinction. *Behavior Therapy*, 1973, 4, 386—91.

Krasner, L. and Ullmann, L. P. *Behavior influence and personality*. New York: Holt, Rinehart and Winston, 1973.

Leitenberg, H., Wincze, J., Butz, R., Callahan, E., and Agras, W. Comparison of the effect of instructions and reinforcement in the treatment of a neurotic avoidance response: A single case experiment. *Journal of Behavior Therapy and Experimental Psychiatry*, 1970, 1, 53—8.

Liberman, R. P. Reinforcement of social interaction group of chronic mental patients. In R. D. Rubin, H. Fensterheim, J. D. Henderson, and L. P. Ullmann (Eds.), *Advances in behavior therapy*. New York: Academic Press, 1972, pp. 151—9.

Liberman, R. P., Teigen, J., Patterson, R., and Baker, V. Reducing delusional speech in chronic paranoid schizophrenics. *Journal of Applied Behavior Analysis*, 1973, 6, 57—64.

Lidz, T., Fleck, S., and Cornelison, A. R. *Schizophrenia and the family*. New York: International Universities Press, 1965.

Lovaas, O. I., Koegel, R., Simmons, J. Q., and Long, J. S. Some generalization and follow-up measures on autistic children in behavior therapy. *Journal of Applied Behavior Analysis*, 1973, 6, 131—66.

Maher, B. A. *Principles of Psychopathology: An experimental approach*. New York: McGraw-Hill, 1966.

Maley, R. F., Feldman, G. L., and Ruskin, R. S. Evaluation of patient improvement in a token treatment program. *Journal of Abnormal Psychology*, 1973, 82, 141—4.

Marks, J., Sonoda, B., and Schalock, R. Reinforcement vs. relationship therapy for schizophrenics. *Journal of Abnormal Psychology*, 1968, 73, 379—402.

Meichenbaum, D. and Cameron, R. Training schizophrenics to talk to themselves: A means of developing attentional controls. *Behavior Therapy*, 1973, 4, 515—34.

Milby, J. B. Modification of extreme social isolation by contingent social reinforcement. *Journal of Applied Behavior Analysis*, 1970, 3, 149—52.

Mischel, W. *Personality and assessment*. New York: Wiley, 1968.

Mitchell, W. S. and Stoffelmayr, B. E. Application of the Premack Principle to the behavioral control of extremely inactive schizophrenics. *Journal of Applied Behavior Analysis*, 1973, 6, 419—23.

O'Brien, F. and Azrin, H. H. Symptom reduction by functional displacement in a token economy: A case study. *Journal of Behavior Therapy and Experimental Psychiatry*, 1972, 3, 205—7.

O'Brien, F., Azrin, N. H., and Henson, K. Increased communications of chronic mental patients by reinforcement and response priming. *Journal of Applied Behavior Analysis,* 1969, 2, 23—9.

Olson, R. P. and Greenberg, D. J. Effects of contingency contracting and decision-making groups with chronic mental patients. *Journal of Consulting and Clinical Psychology,* 1972, 38, 376—83.

Patterson, R. and Teigen, J. Conditioning and post-hospital generalization of nondelusional responses in a chronic psychotic patient. *Journal of Applied Behavior Analysis,* 1973, 6, 65—70.

Paul, G. L. Chronic mental patient: Current status-future directions. *Psychological Bulletin,* 1969, 71, 81—94.

Phillips, E. L. Achievement place: Token reinforcement procedures in a home-style rehabilitation setting for "pre-delinquent" boys. *Journal of Applied Behavior Analysis,* 1968, 1, 213—23.

Phillips, E. L., Phillips, E. A., Fixsen, D. L., and Wolf, M. M. Achievement Place: Modification of the behaviors of pre-delinquent boys within a token economy. *Journal of Applied Behavior Analysis,* 1971, 4, 45—59.

Pomerleau, O. F., Bobrove, P. H., and Harris, L. C. Some observations on a controlled social environment for psychiatric patients. *Journal of Behavior Therapy and Experimental Psychiatry,* 1972, 3, 15—21.

Raush, H. L., and Raush, C. L. *The halfway-house movement: A search for sanity.* New York: Appleton-Century-Crofts, 1968.

Redd, W. H., and Birnbrauer, J. S. Adults as discriminative stimuli for different reinforcement contingencies with retarded children. *Journal of Experimental Child Psychology,* 1969, 7, 440—7.

Reisinger, J. J. The treatment of "anxiety-depression" via positive reinforcement and response cost. *Journal of Applied Behavior Analysis,* 1972, 5, 125—30.

Risley, T. R. Behavior modification: An experimental-therapeutic endeavor. In L. A. Hamerlynck, P. O. Davidson, and L. E. Acker (Eds.), *Behavior modification and ideal mental health services.* Calgary, Alberta, Canada: University of Calgary Press, 1970, p. 103—27.

Sarbin, T. R. On the futility of the proposition that some people be labeled "mentally ill", *Journal of Consulting Psychology,* 1967, 31, 447—53.

Scheff, J. J. *Being mentally ill: A sociological theory.* Chicago: Aldine, 1966.

Shean, J. D. and Zeidberg, Z. Token reinforcement therapy: A comparison of matched groups. *Journal of Behavior Therapy and Experimental Psychiatry,* 1971, 2, 95—105.

Sidman, M. *Tactics of scientific research.* New York: Basic Books. 1960.

Skinner, B. F. What is psychotic behavior? In F. Gildea (Ed.), *Theory and treatment of the psychoses: Some newer aspects.* Washington University Studies, 1956.

Surratt, P. R., Ulrich, R. E., and Hawkins, R. P. An elementary student as a behavioral engineer. *Journal of Applied Behavior Analysis,* 1969, 2, 85—92.

Szasa, T. S. The myth of mental illness. *American Psychologist,* 1960, 15, 113—18.

Tharp, R. G. and Wetzel, R. J. *Behavior modification in the natural environment.* New York: Academic Press, 1969.

Ullmann, L. P. *Institution and outcome: A comparative study of psychiatric hospitals.* London: Pergamon Press, 1967.

Ullmann, L. P. and Krasner, L. *A psychological approach to abnormal behavior.* Englewood Cliffs, New Jersey: Prentice-Hall, 1969.

Wincze, J. P., Leitenberg, H., and Agras, W. S. The effects of token reinforcement and feedback on the delusional verbal behavior of chronic paranoid schizophrenics. *Journal of Applied Behavior Analysis,* 1972, 5, 247–62.

Winkler, R. C. Reinforcement schedules for individual patients in a token economy. *Behavior Therapy,* 1971, 2, 534–37.

Winkler, R. C. A theory of equilibrium in token economics. *Journal of Abnormal Psychology,* 1972, 79, 169–73.

V

The Analytic Listen

CHAPTER 7

The Psychoanalysis of Schizophrenia

It is not unusual to hear the statement that psychotherapy, in general, and psychoanalytic therapy, in particular, have little to offer the so-called schizophrenic patient. But we now have rigorous data from the Michigan State Psychotherapy Project (Karon and VandenBos, 1972) showing that even a small amount of psychoanalytic therapy, an average of 70 sessions over a 20 month period, produce changes that medication cannot hope to produce. Patients who had received psychotherapy as compared to those receiving medication showed less thought disorder (that is, they were more able to think logically when they wanted to), spent much less time in the hospital, and were able to live a more human life in a wide variety of ways. Furthermore, these effects became more marked the longer one followed the patients. Moreover, providing meaningful psychotherapy proved to be less costly in the long run (Karon and VandenBos, 1975a).

Patients had been randomly assigned before treatment to two types of psychoanalytic therapy, one of which used medication adjunctively, or to regular hospital treatment—that is, medication. Patients were evaluated before treatment, after 6 months, after 12 months, and after 20 months by psychologists and psychiatrists not connected with the treatment staff, who did not know what kind of treatment the patients had obtained. Among the unusual measures taken to ensure that evaluations were "blind" was to record the clinical status interviews on tape, edit the tapes to delete clues to type of treatment, and then ratings of clinical status were made from the tapes. Additional hospitalization data were gathered 2 years after the project was over. Other findings of importance were that it did not matter whether the therapist was a psychologist or a psychiatrist, or whether the therapist was a man or a woman, but it did matter whether the therapist was experienced in and trained in treating patients of this sort. By this, I do not merely mean that the therapist must be familiar with the treatment of so-called schizophrenics, but equally important, he must know the problems and resistances of people of the socioeconomic class and ethic sub-group of the patients.

The adjunctive use of medication made it easier to get improved behavioral control and discharge from the hospital, but slowed down fundamental change in the thought disorder. Experienced therapists working in their preferred mode were able to get behavioral control and fundamental change with or without medication; however, it should be noted that the experienced therapist who used adjunctive medication used it initially and then withdrew it as rapidly as the patients could tolerate.

There were also some minor findings: those therapists who were more mature, used supervision more effectively, and were less "pathogenic" as measured by their TAT before beginning the project were more effective, that is, their patients improved more (Vanden-Bos and Karon, 1971). The meaning of "pathogenesis" will be discussed later.

It has been objected (May and Tuma, 1970; Tuma and May, in press) that the evaluations were not blind, that the techniques of data analysis were inappropriate, that the experience of non-medical therapists cannot be considered experience, that arbitrary scores were assigned to untestable patients, and that patients were included who should have been deleted because of organic impairments.

None of these objections are factually correct. (Alternative decisions about statistical procedures or the exclusion of the one questionable case do not alter any of the major findings.)

It has also been objected that there were not a large number of cases in the study nor were there a large number of therapists, that the experienced therapists supervised the inexperienced therapists, that the assignment of patients to therapists was not random, and that these findings conflict with other studies.

These objections are facts. The number of cases and the number of therapists had to be small so that we could be sure that the patients really were appropriate, and that the therapists were practising psychoanalytic therapy. Any number of observations of the wrong patients treated haphazardly would be of little scientific value. That there were only two experienced therapists, who also were the supervisors, was necessary for us to be sure that the experienced therapists really had something to teach and were known to their professional colleagues to be clinically effective. The assignment of patients to treatment group was rigorously randomized, but within the psychotherapy groups it was not random, since the first two cases in each group had to be assigned to the experienced therapists so that the student therapists could observe the treatment of these cases and discuss them as part of their training. Cases were assigned on the basis of the therapists' schedules after that. However, selection of cases was made on the same basis throughout the project by people who did not know to which treatment group the subjects would be assigned, let alone which therapists.

That these findings conflict with those of other studies in the literature is understandable inasmuch as there are some aspects of this project that are unusual, although they ought not to be. First of all, the therapists wanted to do psychotherapy with schizophrenics. There were no reluctant therapists. The student therapists even wanted to work with their particular supervisors as people from whom they thought they could learn. The experienced therapists (who were also the supervisors) had over 10 years' experience, not only in working with schizophrenics, but also in working with poor people and black people (80% of the patients were black). The same therapist worked with the patient on an in-patient and out-patient basis. Any understanding of psychotherapy which takes the concept of transference seriously would lead to such a procedure; yet most hospitals require a change of therapists for purely administrative reasons, without regard for therapeutic considerations.

It may be worth noting that other studies have not shown psychotherapy to be effective with schizophrenic patients because either (1) they have used unwilling therapists (May, 1968)—and you are not likely to do much therapy if you do not want to do it, because psychotherapy is difficult and demanding work—or (2) they have used supervisors who have not had much experience or interest in doing psychotherapy with schizophrenics, and it is axiomatic that you cannot teach what you do not know, or (3) they have not had any therapists experienced with schizophrenia at all (very often in research studies, the word "experienced therapist" is used to refer to somebody who has finished a residency—which is hardly a great deal of experience) (May, 1968; Rogers *et al.,* 1967), or (4) they have not measured the thought disorder with any degree of care (May, 1968; Grinspoon *et al.,* 1972; Bookhammer *et al.,* 1966), or (5) they have examined the patients only on the day of termination of psychotherapy, which is a traumatic day (May, 1968), or (6) they have not followed the patients over a long period of time (May, 1968—at least as far as *published* reports), or (7) they have used therapists who were not familiar with patients of the socio-economic class or of the ethnic sub-group of the patients (May, 1968; Grinspoon, 1972; Bookhammer *et al.,* 1966), or (8) they have done all of these. Under such conditions, psychotherapy is not effective.

However, in some of these studies there are findings which are more consistent with ours than is generally realized. If one looks at ability to stay out of the hospital in the long run or to function outside the hospital in the long run, as opposed to criteria which reflect ward adjustment, then even studies whose findings are supposedly negative, report gains for patients receiving psychotherapy (e.g. Grinspoon *et al.,* 1972).

Incidentally, Rogers and his co-workers, many years ago, showed in a series of studies that on a wide variety of criteria, their kind of psychotherapy was effective with neurotics (Rogers, 1951). The widely publicized article of Eysenck (1952), which suggested that psychotherapy was not effective, did not refer to any of the research by Rogers and his co-workers in the bibliography, because they had already made Eysenck's conclusion obsolete. Moreover, in that study, Eysenck compared patients in the different groups using very different criteria of improvement, so that the cases being treated by psychoanalysis used a stringent criterion, whereas the patients who had received no treatment, or non-specific treatment, were considered "improved" by a very low criterion. Finally, in that study, Eysenck, who, in other places (e.g., 1960) repeatedly makes the point that for no purpose should one include psychopaths with neurotics, in this study included 100 psychopaths in with the neurotics so as to bring the recovery rate down for psychoanalysis. Those were cases of psychopathy treated at the Berlin Institute of Psychoanalysis as an experiment which, predictably, using a very classical psychoanalytic approach, failed. Such handling of data is cavalier, to say the least. More recently, Malan (1973) has demonstrated that psychoanalytic therapy is effective for neurotic disorders.

The Nature of Schizophrenia

But you are only interested in the rigorous data, in that it serves to justify an extended discussion of psychoanalytic therapy and of what is essential and of what is usually not realized to be important.

First, what do we mean by schizophrenics? Bleuler, a long time ago, stated that either schizophrenia was not a disease or it was a group of diseases—a statement which has been largely ignored. In fact, schizophrenics are a widely varied group of human beings. What they have in common is that they are using rather drastic techniques of adjustment. Insofar as they have anything in common, they can be characterized by Bleuler's primary symptoms: autism, a withdrawal from people; the thought disorder, an inability to think logically when they want to; and, an apparent absence of affect or inappropriate affect. They may also hallucinate, have delusions, and show a wide variety of other symptoms which Bleuler called secondary, but which call attention to themselves by the severity with which one's life is impaired.

All of these may be understood as attempts to deal with terror (anxiety seems too mild a term) of a chronic kind. Human beings do not tolerate chronic terror well.

Unfortunately, so-called schizophrenic symptoms, or defenses against terror, have a tendency to make the problem worse. Thus, for example, withdrawal from people reduces one's immediate fear of people, but it makes it harder to overcome the fear of people, or the thought disorder, or the apparent inappropriateness of one's affect by decreasing corrective experience. Similarly, the thought disorder and/or inappropriate affect and/or delusions and hallucinations make it difficult to relate to people. Those people who have tended to use any of these in attenuated form as characteristic adjustive mechanisms are more likely to use them dramatically in the so-called schizophrenic "break". In psychoanalytic terms, they are more likely to use regression as a defense.

Nonetheless, it is clear that schizophrenia is a human potentiality. All of us, under enough stress of the right kind, would develop schizophrenic symptoms. How much stress and of what kind varies from human being to human being. In the Second World War, there was a situation which seemed to "break" every human being who went through it. It was very simple. People were shooting at you and trying to kill you and you quickly dug a fox hole—just big enough for you—and you got in it as quickly as you could because they were shooting at you and trying to kill you. You didn't move, because if you did, you would get killed. You didn't eat; you didn't drink; you urinated and defecated on yourself because there was no other place to urinate or defecate. If this kept up for 2 or 3 days, when the shooting finally stopped and your buddies came up to you, every single soldier who had undergone this experience seemed to show schizophrenic symptoms. In each case, the soldier looked like a "back ward" case. However, if he had been reasonably healthy before this happened, he always recovered spontaneously with rest. This led to the coining of the term "schizophreniform psychosis" for battlefield psychoses meaning they look in every respect like a schizophrenic, but they can't be because they get better (Grinker and Spiegel, 1965; Bellak, 1948). Those were the days when it was assumed that schizophrenics never recovered. Now, of course, we know that schizophrenics do recover, and the term "schizophreniform psychosis" has largely disappeared, mercifully, from the literature.

But most of the patients who break down under the stresses of normal life have been prepared for such a breakdown by their childhood. The patient has suffered from a series of subtle and unsubtle rejections all his life which lead to the formation of a set of fantasies, conscious and unconscious, which then influence how later experience is perceived and the development of further fantasies, which eventually, of course, lead to a way of understanding the world which is intolerable (Karon and Rosberg, 1958a, 1958b; Rosberg and Karon, 1958, 1959).

Genetic and Physiological Distractions

Here it may be useful to review the literature on genetic and physiological findings. The only danger in these studies is that they may lead to psychotherapeutic pessimism (and have in the past), although that is not a rigorously necessary conclusion, even if genetic and/or physiological factors are clearly demonstrated. Every organ system in the human body has been claimed to be the cause of schizophrenia. These findings never last more than 5 years (Bellak, 1948, 1958, 1968; Kety, 1959a, 1959b; Wyatt, Termini, and Davis, 1971), and I would only take them seriously if they did. There is even one investigator who always gets national publicity whenever he discovers the physiological basis for schizophrenia: he makes this discovery approximately every 3 years. In each instance, the data never replicate at other institutions.

What about the genetic data? There are now studies which suggest that there is a genetic component to schizophrenia (Rosenthal and Kety, 1968). What these studies show is not that schizophrenia is inherited or that there is a known mechanism or a known gene for schizophrenia, but that there are some thing or things which are inherited which tend to increase the frequency of schizophrenia. If we assume that schizophrenia consists of extreme methods of adaptation, anything which makes life adjustment more difficult is going to increase the rate of schizophrenia. Thus, it is known that the rate of schizophrenia among the poorest socioeconomic class, is twelve times as high as it is among the highest socioeconomic class, using the Yale five-class system of classification, simply because life is tougher for the poor in our society (Hollingshead and Redlich, 1958). It is also known that the psychosis rate is higher if you are discriminated against (Karon, 1975).

There are many things which are inherited which make adjustment more difficult: a crooked nose, a humpback, an underactive thyroid, and any number of things that we do not know. The sum-total of such effects would well account for the kind of genetic findings which have been reported, namely that about 10% of the variance of the disorder can be accounted for by genetic factors. That is all that has been demonstrated.

The most powerful apparent evidence for a genetic factor are the studies of adopted children whose natural parents were schizophrenic as compared to those whose natural parents were not (Heston, 1970). The rate of schizophrenia is dramatically higher in the adopted offspring of schizophrenic biological parents. While the rate of psychopathology seems higher in the parents who adopted children from schizophrenic natural parents, it is not sufficiently higher to account for the difference in the incidence of schizophrenia.

However, such a finding confuses pathology with "pathogenesis", confuses the degree of one's own symptoms with the degree to which one produces pathology in others. Wynne and Singer in a series of studies (e.g., Singer and Wynne, 1965) have found that parents whose children become schizophrenic tend to show a characteristic thought disorder, which is not identical with that of grossly psychotic people, but which is measurable. Wender, Rosenthal, Zahn, and Kety (1971) gave Rorschachs to the adoptive parents and reported no evidence of increased thought disorder in the parents who adopted children from schizophrenic natural parents, hence the increased incidence of schizophrenia could only be accounted for by genetics.

However, they used the wrong scoring formula; when the same Rorschachs were scored blindly by Singer using the appropriate key, those parents whose adoptive offspring became schizophrenics showed the specific kind of thought disorder found in natural parents whose offspring became schizophrenics (Lidz, 1973, p. 66). Hence no genetic factor would be required to account for the findings. Rather one would begin to ask what are the non-random factors in adoption in Scandinavia that lead parents who are "pathogenic" to be more likely to adopt children born to parents who are "schizophrenic".

Let me put it differently. I have never met a schizophrenic patient whose life history, when I understood it, did not adequately account for the severity of his symptoms. In every case, the individual lived a life which I could not conceive of living without developing his symptoms. In not one case would one need to postulate a genetic factor or a physiological factor to account for the symptoms. That does not mean that if you do a superficial examination of the individual or of his family or of his life that you will necessarily find what that life really was like as experienced by the individual. There are studies in the literature which report that the families and life histories of schizophrenics are not different from that of other people, but in such studies, the patients were not carefully examined. More recently, there are studies like those of Lidz, which indicate that the families are clearly quite different (e.g., Lidz, 1973; Yi-Chuang, 1962).

An Illustrative Case

Some years ago, I was giving a seminar in the psychotherapy of schizophrenia at a State hospital, and they asked me to interview a patient. It is my experience that under such circumstances one usually gets a real gem. The patient that was chosen for me was a back ward patient who was very aggressive, attacked people violently, moved very fast, and was grossly incoherent. When he was not grossly incoherent, he stuttered very badly. The only thing they could have done to make therapy more difficult would have been to choose a patient who didn't speak English at all.

The patient had been in treatment for many years, and there were voluminous psychiatric and social work notes on him. He came from a lower class family—that's tough, but it isn't enough to account for schizophrenia, even though so-called schizophrenia is more frequent among lower class individuals than among those who are less economically deprived. He grew up in Detroit—that's tough, but it still does not account for why he was schizophrenic. His father was an alcoholic. Well, that is more serious, but it still is not enough to account for schizophrenia, since many people have alchoholic fathers without becoming schizophrenic. There was nothing in his childhood to indicate disturbance, until he was a teenager. At that age, he developed a speech disorder which did not respond to speech therapy.

The first indication of real disturbance occurred in the Army where he reported to sick call with a venereal disease, and the site of infection was his mouth. Shortly thereafter, he assaulted a stranger and nearly killed him. He was discharged from the Army and proceeded to repeat this pattern again and again. That is, he would assault someone, nearly kill him, be hospitalized, slowly pull together, eventually be discharged, and, quickly thereafter, assault someone else and go back to the hospital thoroughly disorganized.

He had been in the hospital for some years when I interviewed him.

Now, here was a very dangerous, quick-moving patient that the psychiatric residents had chosen for me to interview; since the vast bulk of schizophrenics are not dangerous to anyone, this represented careful selection on their part. I did interview him, but I insisted that the residents stay in the same room with me. After all, I had experience in dealing with dangerous people and could depend on that experience, whereas they had never been that close to someone who was that dangerous and moved that fast. I felt that if I were scared, they would be and were ten times as scared. (One has to work out one's sadism somewhere.)

In a brief series of interviews with this patient, three facts came to light that nowhere appeared in the voluminous case materials. The first of these came in the first session. The patient had the following symptom: he would crawl up behind other patients and choke them. The attendants would notice the other patient's feet waving in the air. He never killed the other patient; he would always drop him when the man lost consciousness. Nonetheless, he might make a mistake and kill someone. In my value system, you deal with homicide and suicide first—or even potential homicide and suicide first. In working on this, it became clear that as a young child, his mother used to, for minor offenses—like not eating—wrap a cloth around his neck and choke him briefly. Now, innately, when we cannot breathe, we go into a panic. This is a useful, innate mechanism that keeps infants from suffocating: they kick off the blankets when they can't breathe. But choking as minor punishment, of course, left him terrified. We can understand the symptom of choking other patients as an attempt by the patient to master this trauma by himself re-enacting the role of the mother, with the other patient as himself, reassuring himself that his mother never would have killed him. Remember, he choked the other man until his victim was unconscious and then he stopped.

However, a symbolic act, as in this kind of symptom, no matter how often repeated, never does undo the original trauma, because it is not connected consciously with the original problem. Only when the relationship between the symbolic act (or symptom) and the original trauma is re-connected in consciousness can the person really overcome it. In this particular instance, a dramatic change occurred in the symptomatology, namely his choking of other patients disappeared after this session. On a rule-of-thumb basis, such a dramatic change in the symptom may be taken as presumptive evidence that our reconstruction with the patient was accurate.

A second fact came to light in another therapy hour with the same patient. The therapy hour began with his shouting, "Why did you do it to me, Dad?"

"What did I do?" I asked.

"You know what you did! Why did you do it to me, Dad?"

If I were an organic psychiatrist, I might say, "Look how confused the patient is," as if that were an explanation. But, I am not an organic psychiatrist, and it has always been puzzling to me why those people who work with psychotics have been most resistant to psychoanalytic insights. Neurotics like you and me are very subtle, and we make our transference reactions look like realistic adaptations. It took a genius, like Freud, to make us aware of how we transfer. But psychotics are not the least bit subtle. All one has to do is be willing to listen to be struck by the transference.

I asked him what I had done, and he said, "You know what you did. Why did you do it to me, Dad?"

I then asked him how old he was, and he said, "You know I was 8 years old." I asked for further details and finally elicited the fact that "I" had come home drunk when he was 8 years old and anally raped him. Very different from the innocuous life history found in the lengthy but barren psychiatric and social histories!

One more fact not in the histories came to light in connection with his stutter, a serious resistance for a verbal psychotherapy. Now, I do not ordinarily work with speech disorders, and my friends who do work with speech disorders tell me that the genesis of the patient's stutter is very, very unusual. However, it is a kind of traumatic cause of a symptom with which I am used to dealing. Nonetheless, please do not assume that your friends who stutter have, in their past, events at all like that which I shall now relate.

In one session where the patient's stutter was marked, I suddenly heard a sentence or two in real Latin. This startled me. When I was in high school they had told us that if you wanted to go to college, you should learn Latin, and this is the one time in my professional career when it has been of real value to me. How did this uneducated man know Latin? It finally dawned on me that very likely he had been an altar boy. So I asked him, "Were you an altar boy?"

He replied, "You swallow a snake, and then you stutter. You mustn't let anyone know."

Now, if I were a behavior therapist, I would be concerned with his experience with snakes. But I am not a behavior therapist, and I thought I knew what he was talking about. Furthermore, it seemed to me that the very intense guilt associated with the experience and its connection with being an altar boy suggested a very guilt-producing kind of interaction.

So, I said to him (and I hope you will pardon the language within which this communication is carried out, but for many patients such language is closer to the language in which thoughts and feelings occur than is the politely-stilted language of scientific discussion), "I know you sucked the priest's cock, and it's o.k. Anybody who was as hungry as you were, would have done the same thing."

In case you did not notice, this is an oral interpretation of an apparently sexual act. It is characteristic of many schizophrenic patients, that what looks like sexual activity really has an oral meaning. Thus, just as we have learned to consider other things psychoanalytically as symbolic of sexual activity, sexual activity itself, may represent earlier, more basic problems, and in these patients, usually does. The penis may represent the breast; the vagina and the anus may represent a mouth. The basic battles of survival and of nurturance from early childhood may be seen re-enacted in what looks like sexual activity, or sexual ideas and concerns.

The stuttering ceased immediately. Indeed, whenever he started to stutter it was only necessary to say, "I know what you did with the priest, and it is alright. Anyone who was that hungry would have done the same thing." The stuttering would immediately cease, and he then talked intelligibly.

Let us now look at this man's life. We had relatively easily elicited three facts which were not in voluminous studies of the case, because previous investigators probably did not want to hear them. It is not merely that these isolated instances occurred. Think about what kind of a mother would choke her son. What kind of a father would anally rape his son? What does living with such people do to an individual? The patient turns to Mama, and Mama really is, in some ways, rotten. He then turns to Daddy; Daddy, after all, is for most of us the usual and best alternative when Mama is deficient. But Daddy turns out to be rotten. He even turns to God—and God turns out to be rotten. Wouldn't you be psychotic under such circumstances? I would.

Pathogenesis

The reports that there was nothing different about the families of schizophrenics, and, therefore, the pathology must be due to some genetic defect, were so at variance with my clinical experience that I was led to investigate this problem in some detail. From my experience in psychotherapy with schizophrenics, as indeed from that of most people who have done intensive psychotherapy with such patients, there emerges a picture of an interaction between the patient's pathology and certain aspects of the parents, particularly the mother, which seem to lead to the pathology. It seemed to me that the most general formulation of schizophrenia-producing parenting is that the parent met his or her own needs at the expense of the child's when their needs conflicted, whether or not the child could afford to meet the needs of the parent. Let me give you a couple of examples.

A middle-aged mother and her teenaged daughter are talking. One of them is discussing her menstrual distress. The other is suggesting she take aspirins and is giving reassurance. This is a scene which happens hundreds of times every day around the world. But what is peculiar is that it is the mother who is having the menstrual distress, and it is the daughter who is giving the reassurance—a reversal of the natural roles (Rosberg and Karon, 1959). Such reversals occur frequently throughout the life history from very early childhood on, in an emotional and symbolic sense, even from infancy.

Another mother of a very talented boy goes through his notebooks and takes every painting, drawing, or poem that he has completed each night when he goes to bed. The boy cries and says, "They're mine, let me keep them."

To which she replies, "No, I just want to let people know how good you are."

What in fact happened was the boy did not derive any direct benefit other than through his mother from his productions, which indeed showed considerable talent, but the mother derived great kudos from them. As an adult patient, he said, "Nobody thinks I'm worthwhile. If it wasn't for my mother, nobody would think I was worthwhile." It might be added that the patient at that time showed considerable real talent by any adult standard, although he did not know that it was clearly recognizable to others (Karon and Rosberg, 1958).

It also seems clear in my experience that there is either one strong parent who has a destructive impact on the child and the other parent who may be less destructive or even benign, but is so weak as to be emotionally useless, or else there are two destructive parents. What I have called "destructiveness" is not conscious malevolence. It is not that the parents of schizophrenics are evil or bad people. They would not hurt their child, in most instances, if they had any conscious choice in the matter. That is not to say that there are not such things as child-abusing parents, but they are a minority.

Most of the parents of schizophrenics are nice people, who would not intentionally harm their child. Nonetheless, they are destructive in their impact. This destructiveness is an unconscious matter which, if it is real, should be measurable. In order to measure unconscious functioning, one must use either a psychoanalytic investigation or a projective test. The TAT readily suggested itself, and I devised a scoring key which would pick up how the individual, unconsciously, makes use of people who depend on him or her when their needs conflict.

Do they take the needs of the dependent person into account, or do they take what they need whether or not the dependent person's needs are met? If they take the dependent person's needs into account, it is termed "benign", if not, "pathogenic". This is conceived of as an unconscious defense used to solve problems of anxiety.

After scoring stories as either benign, pathogenic, or unscoreable, one can derive a "Pathogenesis" score, being the total number of pathogenic stories divided by the total number of scored stories—pathogenic or benign. Meyer (Meyer and Karon, 1967) investigated mothers of schizophrenics and mothers of normals of the same age and sex and found that when the TATs were scored blindly they seemed to indicate that normal mothers, on the average, run over the child about a third of the time and take the child's needs into account two-thirds of the time when their needs conflict with those of the mother. Mothers of schizophrenics ride over their child three out of four times and take the child's needs into account only a quarter of the time. Nobody is perfectly good, and nobody is perfectly bad, but a lifetime of living with a predominantly pathogenic parent leaves you vulnerable to schizophrenic disorders. This finding has been replicated with larger samples by Mitchell (1968). Mitchell (1969) replicated this a third time using TAT data made available by Wynne and Singer; he found in addition that the fathers of schizophrenics in intact families are also pathogenic as compared to normal fathers, but that they are on the average less pathogenic than the mothers—which fits with the impression of those psychotherapists who have described "schizophrenogenic" mothers. Mothers are, for most children, more important than fathers anyway, and in these families, on the average, the mothers are typically somewhat more pathogenic.

Let me repeat. This does not mean that these are evil people—they are no more to be censured than is the patient who hallucinates or who has a paralyzed arm on a conversion-hysteric basis. It is a kind of symptom. Unfortunately, it is of the very nature of this symptom that it has serious consequences for someone else. Nonetheless, since we can measure it, we can begin to ask not only how do we treat it, but does it, in fact, change with treatment.

Some of my psychoanalytic colleagues, when I discussed the families of schizophrenics, have objected that they have seen neurotic patients whose families were every bit as destructive in their impact as those that I described. As my psychoanalytic experience with neurotics increased, I, too, have seen such families. However, there is a critical difference. For these neurotic patients there is always one or more people outside the family who provided much of what the parents did not. But the families of schizophrenics systematically discourage the person who later becomes schizophrenic from contacts with people outside the family—that is, discourage the identification with and the learning from peers and adults outside the family. Such extrafamilial influences are very important in the course of normal development. All families have warps, but in the ordinary course of development, we overcome the particular warps of our families by identifying with and learning from peers and adults outside the family. This normal corrective process is impaired in the schizophrenic family, thus leaving the individual vulnerable.

Some Unhelpful Treatments

There is not space to review the literature on organic treatments. Needless to say, damaging non-diseased brain tissue only creates brain-damaged patients, and the varieties of psychosurgery do just that. More subtle are the destructive effects of the various shock treatments—ECT, insulin, metrazol, indoklon—which facilitate spontaneous recoveries (as in depression) at a long-term cost. In my clinical experience and that of others, not only is there a greater probability of relapse with shock treatment, but there seems to be a greater subservience to authority (which may lead to following the doctor's orders more carefully) and a greater hostility to people weaker than oneself; a subtle cognitive defect, difficulty "putting the pieces together"; focal memory defects; and most dramatically a gross impairment of the ability to make use of psychotherapy, slowing it by a factor of three to six times. These effects are observable many years afterwards. (An illustrative case history is presented by Roueché, 1974).

Non-Communication and Its Consequences for Treatment

At this point, let me begin to talk about the difficulties in treating so-called schizophrenic people. First of all, the patients are often geniuses at not communicating clearly. For example, a 10-year-old paranoid schizophrenic boy was in treatment with me. Sometime between 8 to 12 months after the treatment began he described a dream. I made some comments about it, and he said nothing. I then said, "Well, maybe I'm wrong."

A slight smile appeared on his lips—"How often do you think you've been wrong, Doc?"

"I don't know," I said, "perhaps half the things I say to you don't fit."

Broader smile—"You haven't been wrong yet, Doc."

What a beautiful statement of positive transference! However, it was 8–12 months after the beginning of treatment, and this was the first time this patient had ever indicated I was right about anything. Therapists who have only worked with neurotic patients are not used to working so long without direct feedback from the patient.

Why should this be? Another child patient made this very clear to me. The child had been adopted by two parents, each of whom independently was sterile. These parents made me believe in psychogenic sterility, because the odds of biologically sterile people meeting by chance and marrying are very slight. Moreover, on a psychodynamic level, each of them was someone who literally could give no one anything. The adopted father was a slum landlord. The mother had adopted the child to save her marriage and had been disillusioned when the child did no such thing. (Of course, such feats are beyond the capability of any child.) By the age of 7 the boy was adapting on a psychotic level.

An indication of the adopted father's pathology may be given by the following conversation. I called both parents in after 6 months of treatment and told them the problem for which they had originally brought the boy was now gone. Originally, he could not be tolerated in school, not even in kindergarten. He now was adapting to the first grade, was doing adequate work, perhaps below his ability, but nonetheless, adequate work. The symptom that had originally concerned them was gone. "However", said I, "he now has a symptom, which is at least as serious—namely, that he can only relate to other children by hurting them or being hurt by them."

"What", said the father, "is sick about that?"

I might add that when the parents first came to see me, they were insistent that the disorder of the child must be genetic. I informed them that under no circumstances would I treat a child that young unless both parents came also for treatment. They were initially resistant but reluctantly agreed when I told them that there were no other circumstances under which such a treatment could possibly be successful; to undertake treatment of a young schizophrenic child without treating both parents would be a waste of their money, and, more importantly, of my time. (The other alternative, of course, is to remove the child from the home if a good residential treatment center is available.)

In dealing with the father, I asked him if he ever hit the child. "No," he said. "Well, almost never."

"How often is that?"

"Almost never."

"Well, how often is that?"

"Well," he said eventually, upon further questioning, "Two or three times a week."

Compared to his own childhood, in which he had been beaten two or three times a day, that, indeed seemed like almost never. Many years ago, Harry Stack Sullivan (1953) said that if you wished to produce a malevolent adult, hurt him every time he wants love. Like so many things that Harry Stack Sullivan said, this statement is true.

In discussing the issue of punishment with the mother, I asked whether there could not be some other method of punishment besides hitting the child.

"But," she said, "You don't understand. He never lets us know what he likes. If we knew what he liked, we'd take it away from him, but he never lets us know what he likes."

This mother clearly let us know why it is that so many of our schizophrenic patients do not tell us things very clearly. They do not even tell us that we are helping them, because they are afraid it will be used against them. As therapists, we are not used to continuing to work for months, or perhaps even years, without clear statements from the patient that "you are helping me in this way," "you are not helping me in that way," "you are doing this," or "this is going on". It is very frustrating.

Assessing Therapeutic Improvement

If one works in a hospital where the mythology that schizophrenic patients cannot be worked with is believed, one can work, and even be helpful, and not know it, and go away assuming that the work was of no value. Very often one gets one's indications that one has helped the patient from the ward staff if the patient is in the hospital, or from the family if not, who may report changes in the patient's behavior. Otherwise, one has to rely on one's past experience or one's supervisor to sustain one's therapeutic effort with little or no feedback from the patient. One needs to know that if one continues to do reasonable things long enough, the patient will get better, even though the patient doesn't say so, and even though one will frequently be wrong since the patient isn't communicating clearly.

In some cases, one knows one is helping the patient from the nature of the patient's complaints. For example, a patient who sounds quite sick in her therapy hours even now, finally says to me, "You know, I don't talk this way anywhere else. You know what would happen to me if I talked this way anywhere else?" She's quite right. But she was not that careful when treatment originally began.

More importantly, she complains, "You haven't helped me because I really don't like the guy that I am now sleeping with, and I really don't enjoy sex very much." These complaints, which should be taken seriously, nonetheless, tell us that she has made enormous progress. When she started treatment, she felt that no man would come within 50 feet of her. She later felt that when she dated a man, if she said "no", he would kill her, and also that if she did go to bed with him, he would kill her. For her to have her present problems means that she had made enormous progress.

Further, she says, "You haven't helped me, because I want more time off from work to take college courses, and they say they can't spare me. And I'm having trouble with my courses and I'll lose my B average." At the beginning of therapy, she was about to be fired. Now, they find her so valuable, they don't want to give her more time off. Moreover, she is taking college courses, and has a B average. Yet, if one were to judge from her communications in therapy, one would believe that she was incapable of such a performance. In a very real sense, she is at her sickest during the psychotherapy hour, which is fine because there we use the psychopathology to gain more and more insight into her life and problems and to enhance the process of growth.

It should be clear from this discussion why one needs to have a great deal of experience, or to have a supervisor who has had a great deal of experience with schizophrenic patients. Only then can one sustain the motivation that if you do meaningful psychotherapeutic work long enough, even without clear feedback, sooner or later the patients will benefit in a clear-cut way.

Understanding and Communicating

It is important for the therapist to let the patient know that he understands. But we are dealing with a patient who is a genius at not communicating. Therefore, it is impossible to thoroughly understand. Luckily, the sicker people are, the more alike they are, even though the patients feel that it is their sickness that makes them unique. The healthier people are, the more different from each other they get to be. Therefore, we can fall back upon our general knowledge of human beings and their problems, as well as our knowledge of psychopathology, to give us clues to why the patient is what he is.

For example, we know the patient is not without affect. The patient *seems* to be without affect, but is actually terrified. Terror is often so chronic that it is no longer noticed by the patient since it is there all of the time, and it can well mask the awareness of other feelings.

I might point out that if you know Freud's psychology of dreams (Freud, 1963), you immediately understand the psychology of hallucinations. Hallucinations are identical in structure with dreams, except that they are easier to understand because the motivation must be stronger if the individual does it while he is wide awake. Much of the hallucinatory activity, delusion formation, symptom formation, and acting out are readily understandable once you take a psychoanalytic position.

There is the view among many psychotherapists that the schizophrenic is fully aware of his unconscious, and that there is no point in increasing his understanding of it. Indeed, there is the view that increasing his understanding of unconscious processes is destructive to his reality testing. These, I believe are errors. The schizophrenic has a consciousness which, like the manifest content of the dream, is dominated by the unconscious. But it is not the raw unconscious itself. The patient does benefit from insight into his unconscious processes, if, and only if, these insights are presented within the context of a strong, warm, protective relationship with the therapist, and in a manner which helps him to understand them, as well as external reality.

It cannot be emphasized too strongly, however, that it is more important to know the nature of the human condition, in general, than of schizophrenic pathology, in particular. Thus, you need to know Freud's view of the human being and mental functioning (1963, 1965) and Sullivan's (1953) view of the human being and mental functioning in order to apply these notions to the understanding of so-called schizophrenics. Nothing that occurs in the worst of schizophrenics violates the general laws of the human being's functioning. What you see in these patients are what you see in yourself, or perhaps, to put it better, dare not see in yourself, only the problems are magnified 100 times because their lives have been worse than ours.

When you communicate what you know to the patient, you will not be right all the time, but if you understand any of it, the patient is amazed: he has never met anybody who understood any of it, and he himself doesn't understand it. These things terrify him, and it is very reassuring to him to find that there really is someone who isn't terrified by them and who does understand at least some of it. And then, of course, the more you work the more you will understand.

Resistance and Transference

This difficulty in communication is only a special part, but an important part, of the fact that one of the differences between schizophrenic and neurotic patients is that in schizophrenics, the resistance is conscious, as well as unconscious. That is, neurotics come for help and do not wish to give up their neurosis because it requires giving up their defense mechanisms that have served them so well. The resistance, nonetheless, is unconscious. With psychotics, their feeling is often that they will die without the kinds of adaptations that we call psychotic. Therefore, they will consciously not cooperate, and we have to deal with their non-cooperation by conscious logical education and by transference gratification.

Understanding the transference with psychotics is very important. First of all, some of Freud's discussions are somewhat misleading, in that he sometimes talks of transference as if it were something that occurred only in analysis. This, of course, is not true, and even in the early psychoanalytic discussions (e.g., Ferenczi (1950)) one clearly finds that transference like other defenses, occurs not only in therapy, but outside it. The difference is that the therapist pays attention to it, studies it, and uses it therapeutically. Indeed, much of the pathology of schizophrenics is nothing but transference to the world at large. Niederland (1959a, 1959b, 1972) has pointed out that in the Schreber case (Freud, 1958), much of the delusional material which Freud does not explain consists of nothing but repetitions of what we would consider torture devices that Schreber's father actually used upon him as a child. (Schreber's father was a famous pediatrician who believed posture was very important, and invented these devices to make children sit or lie straight.)

The transference has three functions in the treatment of so-called schizophrenic patients. The first two of these are the same as in any psychoanalytic treatment. The first function of the transference in therapy is to provide an enormous source of information as to what the life history and problems really were like. Thus, transference means the repetition of events and feelings from the past as if the past were the present. People do this not only in analysis, but in their everyday life. Transference always seems as if it were current reality. As I mentioned previously, we neurotics are very subtle. Psychotic patients are not subtle, as in the patient who called me "Dad". Those people who work with schizophrenics have often been most resistant to psychoanalytic insight, I think, because these patients seem so very sick. We do not wish to recognize that what they are concerned with, we, also, are concerned with, but are trying not to think about. We do not wish to recognize our kinship.

The second function of the transference is to provide gratification which will permit the patient to put up with the annoyance of being in psychotherapy. When Freud said that schizophrenic patients didn't form a transference, he meant they did not spontaneously develop a therapeutically usable transference, that is, a transference of positive, trusting dependence on the therapist which can be used as a motive for therapy. Since the childhood of the patient has been so undependable, the patient has trouble forming a strong, so-called positive transference to the therapist. The therapist for a schizophrenic patient, however, can help this process by being a strong, protective, more gratifying figure than he would be in the therapy of a neurotic. He must actually provide more gratification and protection. It is not necessary or useful to be too subtle, since the patients fill in ambiguities with the destructive aspects of their parents. Reassurance and protection should be stated verbally; the reassurance "I will not let anyone kill you" can often be quite helpful. Providing coffee or cigarettes is useful gratification. The therapist must make it clear that he can and will eventually deal with all those problems that overwhelm the patient, that the problems make sense, and that the therapist is not going to be frightened into leaving the patient.

The third function of the transference is to provide a model for identification, both identification into the superego, and identification into the ego. That is, we want the patient to replace treating himself in the way that his parents treated him with treating himself the more accepting, realistic, and humane way the therapist does. The image of the therapist thus gets taken into, and modifies the super-ego, but it also is taken as a model to some extent for the ego itself. This process is something that occurs in all therapy, although we do not always like to admit it. But in the treatment of schizophrenics, it is of particular importance, because of the defective models for iden-tification available in the patient's early life, and the lack of correc-tive identifications outside the family earlier in the patient's life.

Resistances Specific to Lower-Class Patients

Equally important, with knowledge of the human condition in general, and knowledge of schizophrenic pathology in particular, is knowledge of the particular problems of people of the socio-economic and ethnic sub-group of the patients. There are psycho-logists, psychiatrists, and even such knowledgeable people as Hollings-head and Redlich who argue that psychoanalytic therapy is not suitable to lower-class patients. There are even some people who argue that psychoanalytic therapy is not suitable to black patients. This is nonsense.

But one must deal with the resistances which are specific to such a group of people. The least understood, surprisingly enough, are some of the resistances of lower-class patients—very important because so-called schizophrenia is so much more frequent among the poor.

Lower socio-economic class people are intimidated by doctors. Even many of your friends who are not lower class have gone to a doctor, and when you ask them what they learned, say:

"I don't know. He told me what was wrong with me, but I didn't know what it meant." And they didn't ask.

Lower-class people are very apt to react this way. If they do not understand a professional, they feel as if it's a defect in them, and they won't ask. Furthermore, if you don't understand them, and you well may not, they interpret that as a defect. But if the patient doesn't understand the therapist, no communication is going on, and hence no therapy can go on. A patient can take an appropriate drug that a physician has prescribed, without understanding the physician, but no psychotherapy proceeds without understanding.

The way in which I deal with this problem (clearly not the only way, but it is at least one way), is to tell patients, "You know, I talk funny, and people have trouble understanding me. So if you don't understand me, you've got to tell me. And, furthermore, I have trouble understanding people, so when I don't understand you, I'll try to tell you. But you must tell me when you don't understand me, because I talk funny."

They tend to be amused and don't believe me when I say that I have trouble understanding people but it nonetheless makes it easier for them. They do believe me when I say I talk funny because, in fact, I do talk funny! In fact, all professionals talk funny! No matter what school of psychotherapy you belong to you have a specialized vocabulary that you're used to using which is not the language of your patients. If you have a highly intelligent, well educated patient who is very verbal, he may well have these esoteric words in his vocabulary, or he may learn them very quickly. But, even then you have to inform your patient.

Furthermore, lower-class patients don't know what psychotherapy and psychoanalytic therapy is all about. The whole thing seems very strange. You have to teach them. You have to tell them about an unconscious and about transference and about resistance. You have to tell them why you're doing what you're doing.

There are studies showing that in short-term therapy those therapists who take the trouble, even with middle-class patients, to explain what therapy is about, what they are doing and why, are more apt to have successful cases (Hoehn-Saric et al., 1964; Sloane et al., 1970). Again the well-educated, middle-class patient is apt to know something about psychoanalysis these days, knows something of what's expected of him, and he attempts to cooperate. But the lower-class patient doesn't. Why should he say what comes to mind? Why should talking be helpful? What is going on? Those of you who have read Freud's cases know that, in fact, Freud did a considerable amount of educating his patients as to what he was doing and why he was doing it. Any reasonable person would. But we have become so used to our patients being sophisticated that we forget that we have to teach them what we're doing and why we're doing it (unless they already know), if we expect them to be our allies in the therapeutic enterprise.

The Black Patient

Similarly, in dealing with black patients, there are special resistances that need to be dealt with. It is fashionable, in some quarters, to say black people just do not respond to psychoanalytic therapy. It is fashionable, in other quarters, to say blacks only need to be helped with the effects of discrimination and a sense of identity—black identity—and do not need to deal with such problems as fantasies, defenses, unconscious processes, sibling rivalry, oedipus complexes, and so forth. Such views are most unkind. The fact of the matter is that one needs to deal with discrimination against blacks as a reality and to help your black patient cope with this. You also have to deal with the fantasies, defenses, etc., characteristic of human beings.

A special resistance for a black patient dealing with a white therapist is that your white face arouses anger because of all the white people who have gone out of their way to hurt him or her. You must expect this. You must deal with it explicitly, and make it explicit to the patient—make it clear that you expect him to be angry at you for having a white face, and that it is understandable, given the unnecessary pain to which he has been subjected as a result of being black. Only if you accept his anger toward you as white and the necessary anger at other white people who have hurt him as justifiable, can you then deal with what must be dealt with in the long run, namely, that the deepest and most painful hurts have come from people who have black faces, that is, as with all human beings, from one's own family.

Some Misconceptions About Psychoanalytic Therapy

This ties in with one of the central misunderstandings about psychoanalytic therapy. It is frequently assumed that psychoanalytic therapy only deals with intrapsychic events and does not deal with external reality or the perception of and coping with external reality. This is quite wrong. It is true that if you are dealing with a neurotic who is quite capable and quite knowledgeable about the world, but, despite external success, is internally suffering, you deal mainly with intrapsychic events. With a psychotic patient who has grown up in a family that is bizarre in some respects and whose ability to use people outside the family has been systematically discouraged, we can guarantee there will be deficits which need to be remedied in his coping abilities, in his knowledge of the world, in his knowledge of how to get things done, and how to find things out. The therapist should never hesitate to be educative in these respects. Furthermore, the patient grossly distorts reality, and these distortions must be pointed out and then interpreted.

There is a difference between a psychoanalytic therapy and a common sense approach. According to common sense, there are only two possibilities; either we do not know what to do, or we know what to do and do it. Any real therapist knows that there is a third possibility—knowing what one should do, but being incapable of doing it.

Here is where most of the time in psychotherapy is spent, finding out why it is that the patient cannot do what he believes makes sense.

With psychotics, however, more than with neurotics, we frequently are dealing with people who really do not know what to do. As in child therapy, one should not be afraid to give information, but then one will have to still analyze why the patient cannot make good use of the information he or she now has available to them. It is, of course, an axiom of good therapy that one never does for a patient what the patient is capable of doing for himself, but it is frequently a difficult clinical judgement of what the patient is capable.

Good psychoanalytic therapy increases the ability of the patient to understand and cope with both internal and external reality. It puts the person in the mainstream of his life from childhood to the present. No psychoanalytic therapy is ever really complete. Hopefully, you begin a process which the patient continues for the rest of his life with new resources that he did not have before he met you. That is the sense in which psychoanalytic therapy is and ought to be interminable. What terminates is the overt relationship with the therapist.

Crisis Intervention

Throughout this chapter, psychoanalytic therapy has been talked about as a continuing procedure. But some patients will not accept a continuing psychotherapeutic relationship. I became a convert to crisis intervention as a result of my project on the treatment of schizophrenia described at the beginning of the chapter (Karon and VandenBos, 1972). For many poor people, life is so overwhelming that psychotherapy seems to be a very great luxury, unless you are really overwhelmed by what are clearly psychological problems. The therapist may well know that the so-called reality problems or economic problems are the result of the patient's psychological problems, or at least that the patient could surmount them if, to use the current phrase, he "got his head together", but the patient may not know that. Therefore, many economically poor patients will accept help only when they are overwhelmed.

In the Michigan State Psychotherapy Project, we tried to get the patients to come in on a regular basis, but some of them just wouldn't. They would come in only when "the roof had fallen in"— she was going to kill her husband, her husband was going to kill her, the baby was starving, there was no money, etc. Then the therapist worked frantically until there was some money in the household, she wasn't going to kill her husband, her husband wasn't going to kill her, the baby was being taken care of, breathed a sigh of relief and said to himself, "Now we can settle down and do real therapy." But the patient disappeared.

Incidentally, it is always a good idea to make at least one or two phone calls to see what is going on when a schizophrenic patient doesn't keep an appointment. But when lower-class people disappear, they frequently really disappear; no one seems to know how to get hold of them. Eventually, the patients came in again, but only when the roof had fallen in once more.

Much to our surprise, in many instances, patients who came in on this multiple crisis basis made as much progress as those who came in on a regular basis. I have nothing against patients who come in on a regular basis; in fact, I prefer to work that way, but many patients will only accept help during a crisis, and they can be helped. As you probably know, crises have a natural history of approximately 6 weeks in which they will resolve naturally, but the resolution may be suicide or a chronic psychotic state or some other unnecessary catastrophe. The job of the therapist is to influence the resolution. When people are in crisis, they are wide open, ready to change, and really hear you. You get enormous results for the time put in. As an individual practitioner, it is very hard to be available whenever in the future a crisis might occur, but as a member of an institution or clinic or hospital you can be available. If it turns out that you personally have moved on, the clinic or the hospital or the institution is still available.

Of course, one of the other benefits of crisis intervention is that it allows us to use our insights to be helpful to a large number of people. Crisis intervention by minimally trained individuals is now fashionable; however, in my experience and the experience of others (e.g., McCleod and Tinnin, 1966), the more sophisticated the crisis therapist is in psychoanalytic therapy, the more helpful he can be even in such brief therapy. I might point out that suicide prevention centers do not seem to be terribly effective at preventing suicides, unless they provide more than suicide prevention, unless they provide short-term psychotherapy (in some cases even one session). Most of the people who call suicide centers are really asking for psychotherapy and, unless it is provided, those few who are serious about suicide will not be prevented.

Suicide

I might add a few words about what I think does happen when psychotherapy is provided to people who are suicidal, psychotic or not (Karon, 1964). I think that no one commits suicide if they have a strong hope of attaining something important by staying alive. I think that everyone who commits suicide, whatever other fantasies may also exist, has an aggressive fantasy as well. "I'll eat me some worms, and then I'll die, and then they'll be sorry", is the way the folklore expresses it, and anything which is conscious in every child must be in the unconscious of every adult.

Therefore, the therapist must do two things. He must, on the one hand, make it clear that the aggression will not be successful and, on the other hand, that he is available and the problem is solvable. After all, what do people commit suicide over? The loss of money, loss of a job, the loss of a lover, the loss of a spouse—we know that these are replaceable. People can live poor; people can find other jobs. While, to the patient, it seems as if there never will be another person to replace a lost lover/spouse, you and I know better, if the person stays alive; half the world is of the opposite sex.

We cannot, and must not, falsely say that we can solve this problem today, or that we have any magic, but that, in principle, this is a solvable problem in the long run, and we will talk until we do. That you can reasonably offer the patient, and it is a very great deal.

If the patient makes you his super-ego, if he asks you implicitly or explicitly does he deserve to live or die, you should make it clear that you would decide for life (Jensen and Petty, 1958).

Some Concluding Remarks

It is impossible in this chapter to outline all of the things that would be useful for therapists to know, but obviously a knowledge of psychoanalytic therapy in general, and of the therapy of psychosis is particularly important. Freud (1963, 1965) and Sullivan (1953) certainly are the most important theorists. To help beginning therapists in reading Freud, let me point out that as far as one can tell there is no collective unconscious, that symbolism based on word origins are not necessarily valid, that there is no prenatal memory, that there is no death instinct, the distinction between vaginal and clitoral orgasm is not valid, and that no substance or energy corresponding to libido has been discovered. Hence, the so-called "actual" neuroses are simply neurotic symptoms that need to be analyzed, and that libido is at most a useful metaphor. Much of human experience is as if there were a libido, but the metaphor breaks down in two important respects: (1) the conclusion that psychotics didn't form a therapeutically usable transference, and (2) the notion that self-love and love of others are opposites, whereas they in fact vary together. If I do not like me, I cannot like anyone else, and as Sullivan so aptly said, if all people are pigs, it is little comfort to be the best of the pigs.

With these facts in mind, Freud becomes easier to understand, and more useful clinically, even for the novice therapist. Sullivan writes poorly, but is well worth reading thoroughly. Fromm—Reichmann's book (1950) on therapeutic technique is a good starting point. A number of other writers, e.g., Fairbairn (1954), Searles (1965), Lidz (1973) and many others are of use. Of course, I think my own papers tend to be useful.

In relating this chapter to the others, one might well ask what is the fundamental view of man implicit in psychoanalytic thinking. The answer, of course, is that there is no single philosophy of life underlying psychoanalytic theories. They are basically empirical generalizations. Human beings are seen as developing over time and carrying their past, particularly their childhood, with them; complex individuals with complex thoughts and feelings. Mental functioning is as much unconscious as conscious; current character and defenses are the result of earlier conflicts. Symptoms are to be understood as partially successful adaptations, solutions to earlier unsolvable dilemmas.

What is conscious is modifiable by experience; what is unconscious does not change. Insofar as current problems involve unconscious conflicts, the unconscious must be brought into consciousness to be transformed.

Not everyone needs a therapist, but most people would function better with such help. The processes, conflicts, and defenses found in psychotics may be found in all of us, but the magnitude of the anxiety is much less, the problems less pervasive, and the coping mechanism much more effective for those of us who function at the neurotic level.

While there is not time in this chapter to go into the specifics, some of you may be concerned about the handling of homosexual urges (Karon and Rosberg, 1958) or post-partum psychoses (Rosberg and Karon, 1959), or the oedipal fantasies (Rosberg and Karon, 1958), which, I might add, in psychotic patients almost never are the core problem. Those who are interested in those topics are referred, however, to my papers which may be, I hope, of some value. By the way, the oedipal fantasies in schizophrenics usually cover deeper, more basic, more central problems having to do with survival and the early mother-child relationship as it is relived in various other relationships and fantasies throughout the individual's life.

It would be a serious mistake to assume that there is only one way of working with schizophrenic patients that is successful. That is clearly wrong. I think the Sullivanians were successful; some of the Kleinians were successful, some of the people working within the ego-analytic framework were successful, and so forth. You will find as they talk about their patients and what they do with them, that the less abstractly and the more concretely they talk, the more similarity there really is among the therapists. This is not surprising, because there really is only one real world out there.

In this regard it is clear that my research findings, that psychoanalytic therapy is helpful, generalizes at least to the two kinds of psychoanalytic therapy differing in adjunctive use of medication and somewhat in activity of the therapist that were used in the project. I think it would generalize far beyond this, but only to those therapies which see the patient's symptoms as meaningfully related to his life history, which deal with unconscious processes, anxiety, guilt, defenses, and the parent-child relationship. I have elsewhere said that any real psychotherapy has five characteristics. Let me repeat them: First, it leads to greater insight into the self. Secondly, it gets you closer to your feelings. Thirdly, it makes you free as opposed to being controlled by symptoms or external circumstances, or what seem like external circumstances. Fourth, it leads to more self-control rather than being controlled by other people. And fifth, there is something about the process which is self-corrective, so that, if what the therapist is about or what the patient is about is not what really needs to be done, there is something about the process which leads them back to what needs to be done. Otherwise, therapy would have to be done by gods, and there aren't too many available these days.

In conclusion, let me ask who do we, the professionals, tend to go to when we are in trouble and want help? No matter what we may speak or write about, or recommend to others, overwhelmingly, psychologists and psychiatrists seek out some form of psychoanalysis or psychoanalytic therapy for themselves (e.g., Lazarus, 1971). Why do we not believe our patients deserve as much?

References

Bellak, L. *Dementia praecox*. New York: Grune and Stratton, 1948.

Bellak, L. *Schizophrenia*. New York: Logos, 1958.

Bellak, L. and Loeb, L. *The schizophrenic syndrome*. New York: Grune and Stratton, 1969.

Bleuler, E. *Dementia praecox or the group of the schizophrenias*. New York: International Universities, 1950.

Bookhammer, R. S., Meyers, R. W., Schober, C. C., and Piotorowski, Z. A. A 15-year clinical follow-up study of schizophrenics treated by Rosen's "direct analysis" compared with controls. *American Journal of Psychiatry*, 1966, 123, 602–4.

Eysenck, H. J. The effects of psychotherapy: An evaluation. *Journal of Consulting Psychology*, 1952, 16, 319–24.

Eysenck, H. J. *The structure of human personality*. New York: Wiley, 1960.

Fairbairn, R. W. D. *An object-relations theory of personality*. New York: Basic Books, 1954.

Feinsilver, D. B., and Gunderson, J. G. Psychotherapy for schizophrenics—Is it indicated? A review of the relevant literature. *Schizophrenia Bulletin*, 1972, 6, 11–23.

Ferenczi, S. Introjection and transference. *Sex in psychoanalysis. Collected Papers, Vol. 1.* New York: Basic Books, 1950, pp. 35–93.

Freud, S. Psychoanalytic notes on an autobiographical account of a case of paranoia (demential paranoides). *Complete Psychological Works, Vol. XII.* London: Hogarth, 1958, pp. 13–92.

Freud, S. *A general introduction to psychoanalysis*. New York: Pocket Books, 1963.

Freud, S. *New introductory lectures on psychoanalysis*. New York: Norton, 1965.

Fromm-Reichmann, F. *Principles of intensive psychotherapy*. Chicago: University of Chicago, 1950.

Grinker, R. R., and Spiegel, J. P. *Men under stress*. New York: McGraw-Hill, 1965.

Grinspoon, L., Ewalt, J. R., Shader, R. I. *Schizophrenia, pharmacotherapy and psychotherapy*. Baltimore: Williams and Wilkins, 1972.

Heston, L. The genesis of schizophrenia and schizoid disease. *Science*, 1970, 167, 249–56.

Hoehn-Saric, R., Frank, J. D., Imber, S. D., Nash, E. H., Stone, A. R., and Battle, C. C. Systematic preparation of patients for psychotherapy. *Journal of Psychiatric Research*, 1964, 2, 267–81.

Hollingshead, A. B. and Redlich, F. C. *Social class and mental illness*. New York: Wiley, 1958.

Jensen, V. W., and Petty, T. A. The fantasy of being rescued in suicide, *Psychoanalytic Quarterly*, 1958, 27, 327–39.

Karon, B. P. Some clinical notes on the significance of the number four. *Psychiatric Quarterly*, 1958, 32, 281—8.

Karon, B. P. A clinical note on the significance of an "oral" trauma. *Journal of Abnormal and Social Psychology*, 1960, 61, 480—1.

Karon, B. P. The resolution of acute schizophrenic reaction: A contribution to the development of non-classical psychotherapeutic techniques. *Psychotherapy: Theory, Research and Practice*, 1963, 1, 27—43.

Karon, B. P. Suicidal tendency as the wish to hurt someone else, and resulting treatment technique. *Journal of Individual Psychology*, 1964, 20, 206—12.

Karon, B. P. *Black Scars*. New York: Springer, 1975.

Karon, B. P. and Rosberg, J. Study of the mother-child relationship in a case of paranoid schizophrenia. *American Journal of Psychotherapy*, 1958, 12, 522—33.

Karon, B. P. and Rosberg, J. The homosexual urges in schizophrenia. *Psychoanalysis and Psychoanalytic Review*, 1958, 45, 50—6.

Karon, B. P. and VandenBos, G. R. The consequence of psychotherapy for schizophrenic patients. *Psychotherapy: Theory, Research and Practice*, 1972, 9, 111—20.

Karon, B. P. and VandenBos, G. R. Treatment costs of psychotherapy as compared to medication for schizophrenics. *Professional Psychology*, 1975a, 6, 293—298.

Karon, B. P. and VandenBos, G. R. Medication and/or psychotherapy with schizophrenics: Which part of the elephant have you touched? *International Mental Health Research Newsletter*, 1975b, 17(3), 1—13.

Kety, S. Biochemical theories of schizophrenia, Part I. *Science*, 1959a, 129, 1528—32.

Kety, S. Biochemical theories of schizophrenia, Part II. *Science*, 1959b, 129, 1590—6.

Laing, R. and Esterson, A. *Sanity, madness and the family*. London: Tavistock, 1964.

Lazarus, A. A. Where do behavior therapists take their troubles? *Psychological Report*, 1971, 349—50.

Lidz, T. *The origin and treatment of schizophrenic disorders*. New York: Basic Books, 1973.

Yi-Chuang, L. Contradictory parental expectations in schizophrenia: Dependence and responsibility. *AMA Archives of General Psychiatry*, 1962, 6, 219—34.

Malan, D. The outcome problem in psychotherapy research: A historical review. *Archives of General Psychiatry*, 1973, 29, 719—29.

May, P. R. A. *Treatment of schizophrenia: A comparative study of five treatment methods*. New York: Science House, 1968.

May P. R. A. and Tuma, H. H. Methodological problems in psychotherapy research: Observations of the Karon-VandenBos study of psychotherapy and drugs in schizophrenia. *British Journal of Psychiatry*, 1970, 117, 569—650.

McCleod, J. and Tinnin, L. Special service project. *Archives of General Psychiatry*, 1966, 15, 190—7.

Melnick, B. and Hurley, J. R. Distinctive personality attributes of child-abusing mothers. *Journal of Consulting and Clinical Psychology*, 1969, 33, 746—9.

Meyer, R. G. and Karon, B. P. The schizophrenogenic mother concept and the

TAT. *Psychiatry*, 1967, 30, 173–9.

Mitchell, K. M. An analysis of the schizophrenogenic mother concept by means of the TAT. *Journal of Abnormal Psychology*, 1968, 73, 571–4.

Mitchell, K. M. Concept of "pathogenesis" in parents of schizophrenic and normal children. *Journal of Abnormal Psychology*, 1969, 74, 423–4.

Nichols, N. *The relationship between degree of maternal pathogenicity and severity of ego impairment in schizophrenic offspring.* Unpublished Ph.D. dissertation, University of Michigan, 1970.

Niederland, W. G. Schreber: Father and son. *Psychoanalytic Quarterly*, 1959, 11, 151–69.

Niederland, W. G. The "miracled-up" world of Schreber's childhood. *Psychoanalytic Study of the Child.* New York: International Universities, 1959, 383–413.

Niederland, W. G. The Schreber case sixty years later. *International Journal of Psychiatry*, 1972, 10, 79–84.

Rogers, C. R. *Client-centered therapy.* Boston: Houghton, Mifflin, 1951.

Rogers, C. R., Gendlin, E. T., Keisler, D. J., and Truax, C. B. *The therapeutic relationship and its impact: A study of psychotherapy with schizophrenics.* Madison: University of Wisconsin, 1967.

Rosberg, J. and Karon, B. P. The Oedipus Complex in an apparently deteriorated case of schizophrenia. *Journal of Abnormal and Social Psychology*, 1958, 57, 221–5.

Rosberg, J. and Karon, B. P. A direct analytic contribution to the understanding of post-partum psychoses. *Psychiatric Quarterly*, 1959, 33, 296–304.

Rosenthal, D. and Kety, S. (Eds.) *The transmission of schizophrenia.* Oxford: Pergamon, 1968.

Roueché, B. As empty as eve. Annals of medicine. *New Yorker*, 9 Sept. 1974, 50 (No. 29), 84–100.

Searles, H. F. *Collected papers on schizophrenia and related subjects.* New York: International Universities, 1965.

Singer, M. and Wynne, L. Thought disorder and family relations of schizophrenics: IV. Results and implications. *Archives of General Psychiatry*, 1965, 12, 201–12.

Sloane, R. B., Cristol, A. H., Pepernik, M. C., and Staples, F. R. Role preparation and expectation of improvement in psychotherapy. *Journal of Nervous and Mental Diseases*, 1970, 150, 18–26.

Tuma, A. H. and May, P. R. A. Psychotherapy, drugs and therapist experience in the treatment of schizophrenia. *Psychotherapy: Theory, Research and Practice*, in press.

VandenBos, G. R. and Karon, B. P. Pathogenesis: A new therapist personality dimension related to therapeutic effectiveness. *Journal of Personality Assessment*, 1971, 35, 252–60.

Wender, P., Rosenthal, D., Zahn, T., and Kety, S. The psychiatric adjustment of the adopting parents of schizophrenics. *American Journal of Psychiatry*, 1971, 127, 1013–18.

Wyatt, R. J., Termini, B. A., and Davis, J. Biochemical and sleep studies of schizophrenia. Part I. Biochemical studies. *Schizophrenia Bulletin*, Fall, 1971, 4, 10–44.

Index

213